Bridgebuilders

Bridgebuilders

A Workplace Chaplaincy

Malcolm Torry

CANTERBURY
PRESS
Norwich

First published in 2010 by the Canterbury Press Norwich
Editorial office
13–17 Long Lane,
London, EC1A 9PN, UK

Canterbury Press is an imprint of Hymns Ancient and Modern
Ltd (a registered charity)
St Mary's Works, St Mary's Plain,
Norwich, NR3 3BH, UK

www.scm-canterburypress.co.uk

British Library Cataloguing in Publication data

A catalogue record for this book is available
from the British Library

978 1 84825 036 9

Originated by The Manila Typesetting Company
Printed and bound in Great Britain by
CPI Antony Rowe, Chippenham SN14 6LH

Contents

An index for *Bridgebuilders* can be found
on the industrial mission history website:

www.industrialmissionhistory.org.uk

Acknowledgements

I would like to thank:

My colleagues at the South London Industrial Mission (SLIM), with whom I worked between 1983 and 1988, and particularly Canon Peter Challen. They taught me how to be a workplace chaplain, and encouraged me as I wrote the history of SLIM as my Ph.D. thesis (Torry, 1990);

Bill Jacob, now Archdeacon of Charing Cross, for much help and encouragement as I wrote the thesis;

My colleagues on the chaplaincy team at the Millennium Dome during 2000; those with whom I worked to establish Mission in London's Economy; and the trustees and chaplains of the Greenwich Peninsula Chaplaincy, all of whom have taught me so much about being a workplace chaplain in the twenty-first century;

The officers, clergy and congregations of the parishes which I have served, all of whom have understood the importance of relating to institutions and workers in their parishes;

The managements, trades unions and workers of the institutions in which I have worked as a chaplain or in which I have worked with others to establish chaplaincies - for their welcome, understanding, and co-operation;

Successive Bishops of Woolwich and Archdeacons, for their understanding of the importance of workplace chaplaincy;

My colleagues in the Industrial Mission Association, for their companionship in the task over many years, for their looking forward to new styles of ministry, and for their help with gathering material for this history;

Crispin White, John Hodgson, Liza Filby, and Andy Smith, for acting as a steering group as we established an industrial mission history website and gathered material for it;

All those chaplains who responded to requests in IMAgenda, the Industrial Mission Association's journal, for information about the histories of particular industrial mission teams;

John Hodgson, of the John Rylands University Library, Manchester, for help with the Industrial Mission Association archive;

Crispin and Mary White, for scanning and checking the index of the archive;

The writers of dissertations and theses on particular industrial missions or aspects of the industrial mission movement, for making their dissertations and theses available; those who have helped me to locate dissertations; and Roger Sawtell, for making available Philip Bloy's material on the history of the Sheffield Industrial Mission;

John Paxton, for assistance with the history of SLIM during the 1990s; Tim Scott, for help with locating the SLIM archive; Maggie Lee, for helping to put the archive in order; and the John Harvard Local History Library, Southwark, for receiving and caring for it;

Peter Cope, for interviewing retired chaplains and for writing up the interviews;

Christopher Chessun, Bishop of Woolwich, for granting me a three months sabbatical so that I could write this book;

Crispin White and Michael Atkinson, for their most helpful comments on a draft text;

The Industrial Mission Association's officers, for their enthusiasm for the project;

Christine Smith, and all at the Canterbury Press, for their characteristic help and commitment;

And my wife Rebecca, for putting up with my book-writing.

A note on terminology

The first two major modern workplace chaplaincies were the South London Industrial Mission and the Sheffield Industrial Mission. Their chaplains worked in industry, mainly manufacturing industry, and the movement as a whole thus became known as 'industrial mission'. As manufacturing industry closed and industrial missions turned their attention to retail and service industries, the name still seemed appropriate. During the 1980s the missions directed their attention more to the urban world in all its variety, but industrial visiting was still firmly on the agenda so the word 'industrial' remained as a component of the longer designation 'urban industrial mission'.

The other half of the designation, 'mission', was, as we shall see, a relevant term during and after the Second World War. Because it could be broadly defined to include both pastoral and prophetic aspects, the word continued to be appropriate into the 1980s.

When in some parts of the country manufacturing industry disappeared almost entirely, two adaptations occurred. Chaplains continued to visit workplaces, but those workplaces rarely called themselves 'industry', so 'workplace' replaced 'industry' as the stated location of the chaplaincies' work. 'Mission' was becoming problematic because it was either not understood at all, or, in an increasingly multi faith society, it could be understood as a rather threatening proselytising of people of other faiths. 'Ministry', with its 'servant' meaning, thus replaced 'mission' in the names of some industrial missions: but in common parlance 'minister' can mean a government minister, so it remains ambiguous.

'Chaplaincy' is what chaplains do, so 'workplace chaplaincy' has now become a fairly uncontentious replacement for 'industrial mission'.

Some longstanding chaplaincy teams (as in Liverpool), some new initiatives (as in London), and some denominations (as in the Methodist Church), have increasingly sought more diverse ways of relating to the economy within which workplaces function: so 'the economy' has become the place where the work occurs. In some cases chaplaincy is no longer the main activity, so there 'mission in the economy' is a more appropriate designation than 'workplace chaplaincy'. 'Mission' remains the first term in this designation because, whilst it might need to be explained, its broader meaning is more appropriate than the narrower 'chaplaincy'.

This book is mainly a history of chaplains visiting workplaces. In the earlier chapters I use the term 'industrial mission' because that is the designation used during the period under discussion. In the chapters dealing with more recent history I use 'workplace chaplaincy' for chaplains visiting workplaces and 'mission in the economy' for the more diverse activity of the Church in relation to the economy. In more general discussion, in the introduction, and in the concluding material, the terms 'industrial mission' and 'workplace chaplaincy' might be used interchangeably. Here 'industrial mission' means chaplains visiting workplaces, and if additional meanings are in view (such as chaplains working amongst the unemployed) then I shall state them.

Introduction

The challenge and the response

Since the Second World War workplace chaplaincy has been the Church's most important piece of work. This might appear to be rather a bold claim, but I can justify it. Secularization is the most important issue facing the Church in the longer term; workplace chaplaincy has tackled more varieties of secularization than any other mission activity of the Church has done; and therefore workplace chaplaincy is the Church's most important piece of work. Whether my readers will agree with me by the end of the book is another matter, but whether you come to agree with me or not I hope that you will at least agree that workplace chaplaincy has been a highly significant mission activity, that its lessons need to be learnt, and that it needs to continue to be a priority.

Secularization is the major issue facing the Church. This isn't always obvious because Christians and the media think that other issues face us with more significant challenges. They might be right in the short term, but not in the long term. One reason why it isn't obvious that secularization is the major issue is that in some places, such as in London, congregations are growing. As we shall see in my first chapter, this in no way negates my view that secularisation is such a serious issue. Another reason for it not being obvious that secularization is our major challenge is that there is no shortage of religious belief. Again, this in no way negates my view, as we shall see. A further reason why it isn't obvious that secularization is such a major challenge is that there are many different kinds of secularization. The kind to which I shall particularly draw attention is the growing distance between religious and secular institutions, but I shall discuss other kinds too because the different sorts constantly reinforce each other.

By the end of the first chapter I hope to have persuaded you that secularization is the most serious issue facing the Church.

For over 60 years the modern industrial mission movement has been the Church's most consistent answer to the institutional aspect of secularization. That is why this book is what it is: an exploration of the meaning of 'secularization', a history of workplace chaplaincy, and finally a discussion of workplace chaplaincy's importance for the future.

I have two kinds of reader in mind, and the way you read the book might depend on which kind you think you are. If you are primarily interested in the history of workplace chaplaincy, then you might wish to read just the first couple of pages of chapter 1 and then move on to the beginning of chapter 2. By the end of chapter 9 you will, I hope, understand that workplace chaplaincy is an important strategy for tackling, what I call 'institutional secularization'. You might then return to chapter 1 before reading the book's conclusions. But if you are primarily interested in secularization then you might start with chapter 1 and then carry on through the history of workplace chaplaincy, because after reading the first chapter you will want to learn to what extent workplace chaplaincy has been an appropriate response to institutional secularization. Either way, by the end of the book you should have come to appreciate the significance of workplace chaplaincy, and you might wonder why such an important movement is so little known outside the group of people who do it or experience it. You will also be able to decide whether workplace chaplaincy has been an appropriate response to secularization, and you will be able to ask yourself whether chaplains visiting workplaces should be a priority for the Church in the future.

What this book is, and what it isn't

The chapters on the history of workplace chaplaincy mainly describe what chaplains have done, not what they have thought. The reason for this is that the movement is primarily a practical one.

At its heart is chaplains visiting workplaces. The visiting has often provoked theological reflection, theology has often influenced practice, and you will find some theology in these pages: but it is workplace visiting from which all else springs, so that's what most of the book is about. Industrial chaplains have of course done lots of other things, and you will find many of those activities in the book, too. One of the conclusions which I have drawn while writing this history is that where chaplains have stopped visiting workplaces and haven't replaced it with some other active engagement with a wide variety of people involved in the economy, then no matter what else they're doing the movement has lost its soul and has ceased to be a valid response to secularization. By the end of the book you might like to decide whether you agree with me.

This is not in any sense a complete history of industrial mission. For over 50 years there have been dozens of industrial mission teams in England alone. Chaplains and researchers have written histories of individual teams and dissertations on aspects of the movement, and there is more than enough archive material: in boxes at the John Rylands University Library in Manchester, on shelves in local history libraries, in cupboards at industrial mission teams' headquarters, in suitcases in chaplains' attics, and on the industrial mission history website: www.industrialmissionhistory. org.uk. I have enjoyed reading a great deal of this material. Sadly, I've been able to include only a fraction of it in the book.

I have also had to restrict myself to chaplaincy in industrial and commercial organizations, that is, to chaplaincy undertaken by people who call themselves, and are called by others, 'industrial chaplains' or 'workplace chaplains'. A comprehensive history of workplace chaplaincy would have to include hospital chaplains (Flagg, 2006), hospice chaplains, university chaplains (Collier, 2006), prison chaplains (Tyler, 2006), school chaplains, sports chaplains (Heskins and Baker, 2006), theatre chaplains (Truss, 2007), emergency services chaplains, armed forces chaplains, and the various missions to seamen, because these are all chaplains relating to workplaces. Some of these get a mention in the book, but each of these activities really deserves a history of its own.

This will also be a rather personal history. I was for five years a full-time chaplain with the South London Industrial Mission (SLIM). The space which I give to SLIM reflects my own appreciation of SLIM's work; but I also give it lots of space because throughout its development and decline SLIM has experienced many of the challenges facing the movement and has exemplified many of the wider movement's responses to those challenges.

Sheffield Industrial Mission (SIM) has to be the other mission to which I give lots of space. SIM's impact on industrial mission can't be exaggerated, and the crisis in Sheffield during the mid-'60s was crucial to the way in which the movement developed. An additional reason for the amounts of space which I give to both SLIM and SIM is that they worked with contrasting methods and ideas, and to discuss them both in depth gives a rounded picture of the movement as a whole. It's not that other industrial missions don't get a look in: they do, especially when they typify aspects of the movement's development not exemplified by SLIM and SIM, but also when a combination of information about other missions can make clear the direction in which the movement was going.

Some of my readers would no doubt have chosen to omit some of the material which I have included and to include some of what I have omitted; and I can perfectly understand that some chaplains would have liked me to include far more of the work of their own industrial mission teams. I have chosen in the way that I have in order to typify general trends within the movement, and I hope that by getting to know quite well a limited number of chaplains and their work my readers will gain an understanding of the history of workplace chaplaincy as a whole.

I hope that mine will not be the last book written on the history of workplace chaplaincy, and that future books will take different approaches. In particular, I hope that a historian will one day undertake the kind of comprehensive study which Alan Wilkinson has contributed to our understanding of the Church during the First and Second World Wars (Wilkinson, 1978, 1986). Future historians will find helpful both the website and the lists of references at the end of each chapter.

This book is mainly about workplace chaplaincy in England from 1942 onwards. Scottish industrial mission already has its own history and there's no point in repeating the material here. I give the Scottish history an occasional mention where it sheds light on the English experience, but readers interested in the movement in Scotland should read Donald Ross's excellent book, *God It's Monday* (Ross, 1997).

Wales gets an occasional mention, but here the reason for brevity is different. There isn't much material available. The history of industrial mission in Wales would be an ideal research project for somebody.

Workplace chaplaincy is now an international movement. I don't have the space for a thorough treatment of workplace chaplaincy around the world so I only mention work in other countries where it relates to work in England. I hope that one day a researcher will study the global spread of workplace chaplaincy. (My chapter on secularization relates to the English situation, to some extent to the rest of the UK, and to some extent to Europe. Anyone researching workplace chaplaincy in other continents will need to write a very different chapter on secularization if they write one at all (Davie, 2002).)

The historical chapters in this book are arranged chronologically. There is now a consensus that we can identify four phases in the development of industrial mission:

1 Before the Second World War, mainly evangelistic mission
2 From the Second World War to the 1970s, the classical period of full-time chaplains visiting industry with a broad range of motives and understandings
3 The 1980s, during which chaplains ran projects of various kinds in response to some major issues facing our society
4 The 1990s onwards, during which local economies have become a major preoccupation[1] (Davies, 1991).

The chronological boundaries of my chapters are arranged to reflect this categorization and also such other major changes in the movement as the crisis at Sheffield in the mid-'60s. Some situations, activities and issues don't fit neatly into these chronological boundaries. When this happens I locate the material within just one chapter but make it clear that I am transgressing chronological boundaries.

The industrial mission movement has given birth to numerous projects, such as training and work experience for the unemployed during the 1980s, and also to new organizations, such as Church Action with the Unemployed, the Race Equality in Employment Project and the Ecumenical Council for Corporate Responsibility; and former industrial chaplains have been involved in numerous new enterprises, such as Afghan Action, which trains Afghans in carpet-making. I give some of these organizations an occasional mention because industrial chaplains gave them birth and they resulted from issues arising from workplace visiting: but I can't pay them the attention which they deserve and which I hope other historians will one day give to them.

Similarly, lots of people have thought about the relationship between the Christian Faith and the economy. They have founded organizations, organized meetings, given lectures, mounted campaigns, built websites, and written books. Where such material has informed or sprung from the work of workplace chaplains then it receives a mention here, but not otherwise. Readers interested in this field should begin with the reader *The Church and Economic Life* edited by Malcolm Brown and Paul Ballard.

Most chapters contain comparative material. This will normally be about a movement or an organization which is different from industrial mission but which is also in some way related to it. I include this material because of the light it sheds on the history of workplace chaplaincy and not for its own sake.

Just as my historical chapters provide the most sketchy account of the industrial mission movement, and employ a fraction of the archive material now available, the chapter on secularization is very sketchy indeed. It cannot be otherwise. There is now a huge literature on secularization (Charles Taylor's massive *A Secular Age* is a library in itself), and an adequate discussion of the concept would have to be a book in itself. In my first chapter I discuss briefly a variety of kinds of secularization so that you can understand how workplace chaplaincy tackles secularization. Similarly, in the subsequent chapters, I give a sufficient overview of the history of industrial mission to enable you to decide whether workplace chaplaincy has been an appropriate response to secularization and whether it is a response worth pursuing in the future.

Note

1   Davies, Mostyn, et al, 1991, 'Towards a Strategy for the Fourth Generation of IM', from *Local Economy Based Industrial Mission*, a paper produced by the Theology Development Group of the Industrial Mission Association, quoted in Brown and Ballard, 2006, p. 395.

I

Secularization

There is no such thing as secularization. There are secularizations, in the plural:

1 *The secularization of ideas*: The way we think no longer has religious ideas at its heart, and often has no connection at all with them. For most people, we're here because we've evolved, not because God created a universe.

2 *Cultural secularization*: Religious symbols and ideas no longer control our culture, whether that culture be working class, middle class, music, literature, painting, drama . . . We might still find references to religious ideas, but they're usually ironic.

3 *Desacralization*: Many of us no longer experience a sense of the sacred, of something transcendent, and if we do then we keep it to ourselves and it doesn't affect other areas of our lives.

4 *Practical secularization*: Lots of people don't go to church, or get their children baptized, or get married in church, and a priest only conducts their funeral if the funeral director asks their next of kin if they want one and 'yes' is the only answer they can think of. If someone does go to church then everyone thinks of it as a voluntary activity like any other. It's going to church which is now odd and which someone might be asked to explain. No one needs to explain why they don't go to church.

5 *State secularization*: If a mayor decides to have a chaplain then that's up to them. Nobody expects them to or wonders why they haven't got one. A mayor can decide to hold a civic service, but no one asks why they haven't bothered. In England the Church of England's bishops still sit by right in the House

of Lords, but most of us now regard this as the anachronism which it is. The monarch might still 'do God', but Prime Ministers don't, even if they're Christians.

6 *Institutional secularization*: State schools no longer ask the local curate to lead assemblies, and if the curate asks if they can then schools aren't sure what to do with them. Hospitals have chaplains for all sorts of good reasons, but it's not because we think a hospital to be incomplete without one. There used to be deep connections between religious organizations and other institutions. No longer.

7 *Religious secularization*: Religious organizations are now so influenced by other types of organization that they are less religious than they used to be. Social events can be as important to a church's members as the holding of services, and if a new management method arrives from the denomination's head office then people moan about the time it might take rather than whether it compromises the religious nature of the congregation.

8 *Secularization of individual beliefs*: This kind of secularization occurs when someone no longer believes that there is a God (but see below on why this kind of secularization is listed last).

This is rather a large agenda for a single chapter, but brief discussion of each of these meanings of 'secularization' is essential if we are to understand industrial mission as a response to secularization.[1]

The secularization of ideas

Belief in a God who has created all that is and who sustains it out of love for his creation is of course perfectly compatible with a belief that all living creatures have evolved from single-cell creatures and that cells evolved from chemical reactions around volcanic fissures deep in the ocean. The recent 200th anniversary of Charles Darwin's birth and 150th anniversary of the publication of his *The Origin of Species* has rekindled debate, and much of it that I've heard assumes that religion and science aren't compatible.[2] This isn't very intelligent. Science offers us hypotheses for which there is good evidence and which nobody has yet disproved.[3] It has never offered certainties. Unfortunately, not enough people seem to understand this, and fewer understand that it can be perfectly rational to trust both religious and scientific statements. The sepa ration of religious and secular ideas in this way is what I call the secularization of ideas.

A bundle of ideas about human autonomy, human reason and scientific explanation has affected the whole of Western Europe (McLeod, 1974, p. 285), and we are now suspicious of ideas which ask for our commitment before they will allow us to explore them. We don't realise that we are already committed to a huge store of ideas which we have absorbed since childhood. For instance, we are perfectly happy to be committed to the capitalist system and to consumption as a way of life, but far less happy to be committed to a religion: and we are blissfully unaware of the contradiction. What we now call philosophy, mathematics, and the natural sciences, were once elements of a single science at the heart of which was Christian doctrine (or, in other parts of the world, some other faith's doctrine). Now, university religious studies departments thrive because schoolteachers have to teach the subject, but specifically Christian theological departments are having a hard time of it unless there are church theological colleges nearby to provide them with a captive pool of students. Theological ideas are now in the marketplace along with all the others, and the number of people buying into them is declining, at least in Western Europe.

Cultural secularization

'Culture' is a term with many meanings. At the heart of the concept are the sets of ideas within which we understand our lives and the world around us, but the meaning is also wider than that. It's about the unarticulated attitudes which drive our behaviour, and the symbols through which we reflect on the meaning of reality from the personal level to the global. The media and the arts are what we might call 'crystallizations' of culture. They can show us in a pure or stark form what our culture is. Thus in 'The Archers' the Church is an important voluntary organization and its clergy are interesting if they break with tradition, but not otherwise. In this way 'The Archers' captures well how religious organizations and personnel fit into our culture.

Charles Taylor has shown how we now live within a new 'social imaginary' in which society is an autonomous 'instrumentally rational order of mutual benefit', in which unbelief has 'come of age', and in which the economy is an objectified reality: that is, we talk about the economy as if it's a rather important object, rather than what it really is: a set of behaviours which we have created (Taylor, 2007, pp. 171–81). The economy has replaced God as the framework for our action and thought, consumerism has replaced Christian faith, and economics has replaced theology. Where religious belief and behaviour do happen, they are a private matter with no necessary connection to anything beyond ourselves: they belong to the individual, not to the culture within which we live. We have now been living with this secular culture for some time. Owen Chadwick has found that by 1900 most people didn't believe in miracles, sincerity was more important than religious faith, religious facts were as susceptible to inquiry as any other sort, and, even to practising Christians, Jesus' humanity was more relevant than his divinity (Chadwick, 1975, pp. 17, 37, 194, 225; cf. McLeod, 1981, p. 93; MacIntyre, 1967, pp. 24–26). 'Something happened to religious people which affected their attitude to the world . . . We may have less sense of providence in our lives.' (Chadwick, 1975, pp. 226, 258). This is an attitude which we might legitimately call a 'secular culture'.

Modernization and now globalization, have given every society and every community a diverse moral and cultural landscape within which religion must jostle for attention in the same way as every other set of ideas (Bruce, 1995). Peter Berger suggests that whereas the pre-secularized society was one in which 'religion legitimates social institutions by bestowing upon them an ultimately valid ontological status, that is, by *locating* them within a sacred and cosmic reference' (Berger, 1995, p. 50), the many different cultures, ideologies and religions now available to us locate us in a wide variety of subsocieties, each with its own way of understanding reality. This makes any set of religious beliefs relative to every other set of ideas. Secularization inevitability follows: the process by which 'sectors of society and culture are removed from the domination of religious institutions and symbols' (Berger, 1995, p. 50). In a multi-ethnic and multi-faith society schools quite rightly teach a variety of religions; but to teach many religions leaves students standing outside all of them as observers, being more tolerant of each person's chosen religious position (of which we can only approve) and internalising no single religious tradition for themselves. As Hugh McLeod puts it, we have left a 'Christian country' and now live in a 'civilized society' (McLeod, 2007, p. 215).

The arts, whether music, the visual arts, drama, or literature, were once packed with religious symbols, imagery and references, and were particularly full of references to whatever religious conflict happened to be current at the time. People no longer understand religious references in the arts, so university English departments have to run courses for first year students to acquaint them with the Bible so that they can understand pre-modern and much modern literature. The arts and the media still contain religious references, of course, but they are often ironic and sometimes anti-religious. There is just enough understanding of religious culture left for us to be able to identify with the references, but not a sufficiently internalized religious culture shared by artist and audience for anyone to feel that they are standing on holy ground.

It's not just in university English or sociology departments that this secularization of ideas and of culture is understood, of course. A song by *Faithless* goes like this: 'This is my church. This is where I heal my hurts . . . respect, love, compassion. This is my church. This is where I heal my hurts . . . '.[4]

Desacralization

Closely related to Chadwick's suggestion that there is now less of a sense of providence in our lives (Chadwick, 1975, p. 50) is 'desacralization': a loss of the sense of the sacred, of the 'Beyond', or, as Rudolf Otto put it, of a *mysterium tremendum*: the mysterious, the transcendent, the awesome (in its more traditional sense and not with the sense which teenagers and young adults now give to the word) (Otto, 1923, p. 12). Acquaviva distinguishes between 'secularization' and 'desacralization'. By the former he means a secularized religion which rejects 'the magical use of the sacred': by the latter, the loss of a capacity for 'living a psychological experience of the sacred' (Acquaviva, 1975, p. 35). Urbanization and new technology have changed the ways in which we experience the world, have changed our psychology, and have created an 'irreligiosity to an extent previously unknown in human history' (Acquaviva, 1975, p. 161).

> From the religious point of view, humanity has entered a long night that will become darker and darker with the passing of the generations, and of which no end can yet be seen. It is a night in which there seems to be no place for a conception of God, or for a sense of the sacred, and ancient ways of giving significance to our own existence, of confronting life and death, are becoming increasingly untenable. At bottom, the motivations for religious behaviour and for faith persist . . . the need to explain ourselves and what surrounds us, the anguish, and the sense of precariousness. But [we] remain uncertain whether somewhere there exists, or ever existed, something different from uncertainty, doubt, and existential insecurity. (Acquaviva, 1975, p. 202)

However, the sense of the sacred hasn't disappeared entirely. There is still religious experience, though we generally keep it to ourselves if we have it: unless we're part of a community which values religious experience of a particular sort. The 'rumour of angels' (Berger, 1970) is still very much alive within the Pentecostal tradition (Martin, 2005, pp. 26–43, 141–54), and Martin thinks the Pentecostalist sense of the sacred to be popular because it fits nicely with 'modernity, transnationalism, voluntarism, pluralism, the nuclear family, consumption, modern communication, social and geographical mobility . . . ' (Martin 2005, p. 144). Here the sacred is packaged as an experience which we go out and get because that's what we think we need. (I've recently experienced digital television for the first time. Anyone could be forgiven for confusing the religious and the shopping channels.) This isn't to knock Pentecostal experience. It's the way we are, and if that's how the 'rumour of angels' is going to survive then so be it.

Just as desacralization contributes to secularization, so resacralization can contribute to a growth in religious practice and to religious ideas and culture becoming more widespread. Evangelical Christianity and Pentecostalism can do this, and certain forms of intense Islam can have major cultural consequences. An important question for us will be whether such resacralization can have any effect on institutional secularization.

Practical secularization

Acquaviva follows his discussion of the sacred and of desacralization with plenty of evidence for a growing 'irreligiosity' during the early 1960s, by which he means that in Europe, the USA and Latin America Roman Catholic practice collapsed. Fewer people were attending mass, having their children baptized, or getting married in church. All except one of the indicators headed downwards (Acquaviva, 1975, pp. 49–84): the only increase between 1958 and 1961 was for non-believers who practice (Acquaviva, 1975, p. 69), which suggests that religious practice is now a voluntary activity among other voluntary activities and that it has less to do with religious belief than we might have thought. Callum Brown presents large amounts of data which point to 1963 as the turning point in the UK. Since then substantially fewer children have been baptised, the figures for marriages in church have plummeted, churchgoing has fallen (except among some ethnic minorities), and Sunday schools have declined.

A formerly religious people have entirely forsaken organized Christianity in a sudden plunge into a truly secular condition . . . What emerges is a story not merely of Church decline, but of the end of Christianity as a means by which men and women, as individuals, construct their identities and their sense of 'self'. (Brown, 2001, pp. 1–2)

What both Acquaviva's and Brown's figures show is a deep secularization in terms of individual religious practice. However, belonging to voluntary organizations in general has also collapsed since Victorian times (Yeo, 1976). (Today's increase in voluntary activity is not the same as active membership of voluntary organizations.) So to what extent is the decline in churchgoing a specifically religious issue? Brown suggests explanations for the decline in religious practice, and especially reliable contraception and the automation of housework. These have enabled women to enter the labour market, leaving them with less time for religious activity. Television is also a reason, and so is a generally more individualistic and family-centred way of life (Percy, 2006, pp. 96–7). All voluntary organizations have suffered from these changes, of course, but because Christian religious practice mainly happens on Sundays, it is the increased availability of alternative Sunday activities and greater social and geographical mobility which have posed particular problems for *religious* practice.[5] Christians said that they were opposed to Sunday shop opening because shop workers need to spend time with their families, but vociferous campaigns pursued by church councils and by bishops and clergy might also have had something to do with the competition which Sunday shopping would pose to churchgoing.

Robin Gill suggests another reason specifically related to the Church: that the Victorians built too many churches, that cities have become depopulated, that the result has been churches emptying, and that because empty churches don't feel very welcoming they have emptied even more (Gill, 1992, 2003). Similarly, decline causes defensiveness, defensiveness brings to the surface existing tensions in an organization, and the resulting conflict can drive even more people away.[6] African immigration has halted the decline in churchgoing in some of our cities, and some smaller rural congregations are growing as communities work hard to maintain the few remaining public facilities in villages which have already lost Post Offices, schools and pubs (Jackson, 2002, p. 210): but, for whatever reason, the trend generally remains downwards. This matters, and not only to the churches. Where fewer people attend church there are fewer people to create the social capital which churches have always contributed to their communities (Putnam, 2000, p. 79). A more isolated, beleaguered and privatised religion is the result, and we are left with 'the devoutly observant and the entirely unchurched' (Putnam, 2000, p. 75): that is, with a small group of people more conscious of their religious identity over against the society around them. The boundary around the religious organization thus becomes more difficult for the uncommitted to cross, and we end up with a larger body of people who might or might not believe but who certainly no longer 'belong' (Davie, 1994; Davie, 2000, p. 127). The reduced body of active believers can't provide as many vocations to the ordained ministry, and can't afford to pay for as many full-time ministers. It is often the full-time clergy who form the bonds between religious and other organizations, so if there are fewer full-time clergy then the Church will no longer be able to relate successfully to other social institutions. Practical secularization therefore increases institutional secularization. An interesting general question is whether a decline in practice will lead eventually to a loss of religious belief, and a more particular question is whether fewer children going to Sunday School will mean fewer individuals believing in God as well as fewer people going to church.

It is important to keep this kind of secularization in perspective. People not coming to church is no new phenomenon. Ted Wickham's researches in Sheffield proved that 'from the eighteenth century, and progressively through the nineteenth, since emergence of the industrial towns, the working classes, the labouring poor, the artisan class, as a class and as adults, have been outside the churches' (Wickham, 1957, p. 215). There wasn't enough space in the church buildings and they couldn't afford the pew rents. Similarly, Martyn Percy quite properly asks us not to assume that particular statistics imply an inevitable social process. It isn't true that a 'golden age of Christendom . . . is coming to its end' (Percy, 2006, p. 78). There never was such a golden age (Percy, 2006, p. 69), and statistics which look disastrous aren't necessarily so.

The same number of people going to church less often means that the same number of people going to church show up in statistics on congregational size as fewer people going to church. 'Regular churchgoing is in decline, but the appetite for occasional church attendance seems undiminished' (Percy, 2006, p. 78). I agree. Cathedral congregations are booming at the same time as parish church congregations are declining. If what you want is occasional attendance and you don't want to take any responsibility for running a religious institution then you go to a cathedral and not to a parish church with a declining congregation. It's obvious.

In some countries social disruption has resulted in practical and institutional secularization, but in others the results have been new forms of religion (Taylor, 2007, p. 461). The world as a whole might be 'as furiously religious as it ever was, in some places more so than ever' (Berger, 1999, p. 2), but Europe remains 'an exceptional case' (Davie, 2002). Practical secularization is real. If the children of today's African immigrants become as practically secular as those of the ethnic groups around them, then in a few years' time statistics of religious practice might again fall off a cliff.

State secularization

Since their respective revolutions both France and the USA have been secular states, with their secularity enshrined in their constitutions. This doesn't mean that their citizens or their leaders aren't religious: they often are; but it does mean that there are no institutional connections between the government and any church or churches.

In England there is such a connection. (The situations of Scotland, Wales and Northern Ireland are different from England's, and different from each others'.) Twenty-six bishops sit by right in the House of Lords, the Archbishop of Canterbury crowns the monarch, and the Prime Minister appoints bishops – and even though our current Prime Minister has said he doesn't want to choose between names, it's the Crown Appointments Commission which sends him a name and they're not likely to send him one which he might not want. You can get married in a Church of England building without having to apply to a State registrar first, if you want to remove the pews from a listed church building then a church legal officer can give you permission (although this is largely because the Church's own system is more rigorous than the State's), and a Parliamentary committee has to agree to any rule changes the Church wants and they then become English law – which means that if the Parliamentary committee hadn't agreed to the ordination of women then they wouldn't have been ordained. Over the centuries there has been a good deal of secularization: no longer is the Church Vestry the parish council, and no longer is the Church the registrar of births, marriages and deaths: but the connections between State and Church which I've listed suggest that in many ways the State is not secularized.

Fewer than a million people now attend a Church of England service on an average Sunday, so can the Church still think of itself as some kind of representative of the spiritual aspect of the nation? For that is what the remaining vestiges of establishment suggest that it is. It's certainly difficult to see why the Government should think of the Church of England in such terms (Wootton, 2009). Religion is now plural. There are numerous Christian denominations, thousands of congregations which don't fit into denominations at all, and numerous other faiths. The London Borough of Greenwich can boast every major Christian denomination, black-led Pentecostal churches, independent evangelical churches, and active Muslim, Sikh, Hindu and Baha'i communities. (The few Jews in the borough have to go over the boundary: to Bromley if Reform, and to Catford if Orthodox.) Greenwich is not untypical of the nation as a whole. If asked to justify the Church of England's special relationship with the State, I don't try. In any case, we are now a secularized country, there is little enthusiasm for the establishment (Wootton, 2009) except among those bishops who sit in the House of Lords, and it really is time that we dispensed with the anachronism. Disestablishment would, of course, further secularize the State. While we might regret this, to secularize the State through disestablishment might enable the churches and other faith communities to work together more easily and might therefore desecularize society (Buchanan, 2003).

However, if either the Church of England disestablishes itself, or the Government disestablishes it, then we shall need to take great care not to dismantle the parish system. This is a precious gift which the Church of England offers to the nation, and we need to look after it (Torry, 2004, pp. 201–2). No longer can we assume that everyone living within the parish boundaries is somehow a church member, but we should try to ensure that everyone living or working within those boundaries feels welcome to the Church's services, and particularly to the occasional offices: baptisms, marriages, and funerals. Such a welcome is a distinctively Anglican way of being the Church, and we must continue to offer it, particularly if we don't want to contribute to yet more practical secularization.

One sense in which the State is secularized is that government at all levels has difficulty understanding churches and other faith communities (Davis et al, 2008, pp. 48–56). Religious 'illiteracy' is rife: but whose fault is that? I say that it's our fault, and that the resulting secularization is therefore our fault too. Religious and faith-based organizations ought to be aware how different they are from other organizations, including public sector ones (Torry, 2005, pp. 8, 177), and we ought therefore to be aware that we have an obligation to explain ourselves (Riordan, 2008; Torry, 2008). If faith communities are asking to work with central, regional or local government to tackle social problems, or government is asking religious organizations to help, then if government doesn't understand what religious organizations are like or how they work then the only people who can do anything about that are members of the religious organizations concerned. This really is up to us.

In many respects the State is secularized. We need to complete that process. At the same time we need to desecularize the State by communicating the nature of religion and of religious organizations, and we need to prevent the nation from becoming more secular than it is by churches remaining engaged with every aspect of life: in communities, society, and institutions.

Institutional secularization

> Underlying many of the most nuanced discussions is the idea
> that secularism [a term which here means the result of the pro-
> cess of secularization] entails basic social processes in which
> major societal institutions are differentiated from each other
> and no longer represent the same values or work together to
> provide an overall coherence to social life. (Bell, 1997, p. 198)

We have already discussed how religious and State organizations
are slowly drifting apart. The same is happening rather faster to
religious organizations and secular organizations generally. The
links between religious organizations and all other kinds of organization are not what they once were. When in subsequent
chapters we recount the ways in which industrial missions' relationships with industrial and commercial concerns have changed
since the Second World War, we shall find that the organizations
have become more distant from each other, and in particular that
representative personnel of the different kinds of organizations
no longer relate to each other so easily. The same goes for other
relationships between religious and secular organizations.

I use the term 'institutional secularization' advisedly because
here I'm not just talking about organizations. 'Institution' has a
wide variety of meanings. It means groups of people who work
together in a structured way in order to achieve some purpose
(which is what we mean by 'organization'), but it also means relatively stable arrangements of symbols and practices through which
people relate to each other: so both marriage and the economy are
institutions. Institutions generally are now more distant from religious institutions than they used to be, and an understanding of
this fact is one of the reasons for industrial mission's more recent
attempts to relate the Church to the economy as a whole.[7]

Time was when colleges had religious names and you had to
be a priest of the Church of England to be allowed to teach at
a university. Scientists, scientific institutions, and science itself,
are no longer as closely related to religious institutions and their
people as they once were (Bruce, 1992), the same goes for other

disciplines, and, in general, religious organizations and their representatives no longer provide the structure within which society's institutions function. The result is that 'subworlds' form (Berger, 1995, pp. 133, 137). If religious organizations are in one subworld, and industrial organizations are in another, then people working in industry will find it difficult to understand why they should have a workplace chaplain around, and churches will wonder why they're paying for chaplains to work in industry.

Bryan Wilson puts it like this:

> The boards of large impersonally organized corporations find a place on their agenda for market research, but one may safely speculate that none of them accord time to the discussion of the religious implications of business activity'. (Wilson, 1982, p. 39)

This isn't entirely true, of course: but it is generally true that people now rarely think religion to be relevant to institutional activity. This institutional secularization is likely to reduce religious practice, and declining religious practice will create more institutional secularization. Some of the men and women sitting round the boardroom table might be Christians, or they might belong to some other faith community, but institutionally they are secularized by a 'process by which religious institutions, actions and consciousness lose their social significance' (Wilson, 1982, p. 150). The 'social space' which the board members inhabit has been secularized, so their personal religious commitments become irrelevant (Wilson, 1976, p. 6).

Organizations, the economy, marriage and other such social arrangements are important institutions, but perhaps the most significant institution today is 'the city', meaning both a built environment and London's financial and commercial centre. All of this is now secular (Cox, 1968), and many denominations, both in the United States and here, have fled to the suburbs (Winter, 1961). (Perhaps the Church of England would have done so too if it hadn't been chained to every square inch of the country by its parochial system.) Just as the distancing of the Church and its faith from other institutions is an important kind of secularization, so the Church's distancing of itself from the city is a serious secularization of our society. Urban mission and such publications as *Faith in the City* (Church of England, 1985) are in this context important examples of desecularization

Religion isn't just a matter of individual belief. It is a social institution, so institutional secularization matters at least as much as the desacralization and practical secularization discussed above (Wilson, 1966, p. xviii). In fact, it matters more. Institutional secularization is deeper than the secularization of individual belief and practice, so it's more important than individuals no longer going to church. Because we collect statistics about individual belief and practice and not about institutional relationships between religion and society's institutions, the statistics don't represent the full seriousness of secularization, and therefore secularization is deeper than we think.

In his *Church and People in an Industrial City* Ted Wickham showed that the Church of England parish was in no position to relate to twentieth-century industry (Wickham, 1957, p. 264 and Appendix IV). What he failed to see was that increasing secularization would make it difficult for the Church to create any institutional linkages between religious institutions and industrial and commercial institutions: difficult, but not impossible, as our history of workplace chaplaincy will show.

A 'drawing apart and declining integration of religious and secular institutions and their personnel' (Torry, 2005, p. 51) is probably the least studied, least tackled and most significant kind of secularization. It is therefore imperative that the Church should put as much energy as it can into building bridges across the gulf: but, as we shall see in our next type of secularization, while the church might be able to build bridges between itself and other kinds of organization, it might itself be so secularized that what flows across the bridge is no longer the Christian Faith.

Religious secularization

This subtitle looks like a contradiction in terms, but it isn't. It is possible for religion itself to be secularized: to lose its sense of providence, of the sacred, of the transcendent, and to cease to have theological ideas at its heart. Religion can cease to be about God.

Charles Taylor, in his *A Secular Age*, shows how religion became secularized in the eighteenth century. 'Reason' became the criterion for truth in religion as in much else; and just as scientists such as Isaac Newton studied the world in order to discover truth, so churchmen encouraged Christians to study Nature in order to find out about God (Taylor, 2007, pp. 221–69): a God reasonable and distant and no longer the God of the Christian Faith.

A large part of the problem is that religious organizations are being secularized. Religious organizations such as congregations are voluntary organizations, so in many ways they are like other voluntary organizations; but they also have characteristics all their own. Their purpose and their main activity is worship (Torry, 2005, pp. 70–1), at their heart is a mystery represented by words and actions, it's rarely clear who are and who aren't members (is an atheist who comes every week a member?), (Torry, 2005, pp. 131–2), and the clergy are unique: they preside at worship, chair Church Council meetings, belong to the congregation, manage staff, and are both trustees and paid staff members (Torry, 2005, pp. 146–7). The most important difference between religious and other voluntary organizations is that in a religious organization the final authority is God: an authority outside the organization and therefore one to which anyone can appeal. This means that no one part of a religious organization can control any other part of it (Torry, 2005, p. 177). If a religious organization loses any of these special characteristics then it's no longer unambiguously a religious organization. It will be more secular.

Much of Edward Norman's *Secularization* (Norman, 2002) is about the secularization of the Church. Fewer churchgoers believe that miracles occur (and this includes the clergy) (Norman, 2002, p. 67), so theology is now more secular; churchgoers (including the clergy) now tend to define morality for themselves rather than submit to ecclesiastical authority (Norman, 2002, p. 78); most churches no longer attempt to define doctrine (Norman, 2002, pp. 98–9); and 'the English churches – all of them in some degree –

are being infiltrated by secular ideas, and authentic adhesion to doctrine is becoming displaced by modern secular ethicism' (Norman, 2002, p. 101). Norman is particularly scathing about the 'liberal arts' approach to theological education for the clergy (Norman, 2002, p. 148). Some of Norman's comments are fair, but not all of them; and in particular he doesn't recognise that the individual religious conscience has always had a part to play in the authority structure of the Church. He would have had a better case if he had touched on a few organizational aspects of religious organizations. Denominations (including the Roman Catholic Church and the Church of England) are now run as bureaucracies: a secular import. Congregations might maintain the distinctive characteristics of religious organizations, but because their denominations function as secular bureaucracies congregations can't avoid being bureaucratised. To take an example: bishops and similar office holders increasingly see themselves as line managers, which means that the clergy see themselves as managed: a secular and not a religious organizational characteristic.

Denominations aim at survival (of course). They therefore tend to abandon poorer urban areas, where congregations cost money and absorb human resources and don't contribute much of either to the wider church; and they head for the wealthier suburbs, where congregations contribute skilled people and money to central denominational and other activities (Winter, 1961). If denominations have parish structures to maintain and therefore can't escape inner and difficult urban areas for the more comfortable suburbs, then they concentrate ministerial resources where the wealth is.[8] Again, a secular rather than a religious strategy.

Faith-based organizations aren't quite the same as religious organizations. They are organizations which are related to religious traditions but where the main purpose is not religion: for instance, church schools, church-connected development charities, and housing associations established by churches. These are even more likely to get secularized than religious organizations (Torry, 2005, pp. 17–18). Any organization which relates to another organization becomes like it to some extent (DiMaggio and Powell, 1983), so if a faith-based organization draws its staff

from secular training courses, obtains funding from secular bodies, and a secular government regulates it, then that organization
will become progressively secular. If there are sufficiently strong
institutional links to a religious organization then it might remain
'attached', but if not then it will 'wander', which is why many
church-founded housing associations are now indistinguishable
from other housing associations (Torry, 2008, pp. 17–19).

During the 1970s the Church of England's parish boundaries
across Sunderland were dissolved and a single team ministry was
established to minister to the churches. Michael Northcott, in his
study of Sunderland's churches,[9] found that the change had resulted in a secularized theology and secularized structures reinforcing each other. The boundary changes were a genuine attempt
to relate the Church to the secular world, but the result was a
more secularized Church (Northcott, 1983, p. 189).

If the Church is becoming more secular then this isn't just a
problem for itself. It will also mean that the Church will have less
to offer to society (Chaves, 1993; Bell, 1997, p. 199). The same
goes for workplace chaplaincies. If they become too secularized
then they will have nothing distinctive to offer to the organizations in which they work.

Two questions which we might wish to keep in mind as we
study the history of workplace chaplains are these:

1 Are industrial missions religious organizations or are they faith-
  based organizations?
2 Are they attached or have they wandered? – for if they have
  been secularized by their relationships with secular organizations then what distinctive message or way of life do they have
  to offer?

Secularization of individual beliefs

If you no longer believe that there is a God then your beliefs are
secular. I have listed this kind of secularization last because there
isn't much of it. Belief in God, in life after death, in heaven and in

sin are holding up quite well, in Europe as well as elsewhere. In 2000, 71.6% of the population in Great Britain believed in God (in the sense that they believed that he exists, rather than that they put their trust in him), 58.3% believed in life after death, 55.8% in heaven, and 66.9% in sin. Only 35.3% believed in hell.[10] In 2001 the number of people who declared themselves to be 'Christian' on their census forms was very similar to the number of people who believed in God the year before. Because quite a lot of the population now belong to other religions, and we can assume that most of those believe in God, we must conclude that somewhere between 5% and 10% of those who declare themselves to be Christians don't believe in God, which is interesting.

There are lots of good things in the statistics. More people believe in God in Portugal (96.4%) than in Great Britain (71.6%), but more people believe in life after death in Great Britain (58.3%) than in Portugal (47.3%). This suggests that individual religious beliefs are highly susceptible to cultural, economic and other influences. What we would really like to know is how much individual religious belief influences and is influenced by the other seven secularizations in our list. I suspect not much.

Conclusions

We have already discovered some connections between our eight kinds of secularization. My theory is that they are all connected to each other to some extent, but that we can't be sure precisely how they influence each other. For instance: does a decline in churchgoing lead to a loss of religious belief, or is it the other way round? Probably both. And is it because some of the directors round the boardroom table are no longer active believers that a greater distance has opened up between the company and religious organizations, or does a greater distance between religious and other organizations cause a decline in individual belief and practice? Again, probably both. If so, then within all of these relationships between different kinds of secularization there is going to be mutual reinforcement. Mutual reinforcement between eight different kinds of secularization is going to be a difficult web to untangle. As with all such tangled webs, to do something about one kind of secularization might inadvertently contribute to a deepening of another kind. For instance: an increase in private belief and practice will remain precisely that: private; and the intransigence of the rest of the complex secular net will make such private religion even more defensive, sectarian, and private, thus distancing religious organizations further from secular organizations. This will in turn make churches and denominations even more sectarian than they are now.[11]

In 1969 David Martin suggested that the concept of secularization cannot be defined in a unitary manner (Martin, 1969, p. 4) and that a variety of secularizations occur. 'Secularization' includes 'a large number of discrete elements loosely put together in an intellectual hold-all' (Martin, 1969, pp. 2, 4, 16, 57). By 1978 he had to some extent changed his mind and felt able to write *A General Theory of Secularization* in which he listed factors which lead to secularization: urbanisation, industrialization, geographical and social mobility, and a differentiated society: 'In the modern situation . . . all organic solidarities, whether of nation or religion or class, are partly undermined,' leading to an 'apathy which retires from explicit institutional religion' (Martin, 1978, pp. 3, 83, 92). Similarly, our individual lives are differentiated, which means that we can keep different aspects of our lives separate from each other. We might be religious, but our religion needn't affect the rest of what we do. Here secularization can therefore be thought of as a single complex phenomenon with a variety of causes.

Whether we think of secularization as a unitary but complex phenomenon, or as a bundle of different secularizations, as I have done; and whether we think of secularization's causes as consistent and timeless or as different in every different time and place (Cox, 1982), we can, I believe, continue to use 'secularization' as both the name of a category of different secularizations and as an 'umbrella term' (Chadwick, 1975, p. 266) or 'hold-all' (Martin, 1969, p. 2, 4, 16, 57).[12]

But what should be our attitude to it? Is secularization a problem? Should we try to tackle the problem? If so: given the mutually reinforcing relationships between the different aspects of secularization, desecularization is unlikely to succeed. So should we give in to it? No. If we are religious believers then to give in to secularization would be to deny who we are; and for any of us to give in to secularization would deprive society of an important part of its creative diversity.

We might not be able to defeat secularization, but we can at least build a few bridges: between religion and the secular, and between religious organizations and secular organizations. If greater connectivity can be achieved then both the religious and the secular will benefit, provided that both remain what they are. It is of course legitimate to hope that in this process religious truth and religious ways of life might influence and sometimes change people and institutions in the secular world, and that religious people and institutions might discover God's activity in the world; but whether or not these things happen, what matters is connectivity: the building of bridges between Christian Faith and every aspect of a complex secularization. It is to that task that industrial mission has committed itself.

Notes

1 For a discussion on whether secularization is a 'Master Narrative or Several Stories' see Martin, 2005, ch.9.

2 For broader discussion of the distancing of religious and scientific discourses from each other see Bruce, 1992; Martin, 1969; Martin, 1978.

3 Martin, 2005, pp. 24–25. He is referring to the human sciences, but the same applies to the natural sciences too.

4 The last line is 'God is a DJ'. Faithless, *God is a DJ*, written by Maxi Jazz, Rollo, Sister Bliss and Jamie Catto, published by Cheeky Records, 1998.

5 cf. Wickham, 1957, pp. 212–13. Wickham here suggests that the increasing variety of activities available on Sundays, and the loss of social habits occasioned by moving house – something which was happening rather more after the First World War – were factors in the decline of churchgoing during the 1930s. He could have written almost the same paragraph today.

6 See Snape, 2003. Snape has shown here how in the eighteenth century social changes relating to industrialization and a thriving Methodism

revealed the existing poor state of much of the Church of England. Pluralism and social mobility seem to be having a similar effect in the Church of England today.

7 See chapters 8 and 9.

8 In the Charlton Deanery of the Church of England there is now a single stipendiary priest for a benefice containing two large parishes, one of which is among the ten most deprived in the diocese, whereas nearby there are two small but wealthier parishes each with their own full-time priest.

9 See chapter 6.

10 Data from the European Values Study, University of Tilburg, quoted in Davie 2002, p. 7.

11 On church, denomination and sect see Troeltsch, Ernst, 1911, *The Social Teaching of the Christian Churches*, vol. I, reprinted London: Allen and Unwin, 1931; Niebuhr, H. Richard, 1929, *The Social Sources of Denominationalism*, reprinted Gloucester, Massachusetts: Peter Smith, 1987.

12 The term 'hold-all' is a good description of Martin's most recent book on the subject, Martin, 2005.

2

Navvies and Soldiers: The early evolution of workplace chaplaincy

It is always rather difficult to know where to start a history. Should I start with the beginnings of industrial mission in Scotland, South London and Sheffield during the Second World War? Or with the Industrial Christian Fellowship, founded in 1919? (After all, it has 'industry' in its name). Or with the Navvy Mission, working among the men who built the railways?

No: I shall start with Henry VIII's navy.

Armed forces chaplains

The first priest to travel on a ship for the good of its sailors is lost in history, but we know that chaplains travelled with Henry VIII's navy and that in the seventeenth century Samuel Pepys had a hand in regulating both the chaplains and their terms and conditions. One of the most famous naval chaplains was a Dr Scott, the chaplain of the 'Victory', who cared for the dying Nelson and for Nelson's body as the country mourned.[1] Relationships between the navy and its chaplains were often cordial, but not always. Here is an exchange from William Golding's admittedly fictional account of an eighteenth century sea journey:

'A chaplain, Sir? We have no chaplain!'
'Believe me, I have seen him.'
'No, sir.'
'But law requires one aboard every ship of the line, does it not?'
'Captain Anderson would wish to avoid it; and since parsons

are in as short supply as surgeons it is as easy to avoid the one as it is difficult to procure the other.'

'Come, come, Mr. Cumbershum! Are not seamen notoriously superstitious? Do you not require the occasional invocation of Mumbo Jumbo?'

'Captain Anderson does not, sir. Nor did the great Captain Cook, I would have you know. He was a notable atheist and would as soon have taken the plague into his ship as a parson.' (Golding, 1980, p. 21)

Army chaplains have a similar history. The armies of ancient civilisations took priests into battle with them, army chaplains were common in the time of Henry VIII, and the seventeenth century saw the profession regulated. By the twentieth century chaplains of various denominations were serving in every regiment, caring for the spiritual needs of soldiers of all ranks.[2]

From the point of view of the regiments, ships, hospitals, workhouses and prisons in which they served, chaplains were a recognition of a religious aspect of society and of the established position of the Church of England; but from the Church's side they were simply an extension of the parochial system. In a parish the priest cares for everyone within its boundaries: on a ship the priest cares for everyone on board. If a hospital or a workhouse was located in a parish, and no other provision had been made, then of course the parish priest would visit the inmates: or, at least, there was a general expectation that he would. Often other provision *was* made. In 1695 the merchant John Morden founded Morden College, a quadrangle of almshouses on Blackheath in South East London. He not only built a chapel for the residents but also provided for a chaplain to cater for their spiritual needs.

In hospitals, prisons, workhouses and almshouses the chaplain was there to care for people served by those institutions. The chaplain might also have cared for people who worked for the institution, but that would have been a secondary responsibility. The exception has always been forces chaplains. Army and naval chaplains are there for everyone who belongs to the ship or regiment. The forces chaplain is therefore the nearest early equivalent to a workplace chaplain.

Preachers and groups: John Wesley and Methodism's class meetings

During the eighteenth century working people in urban areas found it remarkably hard to go to their parish church. The number of parishes hadn't expanded with the growing urban areas, the distribution of clergy remained largely as it had been in a previously rural era, and many families couldn't afford the pew rents (Wickham, 1957, pp. 42–4). Sadly, nonconformist chapels also turned to pew rents to raise funds, making it difficult or impossible for people on low incomes to attend.

John Wesley never intended to start a church, but his conversion experience inspired him to preach the gospel wherever people needed to hear it. They weren't in the churches, so Wesley preached in homes and in hired rooms. He was by no means the first itinerant preacher of the time. Whitefield was already preaching in the open air to miners at Kingswood Chase near to Bristol, and it was he who persuaded Wesley to come to preach there as well. He reluctantly agreed (Davies, 1963, pp. 67–9). (On Thursday 14th June 1739 Wesley preached on Blackheath in the presence of George Whitefield, whose pitch it usually was. The rise in the ground is still called 'Whitefield's Mount' (Wesley undated, entry for 14th June 1739)).

The Church of England was an alien institution to the working class of Wesley's day. Its links to the state, its identification with the locally powerful, and its welfare functions, made it rather less than welcoming. Open air preaching, and even more the religious societies which Wesley established, provided a place where men and women could grow into Christian discipleship. Two of the Bristol societies were soon too big for their members' homes, so a 'Society Room' was built. This was soon too small, and the first class meeting was founded to help its members to raise money to extend the building. The class meetings soon multiplied and added Bible study, prayer and discussion to their original fundraising function (Davies,

1963, pp. 72–73). The class meetings soon became Methodism's way of caring for its growing membership and of developing leadership skills among its members. 'There could be no better way to come to a sure, thorough knowledge of each person, than to divide them into classes.' (Wesley undated, entry for 25th April 1742) The class leaders were laypeople, and Ted Wickham, who established a similar system of groups among Sheffield's steel workers during the 1940s, looked back to Methodism's class meetings as his model (Wickham, 1947, pp. 266–72): 'The subdivided structure is required not only for missionary engagement within mammoth estranged populations, but as a permanent structural element in a [Church] set in the highly populated society' (Wickham, 1957, p. 272).

Wesley and his preachers and class leaders were not workplace chaplains, but they were doing then what many workplace chaplains have done since, and for the same reason: the Church needed to relate to people in ways appropriate to them.

Scripture readers and moral welfare: The Navvy Mission

Just as Wesley went to where the workers were, so did the Navvy Mission. By the 1870s Britain's canal-building era was over, and navvies ('navigators') had already built much of the railway network; but large gangs of men were still moving from place to place to extend the system and to build reservoirs, sewage plants, and docks. When navvies arrived in an area there was rarely sufficient accommodation, so they would build a shanty town. Their wives and children would often join them.

Some of the construction companies employed their own chaplains, but often it was the local clergy who did what they could. A Yorkshire vicar, Lewis Moule Evans, held services for a group of navvies working in his parish and raised money to build recreation huts for them and to provide them with a library. Local residents were always pleased to support any charitable endeavour which might reduce the damage which the navvies did to local property and morals, and when in 1877 Evans and a number of clergy, landowners, contractors and women with private means founded the Navvy Mission, the great and the good nationally contributed funds and the great and the good locally were happy to be drafted onto the local committees of the 'new machinery' which mission among the navvies required (Coleman, 1968, pp. 170–8; Lurkings, 1981, pp. 23–5).

The Mission employed working class men as 'missionaries', and women with independent means would sometimes volunteer to work among the women and children. The missionaries organized religious services and meetings, provided financial support for the neediest families, and ran libraries, night schools, recreation huts, and Sunday Schools. The first stated aim was 'to promote the spiritual welfare of navvies,'[3] and the others related to welfare more generally. Scripture readers and missionaries were therefore the priority, and statistics were gathered on attendance at services, the number of huts and homes visited, and numbers at Sunday schools and other events (Lurkings, 1981, pp. 26–7; Coleman, 1968, pp. 176–7). As often happens with such initially evangelistic exercises, the missionaries' and local committees' experience of the lives of navvies and their families led them into a deeper concern for their economic and social welfare. From the beginning, the Mission raised awareness of the importance of the navvies' work in an attempt to reduce widespread prejudice against them and to encourage contractors to provide better accommodation for their families (Lurkings, 1981, pp. 31–3).

By 1885, 24 missionaries were employed serving 27 construction sites; by 1891 there were 40 missionaries and scripture readers; and then after 1904 decline set in as the number of railway and other construction projects declined. In 1914 many navvies joined the army, or the labour gangs building the infrastructure of war in France and Belgium, or the gangs building fortifications at home. Some of the missionaries followed them, effectively becoming army and factory chaplains: a prelude to the future history of industrial mission (Lurkings, 1981, pp. 29–30, 35–6).

Clergy in the trenches: chaplains during the First World War

Philip ('Tubby') Clayton was a curate in Portsea at the beginning of the First World War, and young men he had prepared for confirmation were dying both in France and on the sea. He volunteered to go as a chaplain, and his vicar, Cyril Garbett, eventually gave permission (Harcourt, 1953, pp. 51–2). In 1915 Clayton found himself as chaplain to a temporary hospital on the French coast and was horrified at the effects of war on soldiers' bodies and minds, and particularly horrified when wounded men were sent back to the trenches. By the Autumn he was in Belgium, close to the front line. The senior chaplain there, Neville Talbot, rented a house at Poperinghe which they turned into a welcoming home from home for soldiers going to or from the front. A notice on the door of the 'Chaplain's Room' said 'All rank abandon, ye who enter here' (Harcourt, 1953, p. 68). Seven-hundred men would sometimes pack themselves into 'Talbot House': 'Toc H' to Morse code signallers. The town was often shelled and bombed, but the house survived: sadly, not many of the soldiers who passed through it did.

Clayton's parish was now the trenches, and he would hold services of Holy Communion there with the shells dropping around the congregation. He was not one of the hundred or so chaplains killed during the war, but he could well have been. Just as pastoral care and worship were at the heart of Clayton's ministry in the trenches, so they were at the heart of his work at Talbot House, and particularly in the 'Upper Room', the chapel at the top of the house. On Easter Day 1916 he held ten packed Holy Communion services there, one after the other (Harcourt, 1953, pp. 77–84).

During the war several hundred soldiers had vowed that if they survived then they would dedicate their lives to Christ and to his Church. Clayton founded a college, first in France and then in the old Knutsford prison, to prepare them to enter universities and theological colleges: still the only route to ordination (Harcout, 1953, pp. 93–4, 109–17). Then he founded Toc H, a series of hostels in London and elsewhere designed to recapture the fellowship of Talbot House. In 1925 Clayton became Vicar of All Hallows-by-the-Tower. This became the Guild Church of the now international Toc H movement (Harcourt, 1953, pp. 160–5). The church behaved rather like Talbot House, but instead of soldiers it was city workers who came in their hundreds to early morning

Holy Communion services, for individual prayer during the day, and to eat their packed lunches in the nave. Clayton and his colleagues preached regularly in the open air on Tower Hill.

During the Second World War Clayton, although now into his mid-50s, volunteered as a naval chaplain. All Hallows was bombed but continued to function from the undercroft (Harcourt, 1953, pp. 230–9). After the war the building was restored, Clayton eventually retired, and the new Vicar of All Hallows was Colin Cuttell – but that's for the next chapter.

A second First World War chaplain who knew that he needed to be in the trenches with the soldiers was Geoffrey Studdert Kennedy, known as Woodbine Willy because of his habit of handing out Woodbine cigarettes wherever he went. He was the nearest the Church had to a Siegfried Sassoon or a Wilfred Owen:

> For the voice of the Lord, as I 'ears it now,
> Is the voice of my pals what bled,
> And the call of my country's God to me
> Is the call of my country's dead. (Studdert Kennedy, 1941, p. 135)

For Studdert Kennedy God was a 'comrade God', a 'suffering God' (Studdert Kennedy, 1941, pp. 11, 30):

> Father, if He, the Christ, were thy Revealer,
> Truly the First Begotten of the Lord,
> Then must Thou be a Suff'rer and a Healer,
> Pierced to the heart by the sorrow of the sword. (Studdert Kennedy, 1941, p. 13)

Missions and reports: The National Mission and the Archbishop's Commission

During the First World War Clayton, Studdert Kennedy and many other chaplains had learnt that the Church and its Faith were a foreign land to the men in the trenches. They could build temporary bridges, but mutual incomprehension was still the normal experience (Wilkinson, 1978, pp. 120, 161). The Church of England's councils were not blind to the Church's estrangement from the majority of people, and in 1916 the Archbishops called a 'National Mission of Repentance and Hope . . . to call the men and women of England to earnest and honest repentance . . . to claim that in the Living Christ, in the loyal acceptance of Him as the Lord of all life, individual and social . . . lies the one sure hope' (Lloyd, 1946, p. 239). Studdert Kennedy took the Mission's message to soldiers at the front, archbishops and bishops supported and led the mission at home, and in each diocese sermons were given and meetings were held. Alan Wilkinson comments that 'the remarkable thing is not the comparative lack of success of the National Mission . . . but that it should have been mounted at all' (Wilkinson, 1978, p. 71). It made little difference to anything, but after it the Archbishop of Canterbury appointed five Committees of Inquiry, the task of the fifth being 'to consider and report upon ways in which the Church may best commend the teaching of Christ to those who are seeking to solve the problems of industrial life' (Church of England, 1918). The committee recognized the Church's subservience to 'the possessing, employing, and governing classes', and asked for a 'living wage', an end to casual labour, the prevention of unemployment, an end to the use of the term 'hands' as a description of workers, the training for ordination of men from the working classes, and for the clergy to be trained in economic and social science and in the realities of industry (Church of England, 1918, pp. ix, 54, 83, 161). These were radical suggestions from a generally conservative Church.

Evangelism and reconciliation: the Industrial Christian Fellowship

The Christian Social Union was founded in 1889 to promote the social aspects of the gospel in the form of a mild socialism, and in 1919 this rather catholic and intellectual organization (Wilkinson, 1978, p. 240; Northcott, 1989, p. 37; Edwards, 1984, p. 173–5) merged with the Navvy Mission to form the Industrial Christian

Fellowship (ICF). There were two aims: first evangelism, and second 'reconciliation' between the two sides of industry (Wilkinson, 1986, p. 140). The Fellowship employed lay agents, as the Navvy Mission had done; each area had a clerical director; and the message was individual conversion and social justice. The evangelistic method was 'crusades', mainly open air preaching with 'Christ the Lord of all life' as its theme (Miller and Fletcher, 1930, p. 34); and the content of the social justice agenda was the Fifth Committee of Inquiry's report. The ICF recruited Geoffrey Studdert Kennedy. Its radical individual challenge and its call for justice within a conservative social framework matched well his own interests, and his well-known wartime rapport with soldiers made him a popular speaker (Studdert-Kennedy, 1982, p. 166; Wilkinson, 1978, p. 283). The agents and preachers offered nothing too radical, largely because the ICF needed the financial support of conservative laity and the agreement of employers to hold meetings in their factories. More radical in their effects were the correspondence courses for workers. These helped to create a more informed working class. Another important achievement was the establishment of the annual Industrial Sunday. This helped to keep the industrial world on the Church's agenda and constantly reminded the Church of its alienation from that world (Studdert-Kennedy, 1982, p. 179).

The padre in the Second World War

The Second World War was very different from the First, but again chaplains travelled with their squadrons, battalions and ships to minister the sacraments and to provide pastoral care. There were no trenches, but still of course chaplains died with the men they served, as did clergy who remained in their urban parishes as the bombs fell. No Second World War chaplain became a household name, as Clayton and Studdert Kennedy had done, but there were still heroes among the chaplains, especially in prisoner of war camps and as the allied armies drove the German army out of France and Belgium after the Normandy landings. Soldiers frequently resented having to attend church parade, but they came to know the 'padre' as someone accessible who would do what he could for the men (Wilkinson, 1986, p. 292–5).

Important for our story are the chaplains appointed to arms factories in Britain. Each factory had a huge workforce, often as large as the population of a substantial urban parish, and the workers were often far from home. Each denomination appointed a chaplain to each factory (Bloy, 2001, p. 10), and in the Church of England the bishop would appoint the vicar or curate of the parish in which the factory was located. Thus Ted Wickham, Curate in Charge of the Parish of Swynnerton in Staffordshire, became chaplain of the Royal Ordnance Factory there. The shop floor was regarded as too dangerous for chaplains, so Wickham held services and organized discussion groups in the hostels in which the workers lived (Bloy, 2001, pp. 33–6).

Conclusions

As we relate the history of modern industrial mission we shall find numerous connections with the history recounted in this chapter: a history in which the Church came to understand both the practical secularization of the country's population and its own alienation from working people. Navvy Mission evangelists and army padres now understood that you can't separate someone's spiritual welfare from their economic and social situation, but as yet the Church had little understanding that secularization is a diverse problem which requires a suitably diverse response.

The Church's strategy had two related elements: evangelism of individuals by lay and clerical evangelists, and the extension into new contexts of a parochial pastoral ministry of sacrament and welfare. The theology was conservative, but Studdert Kennedy's poetry hinted at some new directions. Social comment and activity were also conservative, though the recommendations of the Archbishop's Fifth Committee of Inquiry looked as if they might go somewhere new. More new action and ideas would soon emerge.

An uncanonical epilogue: two comparisons

Before anyone leaves this chapter with the impression that I have outlined the precursors of modern workplace chaplaincy, two things need to be said:

The first is that the Navvy Mission, First World War chaplains, and the Industrial Christian Fellowship, have become a 'canon', an approved list of precursors to the equally canonical duo which constitute the beginnings of the modern industrial mission movement: the South London Industrial Mission and the Sheffield Industrial Mission. I say this because the Navvy Mission, army chaplains and the ICF are listed together as the movement's precursors in dissertations, theses and books on individual industrial missions (Lurkings, 1981; Torry, 1990), on the movement as a whole, and on aspects of the movement (Erlander, 1991; Reindorp, 2000). Such canons develop where authors find connections: the same people are involved in different organizations, the same ideas are found in later as well as in earlier movements, and similar activity is discovered in the different organizations. Sometimes we can legitimately conclude that one historical event has caused another, but sometimes not.

The problem with such canons is that a wide variety of people, situations and events will have influenced the activity, ideas and personnel of later movements, and that many of these precursors won't be listed in the canon. In our case there is good reason for the development of the canon. We shall discover numerous connections between the events which I have recounted in this chapter and the history of industrial mission after the Second World War, not least among the people involved. However, other previous events might be relevant too.

In 1936 Chelmsford Cathedral magazine mentioned the 'third Marconi Service', organized for workers at the Marconi electronics factory in the city, suggesting that such events had been taking place since 1934. By 1937 the service had developed into a joint service for three employers. The year 1938 also saw a service to celebrate the 60th anniversary of a local company: 600 people attended. This development was in addition to the ICF-sponsored

Industry Sunday. Clearly good relationships existed between the Cathedral and local industry, but we are not told the content of such involvement (Youings, 2008, p. 37). What is particularly interesting is that the magazine accounts don't suggest that anything particularly unusual was going on. There is clearly a history of industry services, and of related relationships between industry and the Church, waiting to be written: a history which would shed light on the modern industrial mission movement.

The second non-canonical prehistory is industrial mission in Scotland. As I mention in my introduction, this already has a written history of its own (Ross, 1997): but what needs to be said here is that Scotland already had a substantial number of industrial chaplains by the time industrial missions in Sheffield and South London had two each. In the early days of the Second World War Church of Scotland sisters worked among the women who arrived from Newfoundland to work for forestry units. The sisters organized leisure activities for the women, and generally a home from home. In 1942 the Church's Home Board recognised the need to undertake ministry and mission in industry, and it appointed a minister, William Bodin, to 'promote and develop the work of relating the Church to industry and to arrange industrial chaplaincies'. The chaplains were mainly ministers visiting local factories (Ross, 1997, pp. 7–8). By 1946 there were 230 of them. Given the extent of this Scottish initiative it is highly likely that it influenced developments in South London and Sheffield. Also in 1942, Ian Fraser, a minister, took work as a labourer in a paper mill in order to be a 'labourer-pastor', predating the French worker priest movement and the English priest workers.

To some extent both English and Scottish industrial missions were taking ideas from their milieu. Scottish Industrial Mission's magazine was called 'The Bridgehead', a term soon to be used by the South London Industrial Mission to describe its work and one of its own publications. The most likely explanation for the coincidence is that a term frequently employed during the war was thought relevant in both places. However, Scotland isn't far from England, and direct influence of Scotland on England in relation both to this detail and to industrial mission as a whole is really quite likely. Scotland's earlier and more numerous industrial chaplains really ought to be part of the canon of precursors for English industrial mission. I commend Donald Ross's book to my readers.

One final uncanonical note: there were lots of chaplains working in munitions factories, they weren't all Anglicans, and many of them regarded what they were doing as something a bit more than individual pastoral work. In 1941, C. H. Cleal, a Baptist, was visiting factories in Swindon. His aim was to apply Christian principles to industrial life, to call men to return to God, to hold services on industrial premises, to gather Christians working in industry, and to organize discussion groups for enquirers. If a factory was near to the church then it was the minister's concern (Cleal, 1945; Hackett, 1977, pp. 37–9; Elwyn, 1966). This was a year before Cuthbert Bardsley visited the air raid shelters at Siemens Brothers, and three years before Leslie Hunter invited Ted Wickham to visit steel mills in Sheffield.

Clearly further research is required to uncover more of the earliest history of industrial chaplaincy in Britain and to explore the causal links between the different industrial mission initiatives in Scotland and England during the early 1940s.

To the history of one of these English initiatives we now turn.

Notes

1 http://www.royalnavy.mod.uk/training-and-people/rn-life/religion-in-the-navy/about-us/a-history-of-naval-chaplaincy-service, accessed 11/8/09.

2 http://www.bbc.co.uk/religion/religions/christianity/priests/armychaplains_2.shtml, accessed 12/8/09.

3 The Mission's first annual report, quoted in Lurkings, 1981, p. 25.

3

Over the Bridge: South London during and after the Second World War

Into the factories

During 1940 heavy bombing reduced much of South London to rubble. German bombers targeted docks, railways and the Woolwich Arsenal, so worst hit was the south bank of the Thames. Woolwich was at the heart of the devastation, and when Cuthbert Bardsley arrived as the new vicar of the parish he often found himself in the air raid shelters, both for his own safety and because that's where his parishioners were. Believing that people who worked in the parish were as much the vicar's concern as those who lived in it, he began to visit the air raid shelters at Siemens Brothers, an engineering factory. He established a Quiet Room, and in 1942 regular lunch-time services began (Cuttell, 1962, pp. 11–12). Bardsley saw the task in the same way that armed forces chaplains saw theirs: visiting the sick, keeping men in touch with their families when they were at work during air raids, and conducting services. He was the 'padre' (Coggan, 1989, pp. 64–6).

In 1944 Bardsley moved to Southwark Cathedral as its new provost. The bombing had blown out the windows, but a small group of people had maintained regular services and were spending their nights in the cathedral fire-watching. Just before he started his new post, Bardsley met Colin Cuttell in Oxford Street during an air raid. They had known each other 15 years previously at All Hallows-by-the-Tower when Bardsley had been a curate and Cuttell a choir boy (Torry, 1990, p. 68).

Cuttell was now ordained and was on leave from the Church in Canada. Bardsley offered him a job as an industrial missioner. (The process for making such appointments is now just slightly different.) Cuttell moved into the vicarage of St Michael's, Lant Street, in the Cathedral parish, and joined Bardsley on his visits to Siemens Brothers. Hays Wharf was already housing the provost's office on the seventh floor, and the office next door became Cuttell's and remained the base for industrial mission in South London for the next 20 years.

Bardsley was soon spending more time on Cathedral rebuilding and administration, so Cuttell took over the pastoral work at Siemens Brothers, co-operating with the welfare department and the medical officer in the same way as any forces chaplain would do. He visited the vast site weekly, organized Christmas carol services, and included a regular padre's letter in the Cathedral's professionally-printed magazine, *Over the Bridge*, which he distributed among the company's 5,000 employees. The 1946 letter told the factory's workers: 'The world needs a moral code . . . we must have a living faith in God behind this moral code. Many of us turned to prayer when things were difficult; let us not forget prayer when things may appear, on the surface, to be easier.' (Torry, 1990, p. 69)

Cuttell tackled the offices, shops, vegetable market and small printing and engineering firms in the Cathedral parish in the same way that any parish priest would have tackled them: by dropping in with a pile of *Over the Bridge* in his hand. He got himself elected chaplain of the local British Legion branch, which got him into dockyard canteens where he would join the dockers during their often quite extended breaks. Among the large companies along the south bank of the Thames, though, Siemens remained unique in the access which it gave to a member of the clergy. The war was now over, it was again difficult for the Church to relate to industrial workforces, and it was becoming more difficult for the clergy to gain access to factories. Cuttell's strategy was to network. (I'm sure that he would have used this modern term had he known it.) Foremen and departmental managers in one factory would know foremen and managers in another, and Cuttell would ask for introductions, make friends, and begin to visit companies without asking for the site management's permission. He knew that if he had asked there would have been 'refusal or delay' (Correspondence from Colin Cuttell, quoted in Torry, 1990, p. 69). His strategy meant that firms found him on the premises (this was before swipe cards) and by then both junior management and trade union officers had got to know him and it was difficult to ask him to leave. An additional reason for managers not wishing him to leave was that Cuttell was making himself useful. Personnel officers had got to know him and they would phone to ask for his help with bereavement counselling (though they didn't call it that then) and 'moral problems' (Torry, 1990, p. 69). *Over the Bridge* was another reason for companies not wishing to remove Cuttell. Managers would have read his magazine and liked what they saw. Throughout the 1940s almost every issue contained a carefully argued article on the dangers of communism.

'Fellowship'

The bridge which Bardsley and Cuttell were building was designed for two-way traffic. Cuttell visited men (mainly men) in their places of work, and Bardsley expected these men to become 'a network of Christian supporters of the Cathedral' (Torry, 1990, p. 69). Lunchtime services for office, shop, market and wharf workers would often attract congregations of 200, and many would use the Cathedral for private prayer before work. The services, religious dramas, concerts and lectures ('What can a man believe?' 'Unite to put right the post-war world . . .') were all designed to bond together a 'family of God which would attract the great unchurched masses into the warmth of its fellowship' (*Over the Bridge*, quoted in Torry, 1990, p. 70).

'Fellowship' was also an important aim of the group of men Cuttell gathered in the Cathedral's Harvard Chapel on Tuesday lunchtimes 'to help the padre to pray and plan his way through the doors of opportunity' (Cuttell, 1962, p. 194). From 1947 onwards the group held monthly lunches explicitly to recapture a wartime 'fellowship', as Toc H had tried to do following the First

World War. Also in 1947 annual Industrial Harvest Thanks-givings began at the Cathedral. Cuttell was leading sessions in companies' then large apprentice schools, and it was apprentices who carried examples of their companies' products to the altar. Firms gave their employees paid time off to attend the services. Some of the apprentices in the photos clearly wished they weren't there, but the Industrial Harvest Thanksgivings represented a reli-gious celebration of the secular which many across industry were able to understand. Until the end of the 1950s the Cathedral was packed for these annual events (Torry, 1990, pp. 71, 114). No doubt clergy organized such liturgical events in the Cathedral, in parish churches, and in canteens, because liturgy is what clergy do and it's what people expect them to do; but there was also a theo-logical motive: as John Robinson wrote of the Holy Communion, liturgy is 'the most materialistic thing to which the Church sets its hand. At its very centre are pieces of matter, bread and wine, and without them the action could not begin at all. And notice too that the matter concerned is not raw materials but manufactures . . . The physical basis of the Holy Communion is the raw material of God's creation as we have worked upon it. The Eucharist pre-supposes production, and all the means of production, distribu-tion and exchange that lie behind every crumb of bread and drop of wine. No production, no communion' (Robinson, 1960, p. 64). You couldn't get a liturgical offering more obviously material and manufactured than the products of South London's industry. Robinson would later have an important role to play in SLIM's development as well as in the development of the Church's theol-ogy and ordained ministry.

So far, 'the working man' had been the target of Bardsley's and Cuttell's attention: the working man alienated from the Church and needing to be brought into its fellowship; but there were soon signs that the vision was becoming more limited. In 1953 Cuttell published a supplement to *Over the Bridge* called *Bridgehead: Being the Account of an Industrial Experiment*, designed to tell the 'story so far'. When it turned to future strategy it envisaged a team of clergy visiting industry from Woolwich to Battersea in order to form relationships between clergy and the 'artisan community', both rather more restricted notions than 'the Church' and 'the Christian Faith' on the one hand and 'industry' and 'the working man' on the other (Youings, 2008, p. 63).

'Reconciliation'

Just as armed forces chaplains would sometimes mediate between soldiers and their officers, so Bardsley and Cuttell would sometimes mediate between employees and employers (Coggan, 1989, pp. 64–6). This was a 'ministry of reconciliation', and it needed the padre to be 'an entirely neutral source of arbitration and help' (*Over the Bridge*, quoted in Torry, 1990, pp. 78–9). However, when haulage drivers struck during 1945 and 1946 for paid holidays, overtime pay for long hauls, and a 44-hour week, Cuttell sympathized with their case (Torry, 1990, p. 79). Over this particular strike he was rather less than 'neutral'.

The 'reconciliation' which Bardsley and Cuttell were really after was one between the Church and the secular world, and they used both military language and the then familiar term 'reconstruction' to build the linguistic bridge which such a reconciliation required. They rode on the crest of the optimistic wave created by the end of the war, and they genuinely believed that both the conversion of England and the reconciliation of industry's warring factions were possible (Torry, 1990, p. 80).

A council, a team, and a membership

On the 17th December 1952 George Giffin, General Works Manager of Siemens Brothers, chaired a meeting at the Provision Exchange, no.1 London Bridge. Managers, trade union officers, and shop floor workers from a wide variety of industries attended, along with members of the clergy. The outcome was 'The Bishop of Southwark's Industrial Advisory Council'. Bertram Simpson, the Bishop of Southwark, the 'bishop' in the council's title, admitted that he was out of his depth but expressed his wholehearted support (Torry, 1990, p. 94). Less out of his depth was Hugh Ashdown who came to the Cathedral as its provost when

Bardsley went to be Bishop of Croydon in 1947. Ashdown had been Vicar of St Aidan's, Hartlepool, and then Rector of Houghton-le-Spring, in County Durham. In those parishes, and at the Cathedral, his aim was to train the laity, first for administration and evangelism, but also for Christian action in a secular world (Torry, 1990, p. 70). Both he and Cuttell saw the parishes, the Cathedral, and industrial mission, as partners in this training exercise, and Ashdown would often chair meetings of the Advisory Council (Cuttell, 1962, p. 8).

In 1956 the Council defined its aims as 'to assist the Church in South London in bringing the Christian Faith into close relation with the workaday world; . . . seeking to encourage and extend the work of the industrial chaplains . . . training Christian leaders . . . building up a supporting fund' (Cuttell, 1962, p. 60). The need for funds was one of the reasons for bringing so many managers onto the Council, and another was that their presence would make it difficult for any future bishop to abolish the project. It is clear from the minutes that Cuttell regarded it as his task to choose, organize, and educate the Council, rather than to be managed by it in any way. In 1953 the Finance Committee asked that Council minutes should contain no references to chaplains' contacts with political organizations. Cuttell took no notice. The minutes and *Over the Bridge* frequently mention his visits to the Trade Union Congress. After all, trade union officers such as Len Squirrell and Jack Jones had attended SLIM's groups, and Cuttell had come to appreciate the importance of trades unions to the large industrial workforces which he was attempting to serve (Torry, 1990, p. 125).

In 1955 the name 'South London Industrial Mission' was used for the first time (Cuttell, 1962, p. 123), and in 1956 a constitution established a 'membership', a body 'under' the Council. A member undertook to 'bring to bear on my job the Spirit and teaching of Christ. I will try to build good relationships, fair dealing and a standard of sound and honest craftsmanship in my place of work' (SLIM membership card, quoted in Torry, 1990, p. 97). Within a year there were 250 members. (The aim of a thousand members was never attained.) The members' relationship to the

Council was ambiguous. The members constituted SLIM but the Council's members were still invited to serve by the Bishop on the basis of Cuttell's recommendation. Most Council members were managers: most members were foremen, shop stewards, and office workers (Torry, 1990, pp. 97, 125). Not all Council members were members. SLIM thus reflected in its own structures the divisions within industry, which isn't really very surprising.

At the beginning of the 1950s Cuttell was the only chaplain. By the end of the decade there were half a dozen clergy who gave most or all of their time to visiting industry, and there were another 20 or so parish clergy who gave varying amounts of time to visiting industry in their parishes. Not untypical was Robert Gibson who in 1954 came as a curate to St Alfege's, Greenwich, and used his curacy to develop chaplaincies at Molins (which manufactured cigarette-making machinery), a couple of power stations, Telcon (a factory making telecommunications equipment), Redpath Brown (engineers), and the docks around Greenwich. Less typical was Charles Birtles, appointed as a full-time padre to work among apprentices. The first chaplain who wasn't a member of the Church of England was Roy Beattie, a Methodist minister working in East Greenwich. He became the 'assistant' at Siemens Brothers (Torry, 1990, p. 99 102).

None of the chaplains were directly employed by SLIM. Birtles was paid by the Industrial Christian Fellowship, other full-time chaplains were paid partly by SLIM and partly by other organizations, and part-time chaplains were paid honoraria. In 1956 Gibson's honorarium was raised from £50 to £100 'in view of the excellent work he was doing' (Minutes of the General Purposes Committee, quoted in Torry, 1990, p. 100). This looks rather like an incentive bonus.

Most of SLIM's early chaplains had direct experience of working in industry. Gibson was educated at Winchester School, Oxford University, and Wells Theological College, and could hardly have been called working class, but he spent the year before his ordination working at Siemens Brothers and at a food factory in order to understand the life of working men and women (Cuttell, 1962, p. 82). Allan Weaver, Rector of Christ Church, Blackfriars

Road, had been a miner, and others had held administrative or other office-based posts. Those who hadn't experienced industry had been in the armed forces, and Roy Beattie had spent some years as a prisoner of war (Cuttell, 1962, pp. 82–3). It was often these experiences which had inspired these men to become industrial chaplains. Training to be an industrial chaplain doesn't get a mention, presumably because Cuttell and the Council assumed that if you had been to theological college, had worked in a parish, and had either worked in industry or been in the army, then that was sufficient. I can only assume that new chaplains did apprenticeships with experienced chaplains, visiting factories with them before launching out on their own.

In any case, the chaplains all modelled their work on Cuttell's. They visited individuals and natural groups in factories, distributed *Over the Bridge*, visited workers in their homes or in hospital, and sometimes linked workers with their parish churches. Some of the clergy saw their factory visiting as simply normal parish visiting, and those who were visiting sites not in their parishes still saw themselves as parish priests doing parish visiting. Such an understanding of the chaplain's task fitted well with the way in which SLIM's membership was starting to regard SLIM: as a church in its own right. This is no surprise. SLIM's activities included services, social events, day trips, dances, day and weekend conferences, study groups, and meetings to hear speakers (Torry, 1990, pp. 97–8, 104): all very like many parish churches.

Keymen

In 1957 Cuttell appointed 'keymen' in many of the places which he and other chaplains visited. These were either Christians or people who valued a Christian ethic, and their task was to coordinate SLIM's members in their workplaces and to increase the membership. Some of the keymen convened groups, some distributed *Over the Bridge*, and some informed the padre of people in need of pastoral care (Torry, 1990, p. 98).

The relationships between members and the Council, between the keymen and the Council, and between the keymen and members, were all ill-defined. Like members and Council members, keymen were mainly chosen by Cuttell. They, like members and Council members, were there to help the padres: but the chaplains also believed that laypeople in industry were the only people who could really apply a practical Christian faith to their workplaces: 'The lay apostolate was already there, inside the situation as chaplains never could be'. They had their own 'ministry of reconciliation', they were 'active partners with the padres', they were not 'supporters of the chaplains, but an apostolate equally called and sent, with its own authentic ministry' (Colin Cuttell, quoted in Torry, 1990, pp. 120–1).

Groups, courses and conferences

In 1957 Cuttell asked John Hughes, the Diocesan Missioner, to suggest someone to speak at a conference. Hughes suggested his assistant, Cecilia Goodenough. (She, like Cuttell, had worked for the church in Canada: among men, rather than among women and children.) Cuttell didn't want a woman, but finally agreed that she could speak provided she left after lunch. The conference participants insisted that she should stay, and she and Cuttell soon became close friends and colleagues.

SLIM's group work had begun with the Harvard Fellowship in 1944, and this group continued throughout the period, developing a four-week cycle of prayer, talk, Bible study, and discussion. Cuttell still only allowed men to join the group (a 'strategy'), but lunches and social events were added to the programme. SLIM's group work expanded as chaplains found their way into more factories. By the end of the 1950s SLIM was running a substantial programme of groups and conferences and Goodenough was organizing themed courses in factory canteens and other premises. Between 1957 and 1961 she ran 21 weekly courses, each of between three and six months in length: three were topical, three social and political, six industrial, five on general religious subjects, and four on the Bible - often on the Old Testament (Torry, 1990, p. 110). For Goodenough, group work was mission, and the groups' members were SLIM. She ran groups on group work.

In 1954 chaplains organized fortnightly lectures: 'Brass tacks' for beginners, about God and the Bible; and a follow-on course, 'Good News', about Jesus and his 'new order'. Lectures were preceded by a meal and followed by questions (Torry, 1990, p. 112). (Alpha Course: there's nothing new.) As always, the aim was to build up a Christian fellowship and to teach a faith both biblical and relevant.

The year 1956 saw the first student vacation course. Students from Cambridge worked in industry for a couple of months, met for prayer twice a day, and shop stewards and foremen addressed them. The course fulfilled its purpose: some of those who attended became industrial chaplains in South London and elsewhere (Torry, 1990, p. 107). Similarly, a number of ordinands worked in industry for short periods, or in some cases for up to a year, and joined in SLIM activities. For some, the experience informed their work as parochial clergy: for others, it was the beginning of the road to industrial chaplaincy.

In 1958 Cuttell's and Birtles' moral and religious education in apprentice schools bore fruit in a regular day conference for apprentices: theological talks, talks by trades unionists and managers, films, and photo calls (Torry, 1990, p. 108). Throughout the period chaplains ran day conferences on industrial premises. In 1953 70 shop stewards, foremen and personnel and welfare officers heard George Goyder, author of *The Responsible Company*, speak about industry's responsibility to the consumer, to the worker, and to the community. The shareholder came last (Torry, 1990, pp. 112–13). Residential conferences slowly replaced the day conferences. These were impressive feats of recruitment and organization, and they, like the study groups and courses, aimed to build up an intelligent laity by means of discussion and fellowship. Keymen and SLIM members would go to William Temple College in Rugby for Mollie Batten's leadership training. (Batten was the second important woman in SLIM's life. Goodenough would never go to the Rugby conferences.) The clergy led discussion groups, there was always a concert or a sing-song on the Saturday night, and a chaplain would lead worship on the Sunday morning. The Rugby conferences were rather exclusive, but anyone could go to the weekend conferences held at Worthing. A manager, a trade unionist and a 'theologian' would speak, and the theme was usually 'responsibility in industry'. About 40 people attended. Cecilia Goodenough usually summed up (Torry, 1990, p. 113).

SLIM's groups, courses and conferences achieved the sense of fellowship and the intelligent industrial laity which they set out to achieve. They brought together Christians and non-Christians, and they brought together on neutral territory managers, trades unionists, and men from the shop floor. They trained their participants to express themselves, and in this and other ways were similar to Methodism's early class meetings. Denominational allegiances became irrelevant for the duration of a conference. SLIM can therefore claim to have been in at the beginning of both organized lay training and ecumenical activity (Torry, 1990, p. 114).

Relations with the parishes

Many of SLIM's chaplains were parochial clergy, and, where a chaplain was working in a factory in a parish not his own, the relationship between the chaplain and the vicar of the parish was generally good; but this was not always the case. Cyril Bowkett, at St George's in Borough High Street, and Allan Weaver, at Christ Church, Blackfriars Road, were explicit in their objections to Cuttell visiting workplaces in their parishes. In 1953 Cuttell suggested that Weaver 'ought to be brought into the orbit of the new industrial mission'. Weaver responded: 'I am already well immersed in [industrial mission], at least in my own, if not in yours' (Letters quoted in Torry, 1990, pp. 105–6). In 1937 the Bishop of Kingston had invited Weaver to Christ Church as a lay missionary to work among the area's workers. He returned as Rector in 1943. He could therefore with some justice claim that his industrial mission had preceded Cuttell's – and we ought to add his missionary work during the 1930s to our list of uncanonical precursors to modern industrial mission. Weaver and Cuttell eventually came to value each other's work, and by the end of the '50s their relationship had improved sufficiently for SLIM to be seriously considering moving its headquarters to Christ Church (Torry, 1990, p. 106). Nothing came of the plan while Weaver was still Rector.

Cuttell had several reasons for a positive attitude towards the parishes. The main reason was that he thought that it was the Church as it was to which industrial men and women needed to be invited. New methods might be needed to do that, but those methods were simply an extension of the existing parochial ministry, and he saw his own work as extending the frontiers of parish ministry into the world of work (Cuttell, 1962, p. 76). There was no doubt also a practical motive for building good relationships with the parishes. Cuttell needed to recruit part-time chaplains. He was full of praise for the parochial ministry of Stephen Mnason, Vicar of St Alfege's, Greenwich. This evaluation would not have been unconnected with the fact that Mnason allowed his curate to spend large amounts of his time working for SLIM (Cuttell, 1962, pp. 60–61, 82).

Change

By the end of the 1950s change was in the air. In 1957 George Reindorp replaced Hugh Ashdown as Provost of Southwark Cathedral. He expressed his support for SLIM, but it wasn't at the heart of his concerns in the same way as it had been for both Bardsley and Ashdown. McCorquodale, the printing company, had printed *Over the Bridge* and its supplements at their own expense and industrial generosity was now coming to an end. Attendance at the Industrial Harvest Thanksgiving began to tail off. Bertram Simpson retired in 1958 and in 1959 Mervyn Stockwood arrived as the new Bishop of Southwark with a plan for worker priests: men who would be trained while still working in industry and would then be ordained to be priests in their workplaces. He also publicised a plan for bringing ordinands to work in industry in the diocese, but without crediting SLIM with having done this for three years already (Torry, 1990, pp. 116, 118; Bogle, 2002, p. 72; James, 1987, p. 92). He enjoyed being photographed visiting factories with SLIM chaplains, he liked to address SLIM's conferences, and he, like Cuttell, wanted a Church which would 'come alongside' (Stockwood, 1982, p. 123): but he gave SLIM not a single mention in his autobiography (Stockwood, 1982). He was better at valuing the projects which he started, such as the part-time Southwark Ordination Course, than the ones which he didn't: but that wasn't all there was to it. I can only suppose that SLIM was tackling the issues which Stockwood regarded as his own territory, SLIM had got there first, and Stockwood didn't like it.

In 1961 George Reindorp left the Cathedral and Stockwood appointed Cuttell as Acting Provost. On the 14th June 1961 Cuttell invited John Watson, a magistrate whose sentencing Stockwood had criticised, to give a lunchtime talk at the Cathedral. Watson criticised 'a bishop' who had criticised him, and Cuttell published the talk in *Over the Bridge*, italicising the offending paragraph.[1] Stockwood summoned Cuttell to see him and during the interview accepted his resignation (Torry, 1990, p. 158). Toc H offered Cuttell employment, and when Tubby Clayton retired as Vicar of All Hallows-by-the-Tower, Cuttell replaced him.[2]

Workplace change was on the way, too. The universal one hour lunch break, and the standard finishing time, both of which had enabled large numbers to attend canteen courses and Cathedral events, were soon to become less common; the flight to the suburbs had begun, lengthening journey times and reducing the time available for voluntary activities such as SLIM meetings; and the Church as an institution was starting to demand more of its members' time (Torry, 1990, p. 121). Theological change, too, was round the corner. John Robinson was soon to open the Church's eyes to questions which some would rather he hadn't asked (Robinson, 1963b).

The theology: 'Getting alongside'

The future was going to be very different from the 1950s, which had been a most stable time both for South London's industry and for SLIM. Throughout the decade, workplace visiting, courses, conferences, discussion groups and cathedral services were the tactics, and 'getting alongside' was both the theology and the strategy.

Cuttell found that working people had 'a sense of God' which was 'most real'. The difficulty they experienced was matching it to what they knew of the Church. What was needed was a bridge, and this could be constructed by the clergy 'getting alongside' (Cuttell, 1962, p. 32). The task was therefore to 'go out and make friends in Christ's name',[3] and, because the strategy required listening rather than talking, Cuttell became increasingly sceptical of the evangelistic campaigns to which Bardsley remained rather attached (Torry, 1990, pp. 73–4).

Cuttell had learnt the importance of 'getting alongside' from Tubby Clayton's practice and theology, and he also knew about the French worker priests whom we shall meet in our next chapter (Hurst, 2005, p. 38). The theological basis for 'getting alongside' was the incarnation: God becoming flesh, coming alongside us in Jesus Christ: 'a whole-hearted identification with the concerns of the world' (Bardsley, 1967, p. 115). This Jesus could be discovered 'in the most unlikely situations and among the most unlikely people' (Cuttell, 1962, p. 31), but that didn't absolve the Church of a task: 'to bring [God] back into the grey streets, market places and factories from where we have banished him' (*Over the* Bridge, quoted in Torry, 1990, p. 75). Understandably, military language was rife: 'explosive Christianity', 'crusaders', and 'bridgehead' (Torry, 1990, p. 75). There was no sense yet that the Church's message should be shaped by the modern world. Chaplains knew that their language needed to relate to the industrial world in order for the gospel to be heard,[4] but the gospel and its 'moral law' were a given. Industrialists were not averse to this conservative attitude to doctrine and ethics as they thought that it posed no threat to the Empire, or to harmonious industrial production, and that it might even help to promote them. As Sir Henry Self, a member of the Bishop of Southwark's Industrial Advisory Council, put it: '[The Church of England] is the spiritual shrine of the great traditions of the British nation and this nation itself [a focus of] the world's endeavours towards a real spiritual destiny for man'.[5] By using such innocuous concepts as 'responsibility', 'fellowship', and 'values', members, keymen and chaplains sought to reconcile the different sides of industry with each other as well as with the Church and the gospel. Because such ideas looked as if they might also reconcile industry's workers with the industries in which they were working, managements were generally happy to support SLIM. Chaplains liked using the ideas because they enabled them to 'get alongside' industry's workers and draw them to the Church and its gospel.

Given the chaplains' view that the gospel was a given, it's a bit of a surprise that SLIM's theological methods were so inductive: that is, the study groups 'worked from the concrete realities of [the members'] lives and [tried to] show the deeper and underlying reality which lies behind these and the Christian value judgments upon which our actions are, or should be, based'. Cecilia Goodenough liked to juxtapose industrial situations, newspaper headlines, and biblical texts, and see what connections might emerge from a group.[6] The more secular '6os were on the way, and while SLIM retained a healthy respect for a conservative theological position, more inductive methods were soon to be consciously employed.

This more theological section is near the end of the chapter rather than at the beginning for a good reason. Cuttell says that 'at the start, there was no search for theological bases . . . the rationale came later' (Torry, 1990, p. 84). He felt the alienation between the Church and working men to be a scandal, and he set out to do something about it. The gospel of reconciliation, of 'being alongside', followed.

Connections

Tubby Clayton's work at All Hallows-by-the-Tower had first brought Cuttell and Bardsley together, and his strategy of going to where people were and building a 'fellowship' became SLIM's strategy. In many ways Cuttell's work in industry was a post-Second World War equivalent of the post-First World War Toc H (Torry, 1990, p. 93).

At the age of 18, Bardsley met Geoffrey Studdert Kennedy when the preacher came to stay with Bardsley's family during his travels with the Industrial Christian Fellowship; and in 1928, the year of Bardsley's father's death, he heard Studdert Kennedy preach at Oxford.[7] It is always difficult to prove causality, but it is possible that Studdert Kennedy became the father-figure which Bardsley needed, and that his preaching influenced Bardsley's conversion and his commitment to reconciliation between people and God and between the Church and the working class.

The roots of SLIM lie firmly in the First World War and not in the Second, though it was industry's workforce's and management's experience of Second World War chaplains which made Cuttell's work possible.

Comparisons

Parishes and liturgy

During this period the Church of England's parishes and the liturgical life of the Church might have looked rather conservative, but there were signs of change. A major player in the reform of parish church activity was Ernie Southcott, who would follow Reindorp as Provost of Southwark Cathedral. As a parish priest in Halton, Leeds, he held Holy Communion services in people's homes: common now, but not in 1952. French worker-priests were the inspiration (Southcott, 1957; Hastings, 2001, pp. 442–3).

John Robinson was soon to arrive as Bishop of Woolwich, but before he did, both at Clare College, Cambridge, and at Wells Theological College, he contributed to the beginnings of liturgical renewal in the Church. Initially the words of services didn't change, but the words' meanings did, and so did the service's actions and physical elements. The offering of bread and wine by the people became an offering of the world's matter and productivity, and ordinary bread replaced the wafers often used in more catholic congregations. This was a return to biblical and more ancient practice, and it also represented the making sacred of the ordinary (Robinson, 1963a).

SLIM's activity, like these movements for reform in the Church's parishes and liturgy, were attempts at desecularization. The liturgical world had been about the sacred rather than the secular, and liturgical renewal was a secularizing of the sacred and a sacralizing of the secular: that is, the building of a bridge between the two. In the parishes, services in people's homes and a renewed liturgy were bridges aimed at tackling individual practical secularization, but with an eye to the effect which this might have on society as a whole. SLIM's activity too was a desecularization of industrial workers with an eye to a desecularization of industrial society.

The Gossner Mission

Someone else who understood the working class's alienation from the Church was Horst Symanowski. As a young minister his opposition to Nazism had resulted in three prison sentences, but during the war he served in the German army. He was sent home wounded in 1943 and declined to promise not to pray in public for leaders of the Confessing Church (composed of Christians opposed to the official German Evangelical Church's support for Hitler) or to collect money for the Confessing Church. No Evangelical Church congregation would offer him a job. The Gossner Missionary Society employed him. This society, founded in 1836, had sent missionaries around the world, but during the war it turned to supporting Christians who were out of favour with the official church. After 1945 it treated secular Germany as a new mission field.

Symanowski and his family found themselves in communist East Germany, rebuilding villages and congregations; and in 1948 they moved to Mainz-Kastel in the West to establish a Gossner Mission centre in an industrial area. Symanowski thought that he was moving from the 'cold, clear atheist air' to 'Christian fog', and he expressed a preference for the former: but he found that congregations were as small in the West as in the East (Symanowski, 1966, pp. 15–18) and that the West was no more Christian than the East.

Symanowski wanted to end the Church's estrangement from 'industrial man'. For six months of each of the next five years he worked as a labourer in a cement works, and during each Summer

he established ecumenical work camps to build Gossner Haus:
a centre with space for meetings and with accommodation for
over a hundred full-time residents, mainly apprentices and young
industrial workers. Study groups began. The subject matter was
their world. Symanowski believed industrial man's estrangement
from the Church to be too deep for religious language to be helpful, so he didn't use it (Symanowski, 1966, pp. 18–19).

> How can we make it clear to the church-estranged man that
> since Jesus Christ there simply is no longer any separation be-
> tween God and man? Nothing at all is accomplished here by
> theological talk. The preaching of Jesus Christ will have to be-
> come flesh once again here and now in the world of work . . .
> It is much more the very simple matter of being there with
> [the industrial worker], of standing with him in his world.
> (Symanowski, 1966, pp. 34–5)

Symanowski invited workers to eat together, and he held discussion groups at 2 am for the men working late shifts. Out of this
strategy emerged occasional Gossner Sundays during which men
and their families could rediscover, or discover for the first time,
a meaningful liturgy, the relevance of biblical texts to their industrial lives, and the sacraments as both in and of their own world.
The Lord's Supper was celebrated around the same tables as the
common meals.

SLIM placed clergy in industry as chaplains. They didn't belong
there, but they were present. In Horst Symanowski's ministry we find
something very different. While remaining a minister of the Church,
he was alternately present in industry as a worker and outside it as a
minister, in both contexts inviting people in industry to reflect with
him on the meaning of their working lives. This strategy

> is not a way out of the Church, as some people may think, but
> a way into the Church of God. Nor is it a matter of pulling
> people back and organizing them into the Church, but only of
> moving forward and counting on God to build up his Church
> anew in the midst of this world of work and with the men of

our time . . . God can take the mutual conversation of these men, their concern for each other, their common eating and drinking, and many other things, and make them into signs that will show that they are members of one body. (Symanowski, 1966, pp. 55–6)

SLIM was more interested in linking people to the Church as it was, whereas Symanowski was building the Church in new contexts. The ultimate aim was the same: to bridge the gulf between industrial man and Christian faith and practice.

Luton

While a minister in Reading, William ('Bill') Gowland helped to establish the rather aggressive 'Christian Commando' evangelistic campaigns run by the Methodist Church between 1942 and 1947. (One of these took place in Southwark and was hesitantly supported by SLIM.[8]) In preparation for the Reading campaign in 1942 Gowland negotiated to use industrial canteens for evangelistic meetings, and he maintained links with the firms after the event. Slowly a broader chaplaincy activity replaced a purely evangelistic one (Lurkings, 1981, pp. 198–9). In 1984 Gowland moved to Manchester where as minister of a thriving congregation he had too little time for what was becoming his major interest: gathering people from industry and the Church in order to build bridges between the institutions (Lurkings, 1981, p. 200); so he sought a post in Luton where he could serve a smaller congregation. Once there he founded a community centre in church premises, started Luton Industrial Mission, and in 1957 founded the College for Industrial Evangelism in rooms in the community centre. This was a centre where people could gather to discuss the relevance of Christian faith to their situations. Congregation members would put up both church and industrial participants who travelled to attend the courses, and eventually the numbers taking part – 6,000 during the first ten years – made larger premises essential. In 1968 a new college building was opened with room for both residents and courses (Lurkings, 1981, pp. 201–2).

From Gowland's work sprang Methodism's early involvement in industrial mission: a hybrid approach encompassing both chaplaincy in industrial premises and a church centre in which industry and church could meet.

Gowland's motivation was similar to SLIM's, but there was a more explicit hope that the Church would be changed by its engagement with industry: 'not only . . . that those without will be saved but the Church will save herself'.[9] To be properly Christian the Church needed to take the secular into its own life and message, so only by re-engaging with the world could the Church become what it was meant to be.

Conclusions

The secularization which Bardsley and Cuttell was concerned about was an individual practical secularization. Working men were not going to church, so they had to get them there. In this respect SLIM's early strategy was something of a success. There was also a corporate aspect to the early chaplains' understanding. They understood working men to be both individuals and a corporate body, and they saw the Church in this dual way, as both individual Christians and as a Fellowship. Thus both working men and the Church were institutions, and the 'bridge' over which the gospel had to travel had to have a corporate as well as an individual aspect. By locating the secular side of the bridge among working men as individuals and as an institution, the chaplains were tackling institutional as well as individual practical secularization. There is little sense that either industry as a whole or capitalism as a whole were understood as secular institutions in need of desecularization, though of course the chaplains' work did to some extent desecularize these institutions.

Notes

1 *Over the Bridge*, September 1961, pp. 125–8.
2 *Over the Bridge*, December 1961, p. 161.
3 *Bridgehead*, p. 5.

4 This was the theology of *Towards the Conversion of England* (Church of England, 1943), pp. v, 11, 19.

5 Sir Henry Self, *Workers Together*, SLIM, 1955, p. 3, quoted in Torry, 1990, p. 123.

6 Robert Gibson, 'Industrial Mission', in the *Industrial Christian Fellowship Quarterly and Annual Report*, October 1963; *Over the Bridge*, February 1958, pp. 24–5.

7 Cuthbert Bardsley in the *Industrial Christian Fellowship Quarterly*, Spring 1986; Torry, 1990, p. 82.

8 *Over the Bridge*, May 1947, pp. 3–4.

9 Gowland, W., 1957, *Militant and Triumphant*, Adelaide: Epworth, Griffin Press, quoted in Masumoto, 1983, p. 17.

4

Dialogue at Depth: Sheffield during and after the Second World War

It took two to start the South London Industrial Mission: Bardsley and Cuttell. In Luton it was just Gowland. Sheffield followed the Anglican pattern, and the two were Leslie Hunter, Bishop of Sheffield, and Ted Wickham, Sheffield's first industrial chaplain.

Leslie Hunter

Lots of clergy visit the public houses in their parishes, but when he was Vicar of Barking Leslie Hunter thought that 'in an industrial parish it is more in line with [the parson's] job to gain an entry into the local factories and know at first hand the character and conditions of the work . . . and if he can meet both managers and men during the dinner hour' (Hunter, 1931, p. 208). Another uncanonical precursor.

As Archdeacon of Northumberland during the 1930s Hunter came to understand both the severe poverty of the North and the massive and growing gulf between a weakened Church and an industrial world. He arrived as Bishop of Sheffield just as the Second World War began. His first concern was to support the diocese's clergy (Hewitt, 1985, pp. 71–5), but he soon turned his attention to the kind of society which England could be after the war. Industrial society was 'mass producing and mass produced . . . [it was a] limited and limiting routine'. The result was people 'without any feeling of spiritual need' (Hunter, 1943) and a Church so 'out of touch with what is by far the largest section of the community – the manual workers' that it approached social injustice 'not as victims but as spectators, and at best reformers'. 'Christian England' was a 'mission field' (Atkinson, undated a, p. 8), and the necessary 'new evangelism' would need to be 'relevant to the life and work of men and women who have little knowledge of the Bible and the traditions of the Church and have difficulties and hindrances to face peculiar to our time' (Hunter, 1941). The first task must be to make contact with people, and only then to bring them into the Church: that is, 'to speak to the masses of the people and to leave the conversion to God.' Hunter didn't expect the Church to be left undisturbed by such a new strategy: 'The new evangelism will be more than a recall. It will look forward to a new order both in Church and in Society' (Hunter, 1941). He expected a new order for institutions as well as a new way of life for individual workers and individual Christians (Hewitt, 1985, p. 158).

Hunter had known Ted Wickham since his ordination in Newcastle, knew of his work as a chaplain of an arms factory, and wanted to see if such 'works padres' might be possible in peacetime Sheffield. He invited Wickham to Sheffield and took him with him on a visit to the Works Council at Steel, Peech and Tozer in Rotherham, part of the United Steel Companies. The meeting was exploratory: a suggestion that the Church might have something to offer to industry in peace-time Britain, and that an industrial chaplain might be worth a try. Hunter introduced Wickham as his new 'industrial chaplain'.

So that Wickham would be paid, Hunter appointed him chaplain of the Shrewsbury Hospital (almshouses: not a hospital in the modern sense of the word). We hear no more about the elderly people who lived there. Hunter commissioned Wickham to establish a mission to industry, supported him as he did it (Hewitt, 1985, pp. 159–60), and remained closely in touch with the growing team of chaplains, meeting with them once a month for Holy Communion and breakfast. He met with Wickham weekly (Bagshaw, 1994, p. 18).

Ted Wickham

Wickham's working life began at Parker Pipes Ltd., a subsidiary of Dunhill's, and he then spent nine years at Insulators Ltd., administering the production of bakelite mouldings. At the same time he studied for the University of London Bachelor of Divinity degree, entirely on his own and self-motivated. He went to St Stephen's House theological college in Oxford, and then to a curacy at Shieldfield, one of the poorer parishes in the Diocese of Newcastle.

In 1941 Wickham went to be one of the chaplains at the country's largest bomb and shell factory at Swynnerton in Staffordshire. Workers were mainly women, and the only way to meet them was in the hostels where they were housed, so that's where chaplains were to be found – as well as at the hospital at Stoke on Trent where too many of the workers found themselves after explosives accidents. On moving to a new place, Roman Catholic and Free Church workers would often seek out the nearest church of their own denomination, but members of the Church of England generally didn't. The chaplains searched out these lapsed Anglicans and also those who hadn't normally attended church anyway. They organized group meetings, newsletters, pastoral visits, and talks in canteens, and they made themselves available at a flat which they acquired. We would call it a drop-in.

By 1944 there can have been few clergy in the Church of England more fitted to a pioneer ministry in industry than Ted Wickham.

The beginnings of industrial mission in Sheffield

The first Sheffield steel mill to welcome Wickham was Firth Vickers Stainless. The managing director was personally interested in the Church forming a better relationship with industry and he sent a memo round the works saying that a chaplain would be coming round with the aim of trying to relate Christianity to industry. Wickham set out to meet everyone. Steel making was characterised by bursts of intense activity interspersed with long waiting periods. Two kinds of meeting evolved. During the waiting periods Wickham would engage anyone he met in vigorous conversation; and during the defined 'snap breaks' he would gather anywhere between 20 and 100 men for vigorous debate.

After each meeting there would be plenty to talk about when he next met individuals and groups as he wandered the shop floor (Bagshaw, 1994, pp. 12–14).

Later a staff group, containing both men and women, began to meet. They and a shop floor group expressed a desire to take discussion further, so Wickham and his wife Helen invited the two groups to their home. The groups soon coalesced into a single Thursday evening group. The weekly agenda was theological discussion and Bible study, to which Wickham later added a short service in the Shrewsbury Hospital chapel (Bagshaw, 1994, p. 14). Wickham's model here was Wesley's class meetings, and he saw himself as a new Wesley, adapting the early Methodist techniques to a new industrial world (Wickham, 1957, pp. 266–8; Bloy, 2001, pp. 51–2).

In 1946 the Thursday group became the 'People's Discussion Group' and welcomed demobilised soldiers to take part. The group grew and moved to Church House in the centre of Sheffield. Social evenings, coach trips to the seaside, social weekends, and an annual Christmas party were now on the programme, and Wickham added Sunday evening meetings for those who wanted to explore the Christian Faith at greater depth (Bagshaw, 1994, pp. 14–15).

Still at the heart of the strategy was factory visiting, to create a 'web of relationships' (Wickham, 1957, p. 245), and particularly relationships with 'representative persons'. Wickham's main objective wasn't personal pastoral work, and religious services in factories certainly weren't part of it. The objective was 'to train men in the meaning of the Christian Faith and its relation to the life of industry' and 'to render a real service to industry'.[1] Wickham was interested in the institution as a whole, and that meant 'influencing the influences' (Wickham, 1964, p. 19) - managers, shop stewards, and foremen. But Wickham's aim was still to relate to everyone. Whoever Wickham was with, whether men on the shop floor, administrative staff, shop stewards, or managers, 'relevant Christian insights' would be 'discussed in the course of the dialogue, as happens inevitably when men pursue at depth their own secular concern' (Wickham, 1966, pp. 160–1).

Wickham might have been a late starter theologically, but he soon made up for it. Throughout his ministry he read widely. He devoured Kierkegaard's existentialist writings as they were translated early in his ministry (Bloy, 2001, p 90), and particu larly identified with this Danish theologian's description of the Christian Faith as a leap of faith. 'Come on, jump in quickly' (Kierkegaard, 1940, p. 8) could have been Wickham's strapline. Another favourite was Paul Tillich, who identified God as the 'ground of our being' and as the one we discover as we explore our own 'depths':

> The name of this infinite and inexhaustible depth and ground of all being is *God*. That depth is what the word *God* means. And if that word has not much meaning for you, translate it, and speak of the depths of your life, of the source of your being, of your ultimate concern, of what you take seriously without any reservation. (Tillich, 1962, pp. 63–4)[2]

This could have been Wickham's manifesto. Martin Buber's 'all real living is meeting' (Buber, 1966) could have been the mission statement. Central to it all was the incarnation: the belief that God has become flesh in Jesus Christ. For Cuttell this was more a strat-egy, a 'coming alongside', chosen by God and therefore by indus-trial mission. For Wickham the incarnation was a breaking down of the barrier between the sacred and the secular. As Bonhoeffer put it, 'God is the "beyond" in the midst of our life' (Bonhoeffer, 1953, p. 124). The Church's task was therefore not to take people out of the world but to return them to it: 'The churches were fish-ing in muddy waters. They thought that their task was to pull people out and to place them in the clean waters of the Church. By contrast, the task of Industrial Mission was to clean up the water. If SIM [Sheffield Industrial Mission] ever drew people out, it was simply to return them better able to help clean up the pool' (Wick-ham, quoted in Bagshaw, 1994, p. 27). Somewhat more radically, Wickham sometimes wanted to 'change the water', too.[3]

The theology might have looked radical on occasion, but in many ways Wickham's incarnational theology was decidedly orthodox.[4]

Similarly, while many group members thought that the agenda really was the industrial world and their own deepest concerns, Wickham's evangelistic aims were in fact rather traditional. Group members who looked interested in the specifically biblical, theological or spiritual aspects of the Mission's diverse activity would be invited to more specifically religious or committed group activity, and they were counted to have 'crossed the line' if they chose to participate in worship, and particularly if they chose to receive communion. In 1950 the Sunday evening group closed and the Thursday evening group became a more committedly religious exercise. Some communists who had attended it in its more open form decided to leave (Bagshaw, 1994, pp. 22–5).[5] In the light of future developments, it is interesting to note Wickham's description of the Mission's task as it was circulated to the group's members during this transition: 'The task of the Industrial Mission is . . . to build up the Christian Church' (quoted in Bagshaw, 1994, p. 24).

A team of full-timers

In 1948 Wickham started to build a team of full-time chaplains. Some of the money came from diocesan funds, and some from industry, with the latter always paid into the Mission's funds and never directly to the chaplain (Bagshaw, 1994, p. 16). The team's work was intensive and well organized. Every Monday morning there was an early service of Holy Communion. This was followed by a staff meeting, during which a discussion gave the chaplains material for snap-break meetings in their factories. For the rest of the week the chaplains visited factories and ran group meetings. John Rogan's timetable at Samuel Fox was typical:

8 am, arrive
8.30 am, meeting
9.00 am, shop floor visiting
11.00 am, lecture apprentices
12.30 pm, shop floor meeting
1.30 pm, white collar meeting, or lunch with management

afternoon, shop floor visiting
5.30 pm, shift break meeting.

Then he might go home, or he might not.

In the noisier factories meetings on the shop floor weren't possible, so at Hadfields Philip Bloy organized regular discussion groups elsewhere. At Steel, Peech and Tozer a group met at the Bridge Inn in Rotherham because lunchbreaks were too short for effective meetings to take place on the premises. This group's discussion topics were typical: the hydrogen bomb, whether the Bible could be related to modern life, whether the Church had failed, what kind of Church people wanted, and spiritual healing (Bagshaw, 1994, pp. 34–5).

The parishes?

The team at Sheffield was all full-time chaplains. This was very different from South London's team of mainly parish clergy visiting factories in their parishes or nearby. Colin Cuttell might have experienced problems with particular clergy objecting to him visiting factories in their parishes, but he never denigrated parish ministry. He valued it. In Sheffield the situation was rather more confrontational. Wickham believed that the Church needed 'a structure and machinery whereby a continuous impact is exerted within the typical institutions of an industrialised society' (Wickham, 1957, p. 245), and that the parishes weren't up to it: they weren't up to creating the necessary active laity in industry, and they weren't equipped 'to bear upon the social and institutional life of the area and nation' (Wickham, 1957, pp. 242–3). He thought that the parishes were imprisoned by the middle classes, had an inadequate theology, were entirely irrelevant to the social structures of the last half of the twentieth century, and were complacent, introspective, and unwilling to change (Bagshaw, 1994, p. 16). Parochial clergy sometimes challenged Wickham on this (one of these was the father of Peter Challen, who later became Senior Chaplain of the South London Industrial Mission),[6] but Wickham didn't change. In South London good relationships between the Industrial Mission and the parishes benefited both parties and kept the parishes alive to social classes and structures about which they needed to learn. The situation in Sheffield was heading towards mutual incomprehension. It's clear who Cuttell is talking about when he wrote: 'It is a pity that the tag "industrial chaplain" was ever invented. It raises doubts and resentments, suggesting short cuts to the Kingdom-of-God-on-earth by way of a special brand of religion aimed at a new collective called the "industrial proletariat"' (Cuttell, 1962, p. 77). Fortunately most of the chaplains who joined Wickham's team were attached to parishes and they weren't as negative as he was, but the fact that the Senior Chaplain was not shy of expressing his views meant that relationships between Sheffield Industrial Mission and South Yorkshire's parishes were never going to be brilliant (Bagshaw, 1994, pp. 36–7).

Hunter didn't entirely agree with Wickham's assessment of the parish system, but he did agree that the extent of the divide between the Church and the industrial world was so great that it was a lost cause to try to encourage working men into the Church as it was. He therefore agreed that Wickham's network of groups should become a 'church outside the Church' (Bagshaw, 1994, p. 17). They both knew that secularization is complex, that it affects ideas, culture and practice, and that it affects both individuals and institutions, and it's probably true to say that they had a keener sense of the depth of secularization than either Cuttell or Bardsley. They knew that a bridge between the Christian Faith and the industrial world was required, and the Sheffield Industrial Mission was that bridge. Sadly, Wickham's assessment of the parishes meant that he never tried to build a bridge between industry and the Church represented by the parishes. Such a bridge would have been a valuable contribution to desecularization.

Lay projects

One issue over which Wickham and Cuttell agreed was that the chaplain couldn't belong to industry in anything like the same way that the worker does, so the creation of an informed and active laity was a priority. This had always been the Roman Catholic position: hence such initiatives as Joseph Cardijn's 'Jeunesse Ouvrière Chrétiènne' (here known as Young Christian Workers: YCW). Each YCW group has a chaplain, but it's the members who run the group (Taylor, 1961, p. 47). From 1955 onwards, Wickham and other chaplains gathered workers with leadership potential on Saturday evenings for discussion of theology, social issues, and leadership skills; and a conference at William Temple College that same year was for 'the second line': those lay members who would support 'front line' workers in industry. By 1961, 40 out of 250 regular meetings in Sheffield's steel mills and other industries were 'lay projects': that is, convened and led by workers (Lurkings, 1981, p. 161). The main support structure for the lay projects was an Industrial Mission committee in each company, with the chaplains offering support only as necessary. The evidence is that steelworkers were taking genuine responsibility for the Church which was emerging in their places of work (Bagshaw, 1994, pp. 30–1). Working men were also taking financial responsibility for the Mission's work. In 1951 Wickham wrote a letter to employees at Samuel Fox asking for their support for 'The Church in Action', which is how chaplains described the Mission's work in the steel mills. The letter asked workers to form meetings in their departments, and also asked them for money: 1d a week each (one old penny, that is: there were 240 to the pound), to be deducted from their wages. The letter explained that 1,600 men, about a quarter of the workforce, were already contributing in this way.[7] That makes about £320 a year: a lot of money in those days. Even more remarkable is the non-computerised administrative burden which the company's salaries clerks would have had to carry in order to make the collection possible.

New initiatives during the 1950s

The early concentration on shop floor and office visiting needed management's support, but early on that's as far as interest in management went. From 1954, however, Wickham organized special meetings for managers (Lurkings, 1981, p. 163). At the same time he started to take less interest in the social fracture between the working and middle classes, and more interest in the effects of urbanisation and new technology on everyone in the industrial world. Did Wickham develop this new way of looking at things because he needed to negotiate new chaplaincy opportunities for his growing team of chaplains and therefore needed to be seen to be sympathetic to management's concerns? – or because he was coming to understand industry as an institution alienated from Christian Faith and the Church? – or because he was affected by a general theological shift from a theology which sees the secular world as God's field of action to one which affirms the secular world? (Reindorp, 2000, pp. 26–7) Whatever the reason, managers' groups met, and Roger Sawtell, a manager at Spear and Jackson, convened them.[8]

Works visiting began to spread beyond the steel mills and other large factories. In 1958, following a period of negotiation with both management and trades unions, SIM chaplains began to visit the larger railway depots in South Yorkshire. Each of the steelworks had a workforce of several thousand in a single large plant, but railway workers were more scattered. Chaplains organized a network of lay groups which all came together once every six months. The 'Sheffield model' thus proved itself adaptable to new circumstances (Bagshaw, 1994, p. 36).

In 1950 Hunter chaired a conference for 50 ordinands.[9] Wickham addressed it, as undiplomatically as ever: 'The clergy are not good, as a result of the kind of training they are given, at making contacts outside their immediate entourage' (Bloy, 2001, p. 55). The Mission placed numerous ordinands in industry for periods of six months: Philip Bloy and then Michael Atkinson at Hadfields, Peter Challen at William Jessop's, Michael Jackson at Firth Vickers . . .

To support the work of the Mission, Hunter organized an Advisory Committee to raise funds, sponsor conferences, and review progress. The Committee suggested that the Mission should have an office base. Wickham declined. The Committee suggested booklets and leaflets. Wickham again declined. The Committee was clearly 'advisory', and not just to Hunter (Bloy, 2001, p. 57).

Sheffield Industrial Mission, like the South London Industrial Mission, was an early context for women's ministry. Kathleen Ellerton joined Sheffield's full-time team in 1953 and worked in Batchelor's (peas), Bassett's (liquorice allsorts) and other companies, mainly among women; but she also gathered 24 members for a city centre group of young workers on Sunday evenings. Margaret Kane was the second woman to join the team. Her experiences at Sheffield were a major influence on the theological contribution which she later made to the industrial mission movement and beyond when in 1969 Ian Ramsey, Bishop of Durham, invited her to be a theological consultant for the North East: 'If it is to be effective, the word must be addressed to men and women in the whole of their lives. The gospel is not an unchanging word but is good news for people where they are.' She, too, looked back to Wesley as her model (Kane, 1980, p. 153).

Kane was one of those chaplains whose shop floor visiting came under management suspicion. She was chaplain at Balfour's, and the management weren't pleased when she helped another of the company's workforces to establish a branch of the British Iron, Steel and Kindred Trades Association. There was always an implicit contract between the Mission and management that overtly political activity was off limits. Kane had broken the contract (Bagshaw, 1994, p. 36).

The movement spreads

The Mission's early relationship with Steel, Peech and Tozer had not blossomed. After the initial meeting in 1944 Wickham had maintained contact and the company had sent people to conferences, but that was all. In 1954 Scott Paradise, an American, joined the full-time team and started to visit the firm. Shop floor meetings multiplied rapidly. By 1958 500–600 men were attending regularly, and by 1959 there were 20 lay leaders of groups. Paradise returned to the United States to join the newly founded industrial mission in Detroit (Paradise, 1968; Tonkinson, 2009, p. 28).

Numerous other Sheffield chaplains moved elsewhere to start new industrial missions, mainly in the UK. (The next long-distance transfer was Philip Bloy's to West Africa in 1962 (Bagshaw, 1994, p. 47)). In 1957 Michael Brooke moved to become Rector of Trafford Park and to start industrial mission in Manchester (Taylor, 1961, p. 34). Brian Cordingley soon followed him and until the 1980s ran the chaplains' residential training courses based in the city. Bill Wright went to Stockton to form the Teesside Industrial Mission, of which more later (Lurkings, 1981, p. 197; Northcott, 1983). John Ragg was appointed to Bristol in 1950 where the model was different. A team of 'advisors' got themselves known, ran groups, organized conferences, took part in apprentice training, got to know people in influential positions in the different sectors of the economy, and generally helped industry and the Church to get to know each other better. Shop floor visiting wasn't part of the plan (Taylor, 1961, pp. 31–2; Lurkings, 1981, pp. 189–95). Nearer to the South London model was Simon Phipps' industrial chaplaincy in Coventry (he, like Cuttell, was on the Cathedral staff) (Phipps, 1966), and Ralph Stevens did industrial mission in Birmingham from a base as Vicar of St Paul's Church in the Jewellery Quarter. This was the personal approach of the vicar in his parish, and not the organized strategy of a Ted Wickham (Claringbull, 1994; Taylor, 1966, p. 33).

Ted Lurkings suggests that 'independent missions tended to define their independence as independence from Sheffield. None of Wickham's detractors ever worked out their ideology and rationale of mission with the same degree of clarity. There was one rationale and one ideology, namely Wickham's, and the others were for it or against it in varying degrees' (Lurkings, 1981, p. 197). This is true of missions which were for the Sheffield model: after all, it was mainly Sheffield full-time chaplains who had founded them. It wasn't true of the Missions which employed alternative models. Neither Cuttell nor Gowland would have measured their strategies against Sheffield's methods. Cuttell visited Sheffield for three days in 1953, noted the differences between their industries and their methods, and expressed genuine praise for Wickham's work: but he believed that SLIM's approach was right for South London, and certainly wouldn't have seen it as worked out in opposition to Wickham's understanding of the task. SLIM regularly sent its chaplains to Sheffield and to other missions to learn from people who were doing the task differently. They never thought of any of the models as normative. They were simply different.

SLIM helped to establish new missions in Rochester and Belfast, but without contributing chaplains; Alan Christmas left SLIM's employment to start an industrial mission in Slough; and in 1969 a SLIM chaplain, Alan Griggs, went to Leeds to start an industrial mission there (Torry, 1990, pp. 119, 215). The methods in Slough and Leeds remained more like SLIM's than like Wickham's. Sheffield was influential, but it didn't have it all its own way.

New industrial missions, like South London's and Sheffield's, were normally episcopal or cathedral initiatives. When a diocese wanted to establish an industrial mission it would look to existing missions for personnel or advice: hence the spread of both the Sheffield and the South London models. A new initiative which ought not to have happened at all was the Bishop of St Albans' appointment of H. M. Jenkins as the industrial chaplain to Luton in 1955. Bill Gowland thought that that's what he was, and it took much effort on the part of Jenkins' successors to mend the broken ecumenical relationships (Lurkings, 1981, p. 196).

By the end of the 1950s most major cities had an industrial mission of some kind, generally mainly Anglican, but sometimes Methodist and sometimes with a mixture of denominations represented among its chaplains. Sheffield Industrial Mission had given birth to much of it.

Bridges to the secular world

But what of how the instigators of industrial mission at Sheffield understood secularization? Hunter and Wickham were both interested in the gulf between the Church and the working class, and for both of them this interest evolved during the '50s into one in the secularization of the industrial world as a whole (Lurkings, 1981, pp. 162–3): hence the increasing interest in urbanisation and technology (Wickham, 1964, ch.2). The secular had taken on its own value and had become an autonomous field for God's activity and thus for ours (Lurkings, 1981, p. 166). From

this flowed Wickham's commitment to lay leadership. The layman, belonging to industry, could properly influence it for good
and for Christ, whereas the priest, belonging to the institutional
Church, could only facilitate the lay role. (Wickham's objection
to worker priests – whom we shall discuss below – was that they
confused the roles.) Thus bridges were needed, not the dissolution
of the secular into the spiritual. The Mission's activity was one of
those bridges. Another bridge was 'middle axioms', an idea which
underpinned much of the chaplains' conversation with workers
(Lurkings, 1981, p. 168). This method, recommended by William
Temple, looks for principles and values which might bridge the
gulf between the particular situations of today and the Bible's
particular texts and presuppositions. The axioms which the chaplains actually employed tended to be such ethical or social principles as 'justice and fair dealing among men . . . justice slanted
to the weaker, that the human race is one . . .' (Wickham, 1957,
pp. 259–60). The problem with this approach is that the axioms
themselves never prescribe what is to be done in particular cases:
but having said that, there are few other candidates for expressing
the Christian tradition in practical terms in relation to institutions. Many chaplains have found the middle axioms approach
helpful in forming their questions even if not in forming answers:
and where prophetic statement can be difficult, to formulate
and offer questions can be prophetic (Lurkings, 1981, p. 169).
Wickham himself found Marxist analysis helpful in understanding the situation of the working class (Bagshaw, 1994, p. 28), but
during the 1950s he wasn't going to say that. Chaplains discussed
important questions, groups studied the Bible, and conferences
debated middle axioms, but chaplains rarely said anything very
specific. This was partly because the layman and not the priest
was the missionary in the workplace, and chaplains saw themselves in a supporting role; but it was also because the middle axioms method doesn't get us very far. It is perhaps significant that
a questioning and middle axioms method was unlikely to alienate
either management's support for chaplaincy or their occasional
funding of it (Lurkings, 1981, p. 169).

Comparisons

Worker priests in France

During the Second World War Germany conscripted French workers. Priests were not allowed to accompany them, so during 1942 and 1943 a number of priests travelled as workers so that they could continue to minister to workers' needs. By the end of the war there were 275 French worker priests in Germany, and all of them had come to understand better the working class and its alienation from the Church (Erlander, 1991, pp. 17–19; Ward, 1949). The term 'La France pays de mission' (France a mission field) was already in circulation, and after the war it took on a clearer meaning for the worker priests. Some of the Church's bishops, and particularly Cardinal Suhard, were also asking themselves how the Church could re-establish contact with working men and women. Suhard was appointed Archbishop of Paris in 1940 and established the Mission de France at Lisieux to train clergy to serve working men and women. Suhard himself ate with workers' families, tried to understand working class culture and the largely communist trades unions, and actively supported those priests who chose to remain workers after returning to France at the end of the war (Melton, 1961, p. 17). Among the best known of this group of men was Henri Perrin. His diary records the friendships which priests and workers formed in Germany, the 'cells' within which workers met each others' needs, and his own verdict on working people's religion: 'De-christianised, yes, but they are not against Christ. And the smallest thing will sometimes uncover Christ's face for them and by slow degrees awaken their love' (Perrin, 1947, pp. 19, 59, 230). After the war, worker priests often chose to work in the most dangerous of industries, and because they were educated and socially concerned they were frequently active in the volatile trades unions. Many in the Church's hierarchy felt this to be even less appropriate than priests becoming workers (Collange, 1961, pp. 45–6). An additional problem for the worker priests was that while their relationships with the parishes in which they lived were often friendly, and their own spirituality was still focused on the mass, they rarely related to the parish's congregation or to the diocese (Perrin, 1965, p. 114). In many cases priests and bishops had become strangers to each other (Collange, 1961, p. 57), and when employers lobbied the Vatican, and the Vatican didn't like what it heard, the worker priests found that they had too few ecclesiastical defenders. First they were forbidden to join in trade union activity (at which point some of them chose excommunication rather than lose their fellow workers' trust), and then in 1954 they were told to cease working in factories altogether. In October of that year Perrin was killed in a motorcycle accident involving no other vehicles. He had in his pocket a letter requesting laicisation (Perrin, 1965, p. 245). The movement's seminary was eventually reopened at Pontigny, and worker priests were again permitted (Collange, 1961, pp. 72–3), but in 1959 Pope John XXIII again forbade priests to work in industry. The Holy See's letter suggested that the priests were in danger of thinking like working men.

The worker priests experienced intense role conflicts (Lurkings, 1981, p. 385), between on the one hand a conservative Catholic faith and on the other an 'ethical clarity' and a deep involvement with the lives of working people. In the French anti-clerical context theirs was a brave and appropriate experiment. They had built a bridge and a great deal of two-way traffic had gone across it.

England's worker priests

During the 1950s, industrial mission in Britain followed the fortunes of the worker priests closely because the chaplains believed their task to be the same but the strategy necessarily different in a different context. Sheffield's chaplains were perhaps closer in outlook to the French worker priests than many others because they felt more keenly than did SLIM's chaplains the inability of the Church to relate to working people (Erlander, 1991, pp. 155–8). From 1959 onwards SLIM was even less enamoured of the idea, but that was because Mervyn Stockwood had arrived with a plan to train worker priests for the Diocese of Southwark. Cuttell and the officers of the South London Industrial Mission believed this to be inappropriate in the British context, because in Britain clergy could serve the laity at their workplace without becoming workers, and workers could remain the laity which they were meant to be.

However, that didn't stop Cuttell from writing approvingly of two English worker priests, Michael Gedge and Jack Strong, then working in the Kent coal field.[10] Gedge and Strong were different from the French worker priests in that they remained parochial clergy, firmly related to the Church as it was. They were thus building bridges not only between the Christian Faith and working men but also between industry and the Church. Of this SLIM could approve.

Gedge trained for ordination at the Community of the Resurrection in Mirfield and was ordained in 1927 to a parish in Southampton. He remained in parish ministry until in 1943 he took employment at Benham and Sons, formerly a heating and engineering company but by then manufacturing armaments (Mantle, 2000, pp. 99–102):

> I have always wanted to work with my hands . . . I felt half consciously that I was not a man, because I have never done what the world calls 'useful' work. I suppose only a celibate would feel this – not a man with children; certainly I felt it, and was glad at last to be a man among men at work. Something of the same joy was being felt almost at the same time by my opposite numbers (if I may call them so) in France. (quoted in Mantle, 2000, p. 96)

Gedge's spirituality remained traditional and catholic: the Eucharist every morning before going to work, and prayer according to the monastic offices while operating his drilling machine. He remained firmly attached to his parish church and in 1944 began a youth club there; and on VE day he invited the firm for a thanksgiving service in the church. It was packed (Mantle, 2000, pp. 102–5).

At the end of the war Gedge moved to Hoe-Crabtree, a company making printing equipment; in 1949 he returned to parish ministry; and in 1951 Canterbury's Diocesan Missioner asked him to lead a mission in Eyethorne, in the Kent coalfield. The Vicar of Eyethorne died and Gedge formed a plan to serve the parish at the same time as working in a local coalmine.

John Strong had worked in parish ministry in London for eight years. The Bishop of Southwark introduced him to Gedge, and for three years they were both employed as conveyor belt cleaners at Tilmanstone colliery while at the same time serving the parish of Eyethorne. Strong's health suffered, and in 1954 he visited Bristol to see if there might be some way of working on the shop floor, serving a parish, and co-operating with John Ragg's industrial mission. Ragg wasn't enthusiastic (Mantle, 2000, pp. 113–5, 120). Strong moved to Luton, worked as an oil meter calibrator at George Kent's, and in 1956 became priest in charge of Harlington, a small community within commuting distance of his work. Conservative attitudes among a middle class contingent in the village ensured the end of the experiment and Strong's departure four years later. Michael Gedge eventually became a Roman Catholic and tried to interest the English Roman Catholic hierarchy in worker priests (Mantle, 2000, p. 125, 130–3).

Ragg wasn't the only industrial missioner sceptical of English worker priests. Industrial mission in England had had considerable success with its own models of engagement, and Wickham thought that worker priests in England could obscure 'the first priority of mission appropriate to the British scene and a reformed Church, namely the engagement of the Church with the world through the laity' (Wickham, 1957, pp. 146–7). It's a pity that industrial chaplains never tried to see worker priests as a complementary way of building bridges between the Church and industry, particularly because in the case of the English worker priests relationships with the territorial parish remained strong and there was potential to change the Church as well as influence the working world. Only Cuttell seems to have viewed the English experiment in a positive light. The French experiment, however, was the other side of the channel and in a very different place, so Wickham could say of it: '. . . whenever the question of the church and the poor or the church and the workers is raised, the worker-priests of France will trouble the conscience of a comfortable church just as the Poor Man of Nazareth does himself' (Wickham, 1961, p. 131). Perhaps English worker priests were troubling his conscience, too.

As with SLIM in its early days, the early English worker priests had no carefully worked out theoretical strategy. They simply wanted to be where the members of their community found themselves (Mantle, 2000, pp. 121–5). While a few other members of the clergy followed Gedge and Strong into full-time employment during the 1950s, and during the 1960s many men were ordained to serve their parishes part-time and at the same time remain in full-time employment, few would seek the substantial combined commitments of full-time employment in a coal mine and pastoral responsibility for a parish which the two pioneers had taken on. The clergy trained on the Southwark Ordination Course called themselves 'priest workers'. They remained in their chosen professions during training and after they were ordained, so they were workers who were also priests. They saw themselves as very different from the French worker priests who were priests who became workers (Hurst, 2005, p. 39). Gedge and Strong were worker priests.

Conclusions

Gregor Siefer's verdict on the French worker priests was that 'this particular expedient for overcoming class antagonisms has only confirmed and strengthened them. That was not the fault of the worker-priests; on the contrary, their experiment has simply shown that it did not work because the Church, in the mass of her faithful, felt herself only perturbed by it, not called to action. The consciousness of the gulf had only been deepened by the change of sides on the part of the worker-priests' (Siefer, 1964, p. 9).

Sheffield Industrial Mission's chaplains remained firmly related to the institutional Church. Wickham might have been less than complimentary about the parishes, but Sheffield's chaplains remained on one side of a gulf, and from their relatively secure position they attempted to build bridges to an industrial world to which they knew they didn't belong. As we have seen, these were remarkably successful bridges, as in their different way were SLIM's. Industry, industrial workers and the Church were all changed by the chaplains' activity. The chaplains were able to build their bridges into industrial territory because management and trades unions shared a widespread belief that the Church had a place in the life of the nation and that therefore it wasn't unnatural for the Church to be involved in industry. Sheffield's chaplains, like Cuttell and his colleagues, were padres: a category of priest which many of the men working in the steel mills could recognise.

In 1943 the British Council of Churches conducted a survey of the churches' relationships with industrial premises. Fifty-three responses revealed a mixture of religious services and pastoral visiting, all with the aim of creating 'fellowship', not of taking religion into the workplace. A subsequent pamphlet recommended that clergy should regard local factories as part of their normal responsibilities, that the churches should treat full-time chaplaincies as experiments to be handled carefully, and that the chaplain's task was always subordinate to that of the layman.[11] Near to the end of the period under review, in 1958, the British Council of Churches published another report: *The Church and Industry*. This, too, recognized that the Church is already 'in industry in the persons of its members who work therein and thus . . . ordained ministers would see their rôle as primarily one of helping Christians in industry better to understand and exercise their responsibility there' (British Council of Churches, 1958, p. 7). The report hoped that in relation to industry the churches would act together, not separately (British Council of Churches, 1958, p. 31).

Not entirely in the spirit of this British Council of Churches report, in 1959 the Church of England published *The Task of the Church in Relation to Industry*. This encouraged the Church to take industry seriously, to recognise that the Church is already in industry in the form of its own laity, to maintain full-time chaplains in large-scale industries, to do theology with 'a secular cutting-edge and clear social orientation', and to plan a national strategy for industrial mission: a 'central machinery' with a 'competent and experienced secretariat' (Church of England, 1959, pp. 7–9, 14–25, 27, 34). This was largely Wickham's report. He had been feeling for some time that it was time to move on, and from the mid-'50s onwards did less and less shop floor visiting. In 1955 he was appointed a research fellow at the University of Sheffield so that he could write his book *Church and People in an Industrial City* (which showed that the Church hadn't lost the working class: it had never contained it) (Wickham, 1957); and thereafter he sought influence on the national stage rather than in South Yorkshire. He desperately wanted to found and run a national agency to co-ordinate industrial mission: the agency for which *The Task of the Church in Relation to Industry* was asking. He didn't get the agency, largely because it would have removed industrial mission from the control of the bishops, and they didn't fancy that. The Church did what it often does when it wants to silence somebody: Wickham was asked to be Suffragan Bishop of Middleton. Leslie Hunter wrote at the time that Wickham had been 'urged to undertake the office of a Bishop in the Church of God on the understanding that he will continue to advise and promote work in that sphere with which his name will always be associated' (quoted in Bagshaw, 1994, p. 41). Wickham agreed to take the post, and his influence on the movement came to an end.

Notes

1 A report of a survey on 'Work on the Shop Floor in Industry', British Council of Churches, 1952, unpublished, in Hackett 1977, pp. 51–3. Hackett calculates that 22% of the whole report is about Sheffield Industrial Mission.

2 According to correspondence from Michael Atkinson, Wickham's favourite Tillich text was 1951, *The Protestant Era*, London: Nisbet.

3 Correspondence from Michael Atkinson.

4 Van Buren, 1963 was similarly orthodox in spite of its radical title.

5 According to correspondence from Michael Atkinson, there was less of such Church-related definition of the task during the later 1950s.

6 Notes from Peter Challen on the first draft of Torry, 1990.

7 'A note from the Padres in the Works on the 'Church in Action' – in industry', Spring, 1951.

8 Roger Sawtell later left Spear and Jackson and after working for Trylon (a canoe manufacturer) and founding the Neighbours Community in Northampton he drew up model rules for co-operatives and contributed to the founding of the Daily Bread Co-operative (Kerr, John, 2005, *25 Years Already? – Crumbs*, Northampton: Daily Bread Co-operative). Sawtell's father, H.D. Sawtell, had been instrumental in establishing one of Wickham's early chaplaincies at Samuel Fox and Co. Ltd. (Sawtell, Roger, 'A note about H.D. Sawtell and the emerging industrial mission in Sheffield 1947–1950', unpublished paper).

9 The list of attendees included Bloy P, Blows D, Bowlby R, Gledhill J, Grindrod J, Grubb M, Janet Gulland/Jackson, Jackson M, James E, Jenkins D E, Lambert C, Lees-Smith C, Pickering W, Ward J, Wise R, Wright W. (From a list in Michael Atkinson's papers in the Sheffield City Archive). Readers will find most of these names in other parts of this history.

10 *Over the Bridge*, September 1953, p. 117.

11 British Council of Churches, 1943, *Summary of Industrial Chaplaincies Enquiry*, C.M.H. no. 4/44, London; an British Council of Churches, 1944, *Industrial Chaplaincies*, London: both discussed in Hackett, 1977, pp. 32–4.

5

The Secular Sixties: Institutional change in the early 1960s

The world's agenda in Croydon and Coventry

Cuthbert Bardsley was a Freemason. This would have been no surprise then: it was the way to get things done, and provosts and bishops were as likely to be Freemasons as anyone else in a position of responsibility. When he became Bishop of Croydon Bardsley wanted to do for industry in Croydon what he had done for industry in South London, so he persuaded 30 Freemasons to contribute to a fund to pay for a chaplain to work in their companies. A series of former forces chaplains filled the post. The managers treated them rather like welfare officers – for that's what they thought they were paying for – and by 1961 the task had become more than a full-time job. Roy Parsons, the chaplain at the time, took the problem to the new Bishop of Croydon, John Hughes. He invited three or four curates to help with the task. They were all called 'padre'.

One of those curates was Denis Claringbull, who was by then in the final year of his curacy. He visited Bourjois, a perfume company. When Parsons moved on, Claringbull took his place. The team of curates visiting companies grew, conferences and evening meetings multiplied, ordinands were placed in industry, Industrial Festival Services were held, and chaplains contributed to apprentice training. The job for life was on the way out, so meetings and conferences frequently discussed 'retirement' and 'redundancy'; change was in the air, so 'change' was discussed; and because industry was interested in 'productivity', that was increasingly on the agenda. T-groups ('training groups'), designed to teach their participants group skills, were now in vogue, so the industrial mission taught people how to organize them; and chaplains ran school leaver conferences to prepare young people for their first job. In order to understand industry better, Claringbull joined the Institute of Personnel Management.[1] 'Industrial democracy', 'human relations at work' and 'industrial relations' then found their way onto conference programmes. In response to demand, the chaplains ran in-service training for managers. Purely in terms of numbers attending events, and the benefits which participants gained from being there, the conferences, meetings and courses which the Mission ran were a considerable success (Claringbull, 1994, p. 89).

Many of the events were organized in partnership with others: with the Institute of Personnel Management, the Productivity Association, the Chamber of Commerce, and the Croydon Commercial Clubs Association: an organization for promoting inter-company sporting events of which Claringbull eventually became chairman. Croydon Industrial Mission shared weekend conferences at William Temple College with the South London Industrial Mission. (Bizarrely, Croydon was then a detached part of the Diocese of Canterbury, rather than in the Diocese of Southwark, which is the main reason it had its own industrial mission.)

In 1967 David Curwen was appointed as a second full-time chaplain. By then the control which industrial managers exercised over chaplains was becoming rather burdensome. Industrial managements were paying the salaries, so it was difficult for chaplains to address contentious issues in the companies they visited. It was also difficult to work for the 'reconciliation' which they thought they were there to create because shop floor workers thought they were in the management's pocket – which of course they were. To solve the problem, Claringbull asked the Diocese of Canterbury to pay the chaplains. The diocese agreed.

The theology was trinitarian. God the Father cares, and so that is what chaplains do; Jesus is a reconciler, between God and us and between one person and another, so that is what industrial mission must do; and the Holy Spirit leads us into truth, so training and education must be part of the task. As with industrial mission theology in the 1950s, there was plenty about the incarnation, which meant to the chaplains that God is at work in every aspect of life and we can discover his presence in any situation.[7] In Croydon incarnation didn't seem to mean that God is come among us in the flesh and that we too must be alongside people.

Coventry was a very different place from Croydon, but the ethos of its industrial mission was in many ways similar. During the late '50s and early '60s Simon Phipps' base was Coventry Cathedral, his work was industrial chaplaincy, and 'partnership' was a frequent theme: this time partnership with the agencies of the welfare state, with which we need to co-operate because 'all too often the clergy are trying to run a pastoral ministry less well-informed, less well-documented, less well-manned and far less well-financed than the considerable pastoral ministry already being rendered by departments of the local authority, and national agencies and voluntary bodies consciously integrated with them' (Phipps, 1966, pp. 79–80). The chaplains' view of society and its institutions was optimistic, to say the least, and the theology equally so: 'The world as man's means of freedom . . . The world as God's means of communication . . . The world is man's means of response . . . If the Bible's theology says that God speaks in and through the secular world, then it is in the secular world that man must stand and listen for what He says' (Phipps, 1966, pp. 12, 14, 17, 37).

Teesside Industrial Mission

When Bill Wright completed his ordination training in Durham he deferred ordination and went instead to work in a factory in Sunderland. In 1955 he was ordained and joined Sheffield's full-time team of chaplains with the intention of returning to start an industrial mission in the North East. In preparation for that return Mervyn Armstrong, Bishop of Jarrow, and Ronald Bowlby (Vicar of St Aidan's, Billingham) approached a number of iron and steel works, some British Rail workshops, ICI, and other industries, to explore the possibility of Wright working as a chaplain among their workforces. In 1959 Wright took up the negotiations himself, telling the firms that his aim was to contribute to industrial relations as well as to undertake pastoral work among the workers (Northcott, 1989, p. 41). Neither management nor workers were very keen, but he eventually persuaded ICI to allow him onto their premises. He was soon training apprentices, making contact with 'key people', forming groups, and stimulating discussion about the relationship between Christian faith and industry, and particularly about industry's human relations.

Bowlby, Trevor Beeson (Vicar of St Chad's, Stockton) and other clergy did what they could to support Wright's work, but sadly he wasn't very complimentary about theirs, telling a meeting of Stockton clergy that their pastoral work was inadequate as a means of relating the gospel and the Church to the working classes. A course which Wright organized to educate clergy in the realities of industry closed after two years through lack of demand (Northcott, 1989, p. 43).

In 1961 the mission's work was extended into the Diocese of York to the south of the Tees, and part-time Methodist and Anglican chaplains joined the team. Chaplains were now visiting factories in Stockton, Billingham, Middlesborough and Redcar, as well as a variety of British Rail depots. Discussion groups and work among apprentices multiplied, as did school leaver conferences. An additional full-time chaplain was appointed in 1962, and further part-time chaplains followed.

By the early sixties unemployment was growing in the North East and discussion groups which the chaplains had established frequently debated the topic. They also debated technological change and styles of management. Wright organized exchanges between ICI and a steel company in the Ruhr so that they could learn from each other, and particularly so that ICI could learn from the industrial democracy which was now developing across Europe. Two further full-time chaplains joined the team in 1965 and 1966, but by then Armstrong, Bowlby and Beeson had left the area and a sense of isolation from the rest of the Church contributed to frequent internal debate about the purpose of industrial mission. Unfortunately Wright was as unable as usual to appreciate the dedication and relevance of parish churches to their communities, and complained that neither bishops nor the parishes understood what industrial mission was about: 'We do not set out primarily to do pastoral work among individuals'.[3] The chaplains' task was to influence the structures of industry, and also to educate laypeople at work so that they could relate the Christian faith to their working lives. 'The good news is . . . that God's will can be done in secular life' (Northcott, 1989, p. 50).

The sense of isolation lifted when Ian Ramsey was appointed Bishop of Durham in 1966. He got to know the chaplains, joined in the mission's study groups, and arranged for a constitution to be drawn up; but his suggestion that he should help the Teesside Industrial Mission (TIM) with its theological development seems to have been more promise than actuality. Wright, like Claringbull, became an evangelist for T-groups, and he later espoused the more complex 'organizational development' process and employed it in the companies in which he worked. The secular world also formed the agenda for the chaplains' 'frontier' groups and determined their timing. Some of these liturgy-free discussion groups took place on Sunday mornings (Northcott, 1989, pp. 52–3).

Continuity and change in Sheffield

When Wickham left Sheffield in 1959 Michael Jackson became Senior Chaplain. He looked like the right candidate. In 1949 he was in France and was inspired by the worker priest movement; in 1950 he took part in Sheffield's first theological students' summer course; and following ordination training he worked at Firth Vickers. Two years later, in 1957, Leslie Hunter agreed to ordain him deacon while he remained at Firth Vickers (so he was the nearest Sheffield ever had to a worker priest), and when he was ordained priest he joined the full-time chaplains' team (Bagshaw, 1994, p. 45).

Jackson faced a number of problems in his new post. The industrial world was changing. Mechanisation was causing the number of men on the shop floor to fall, shift patterns were changing, and waiting times were shorter, so chaplains had fewer opportunities to gather men for discussion. An equally serious problem was that Hunter wasn't sure that Jackson was up to the job. He was only 34, and he had been in priest's orders for only two years. Hunter therefore appointed three members of the Advisory Committee to keep an eye on him. This was no way to provide a Senior Chaplain with the necessary self-confidence (Lurkings, 1981, p. 228). It is no surprise that under such circumstances a young man like Jackson, feeling his authority threatened, sometimes behaved rather badly. In 1963 he imposed himself on arrangements for a television programme being made at a company where Michael Atkinson was the chaplain, putting at risk relationships in the company which Atkinson had carefully nurtured; and soon afterwards he imposed himself on a staff meeting which Brian Cordingley was supposed to be leading. On that occasion Jackson had decided that he needed to talk to them about loyalty, and about the circumstances in which chaplains might be dismissed (Lurkings, 1981, pp. 229–30). A third problem which Jackson had to cope with, and one which was nobody's fault, was an almost complete turnover in the chaplains' team. Philip Bloy left for West Africa, Bill Matthew for a parish in Leicester, and John Rogan for the Industry Committee of the Church of England's Board for Social Responsibility. (This subcommittee was all that was left of Wickham's idea for a national agency.) Margaret Kane and Brian Cordingley had only recently joined the team, and Michael Atkinson arrived in 1960. The first two of these had worked with the team part time, Kane for seven years and Cordingley for three, but they were still a new team. Ian Mackay joined in 1960, John Rhodes in 1961, and Barry Parker (the first Free Church chaplain) in 1962.

In spite of these three problems, the 1960s got off to a good start. By 1965 there were eight full-time chaplains working in 20 firms which between them employed 70,000 people. Chaplains did what they'd always done:

One would be in the snap-cabin and the chaplain or one of our friends would call for silence or beat the table with a mug and then there would be either a harangue from the chaplain, or, much more often, four or five sentences of introduction and then a free-for-all discussion, or the 'audience' might chuck a question in. Sometimes the themes would be religious, especially near the great festivals, but most often they would be social and cultural and political. (Atkinson, undated b)

The chaplains generally worked well together, and their own theological and sociological discussion was vigorous. When chaplains faced problems in their companies Jackson supported them and found solutions: so when at Hadfields Michael Atkinson found himself involved in some industrial politics which he wasn't supposed to know about and a manager asked him to leave, Jackson went to see the manager and simply presented him with the company's new chaplain, John Rhodes (Atkinson, undated b). The chaplaincy continued until the firm was broken up. Members of the team wanted Jackson's leadership to work, and they seem to have understood his insecurities and to have forgiven their effects.

A sign of things to come, though, were the questions which Hunter was asking Jackson: questions which he had felt less able to ask Wickham. Hunter was nearing retirement, and as people often do in that situation he wanted to see the industrial mission being the success which he had hoped it would be. Although during the previous fifteen years he hadn't asked how many new converts and church members the industrial mission was reaping, he had clearly been hoping that one of the outcomes of the Mission's work would be more working class people coming to church. Such questions would become more insistent under Hunter's successor.

Hunter retired in 1962, and was replaced as Bishop of Sheffield by John Taylor, an academic evangelical who had a stroke just before he came as the diocese's new bishop and decided to come anyway (Bagshaw, 1994, pp. 46–7; Atkinson, undated b).

Continuity and change in South London

After Colin Cuttell left SLIM, the General Purposes Committee recommended that Robert Gibson should be appointed

Senior Chaplain. Gibson had worked with Cuttell for six years and shared his theory and practice. He was a good organizer, he was easy to get on with, and he was still on the staff of St Alfege's, Greenwich, and committed to maintaining good relationships between SLIM and the parishes. He was a known quantity, and after Cuttell's rather traumatic departure a period of untroubled consolidation was what was required. Mervyn Stockwood readily agreed to Gibson's appointment.

Gibson, impressed by the commitment which Sheffield's full-time chaplains were able to offer, asked for a team of full-time chaplains for South London so that 'penetration in depth' might be achieved, especially in such large industries as British Rail, the docks, and the Central Electricity Generating Board (Torry, 1990, p. 161). He eventually got what he wanted, but in a rather roundabout way.

Bill Nightingale came in 1962 to be Allan Weaver's curate at Christ Church, Blackfriars Road, and he, like Weaver, visited in the parish. His chaplaincy to the printers at Fleetway Press began when workers there mocked him for visiting elderly ladies living in the nearby flats. He said that he would visit them if they invited him, so they did, and he did. For Nightingale, as for Weaver, visiting local industry was part of the parish church's work and it wasn't SLIM's work, but this changed when he became a full-time SLIM chaplain at the end of his curacy in 1965. He served as chaplain to a rather larger printing company, the International Printing Corporation (IPC) and the company's donation to SLIM's funds paid his stipend. He also visited Bankside Power Station (now Tate Modern), the Central Electricity Generating Board's headquarters, Sainsbury's headquarters, and a few other smaller companies. Alan Griggs was another chaplain who made the transition from part-time to full-time. He joined the Cathedral staff in 1963 and visited Dewrance and Co., and in 1966 he became a full-time chaplain visiting power stations at Blackwall Point, Deptford, Bankside, Wimbledon and Kingston, and also the Central Electricity Generating Board's apprentice school and regional headquarters. Eric Blakeborough, a Baptist, was paid half and half by SLIM and the Baptist Church, and was chaplain to Redpath Brown (engineers) and the South Eastern Gas Board. He was the first full-time chaplain who had not previously worked as a chaplain part-time (Torry, 1990, pp. 160–2).

There were still plenty of part-time chaplains. Two of them, Robert Hughes and then the Methodist Ray Billington, were members of the innovative team of clergy which Nicholas Stacey had put together at St Mary's, Woolwich. They visited G. A. Harvey and Co. and J. Stones, both large engineering companies. SLIM contributed towards their stipends. Sometimes it's only in a crisis that we discover how much people appreciate a priest's work. Hughes had a serious accident on his motorbike, and if it hadn't been for the surgeon's skill he would have lost a foot. So many wellwishers from the parish and its factories wanted to visit him that the hospital had to guard his room. He was meant to be moving house at the weekend, and 20 men from the shop floor he had visited the day before the accident made sure that it happened (Stacey, 1971, pp. 85–6, 181–4; Torry, 1990, p. 162).

The Cathedral still provided part-time help, too: Anthony Baxter-Shaw replaced Alan Griggs when Griggs became a full-time chaplain. Baxter-Shaw edited *Over the Bridge*, which was still largely a SLIM publication.

While there were still part-time chaplains, Gibson's strategy was a full-time team of specialists. Alan Griggs specialised in electricity, Bill Nightingale in printing, etc. This was a conscious imitation and development of the Sheffield model, and, as in Sheffield, the larger chaplains' team made new chaplaincies possible. In 1960, 19 chaplains were visiting 42 workplaces representing a working population of 40,000. By 1966 chaplains were visiting 50 companies representing 45,000 employees (Torry, 1990, p. 165). By then, though, the expansion had ceased. SLIM said that it wasn't seeking new chaplaincies so that the chaplains could 'deepen' the work they were already doing. The real reason was that firms were starting to close. The first major closure was at the Woolwich Arsenal in 1964; 3,800 workers lost their jobs, and few of them found alternative employment. There were other reasons for chaplaincies closing, too. British Rail asked John Gingell to leave after he had an argument with the Welfare Department.

Generally, though, relationships remained good, and now that most chaplains were full-time they were able to attend works and trade union meetings, address staff induction courses, and contribute to company conferences, as well as walk the shop floor and facilitate discussion groups. This kind of greater involvement faced chaplains with a problem: co-option. The Mirror Group, glad of Nightingale's contribution to industrial peace, provided him with a car (the justification being that he was sometimes called out at night), gave him an office in the building, and asked him to give up his chaplaincy to the Royal Eye Hospital and made up the fee which the hospital had paid. Unfortunately Nightingale didn't see any of this as a problem (Torry, 1990, p. 166).

Just as the firms' managements were looking for more accountability from their chaplains, the fact that SLIM was paying more of its chaplains meant that the General Purposes Committee was hoping to manage the chaplains more closely. It had tried to manage part-time chaplains, but the only sanction available was the reduction or withdrawal of SLIM's small honoraria, so all the Senior Chaplain or the Committee could do was to ask for information and put up with whatever the chaplains chose to offer. Unfortunately for the committee, the situation was much the same when it came to full-time chaplains. Eric Blakeborough had founded a youth club in a disused night club and was spending rather a lot of time there. The Committee thought that he was spending rather too little time on factory visiting. He declined to fill in Gibson's questionnaire on the use of his time, and because he was accountable both to SLIM and to the Baptist Church, and thus effectively to neither, there wasn't a lot anyone could do about it. In 1967 he returned to the ministry of a local church where he could develop his ministry among young people without interference (Torry, 1990, pp. 163–4). Superficially it looked as if Gibson was in a managerial role in relation to the chaplains, but as there was no uniform means of appointing chaplains, and their stipends generally came from a number of sources, it wasn't at all clear to whom any of them were accountable. In Sheffield Wickham appointed the chaplains and himself raised their salaries, so accountability was somewhat clearer.

One point of continuity with the SLIM team of the 1950s was that there was plenty of industrial experience among the chaplains: Nightingale had been an accountant, Griggs had worked at GEC in Croydon for a year after army and university, and Baxter-Shawe had edited technical journals. Some of the influences were the same, too. Baxter-Shaw had been in a mining village in 1944, had attended an Industrial Christian Fellowship mission addressed by Ted Wickham, and had been deeply affected by Studdert Kennedy's poetry. However, new theological influences were also at work. Bonhoeffer's writings were an influence on a number of chaplains, and unfortunately for Billington the Methodist Conference didn't think much of Bonhoeffer's 'religionless Christianity' or of his idea that we have 'come of age' and should live as if we can 'get along very well without [God]' (Bonhoeffer, 1953, pp. 123, 163–4). Billington ceased to work for either St Mary's Woolwich or SLIM, ceased to be a minister, and took a lecturer's post at Woolwich College of Further Education. Such continental theological currents would continue to influence the full-time chaplains just as they had Sheffield's. The influences on the part-timers remained rather more conventional.

Groups of various kinds continued, and there was now more diversity. Bill Nightingale gathered groups of managers and trade union officials (Fathers of chapels) at Mirror Group Newspapers, then part of IPC, and these developed into conferences at St George's House, Windsor. They were an attempt to improve communication within the industry. Other groups continued to meet on industrial premises, and particularly in the power stations, where something like Sheffield's early pattern re-emerged. Power station workers, like the earlier steel workers, experienced periods of intense activity interspersed with long waiting periods (Torry, 1990, p. 164–5).

SLIM's list of groups, conferences and events was now published in *Over the Bridge* as an annual 'syllabus'. In 1961, 12 regular groups were listed, many of them 'lay-led': which in general meant Cecilia Goodenough, who was now sufficiently in control of the groups to be setting the agenda for all of them. 'Decision' and 'the acceptance of responsibility for decisions' were the topics in 1960, and 'politics' and 'authority' in 1961 (Torry, 1990, p. 167). By 1965 her grip had loosened and variety had returned: one group was studying Harvey Cox's *The Secular City* and another Richard Taylor's *Christians in Industry*. The groups still echoed the early Methodist class meetings. They gave people an opportunity to discuss the Christian Faith (not something which happened in many churches), they gave laypeople a voice, and they developed lay leadership. Thus the Mills canteen group gave Peter Jolly the confidence to discuss nuclear waste with his colleagues in the Central Electricity Generating Board (Torry, 1990, p. 168). A rather different group was the 'dining and discussion club' which Peter Ruff and Peter Pounsford, both of Sainsbury's, convened at the Royal Commonwealth Society. Each month, 20 to 25 managers attended to hear such speakers as Bishop Leslie Hunter and Sir Fred Catherwood (then of the Department of Economic Affairs). Some of SLIM's members raised questions about this group. Neither SLIM's Council nor its membership had debated it before it happened, and it was clearly quite exclusive. They wanted to know whether the fact that it might have been the only way to get that particular group of people to discuss serious ethical issues justified such elitism (Torry, 1990, pp. 168–9). The issue was not resolved. The group carried on.

The Worthing conferences remained inclusive, and they were such a success during the early '60s that each year four had to be held, with 35 people attending each one. (One of the four was mainly for apprentices who had already attended SLIM day conferences.) 'Reconciliation' was still a common topic, but change was on the way. In 1962 Cecilia Goodenough suggested that 'the Christian duty . . . was to do everything to bring the two sides together,' but others favoured 'creative conflict', and in 1963 'much conflict raged as [participants] discussed piecework, different canteens [for managers and workers] . . . and the varying length of holidays between works and staff members' (Torry, 1990, p. 169). By 1965 it was becoming harder to recruit for the conferences as people had either been before or were too busy. Firms were no longer sponsoring places because economic pressures were greater, industry had developed its own training provision, and managements were becoming more distant, more 'professional', more 'scientific', and less paternalistic (Torry, 1990, pp. 169–70).

In 1963 the Rugby weekend conference studied 'change in industry' (a new topic for SLIM). In 1964 Redpath Brown announced sizeable redundancies, so that year 'redundancy' was the topic for the conference. By the late '60s fewer people wanted to make the long journey to Rugby, more wives were employed so weekends were precious, few chaplains had the necessary charisma to persuade workers to attend conferences, and life in general was becoming more privatised. The 1968 conference was cancelled through lack of interest, so 1967 was the last conference SLIM held at William Temple College, and also the year of the last apprentices' conference. The more secular sixties no longer required SLIM's 'moral law'. A new and successful initiative in 1962 was Goodenough's gathering of ten people from industry and ten from parishes. They discussed 'lay leadership'. Mervyn Stockwood spoke at a similar conference on technological change in 1963. The conferences became annual events. Another successful new initiative was Eric Blakeborough's 'Fresh Look at Life' courses for younger unskilled, semi-skilled and clerical workers. The courses were somewhat unusual as the programme contained films, theatre visits, discussions, and dances. Firms were happy to sponsor places on such educational conferences, though after the first conference in 1965 they said that they would only send workers to the next one if there was a bit more education and a bit less culture. The 1966 course contained discussions on politics and religion and a jazz concert. Blakeborough thought these courses to be a matter of simple justice. If it was right to make generous provision for undergraduates to enjoy debates and social functions, then it was right to do so for young workers too (Torry, 1990, pp. 170–71).

Equality also became an issue at SLIM's Industrial Harvest Thanksgiving. In 1961 a female secretary wrote to *Over the Bridge* objecting to the male domination of the service. She had looked in vain for a symbol of her own secretarial work on its way to the altar, and had listened in vain for some reference to women's place in industry (Torry, 1990, p. 171). The world was changing and the organizers hadn't noticed.

The Industrial Advisory Council was doing its best to keep tabs on all of this activity, though it only caught up with the dining and discussion club, Goodenough's new conferences and Blakeborough's courses after the event. The SLIM dances, long held at Greenwich, had by now taken on a life of their own, and they were no longer connected to anything else SLIM was doing. *Over the Bridge* went the same way. In 1964 the Council expressed the view that the magazine had gone 'a bit pink' (meaning left wing), and that same year the General Manager of Courage and Barclay's banned the magazine from his firm (Torry, 1990, p. 172).

Now that there was a team of full-time chaplains, the Council's main task was raising the money and housing required. The money was still coming from both industry and the Diocese of Southwark, with a particularly generous donation of £10,000 per annum from IPC. The early '60s was a period of economic growth and firms could afford to be generous (Torry, 1990, p. 156). But from the mid-'60s onwards, as firms began to close, industrial financial contributions declined and contributions from the Church Commissioners and from the Diocese of Southwark rose so that SLIM could continue to employ a team of full-time chaplains. The churches in London still seem to have had money to spare and were sufficiently interested in industrial mission to be willing to pay for it.

A matter which had been a matter of concern for the Council, Mervyn Stockwood's plan for training men for ordination while they were still working, became less a matter for concern once the Southwark Ordination Course (SOC) was running. The stipendiary and non-stipendiary ministers emerging from the course often became good friends of SLIM. Tom Field, an inspector with London Transport, not only conducted a pastoral ministry within his own workplace but also organized discussion groups in the canteen of A. J. Mills and Co. and held a service in Southwark Cathedral for the firm's staff. Most of the men trained on SOC concentrated on ministry in their parishes, which hadn't been Stockwood's intention (Bogle, 2002, p. 74), but at least it gave the Council and chaplains less to worry about.

A frequent topic of conversation at Council and General Purposes Committee meetings was Christ Church, Blackfriars Road. The old church had been destroyed during the war and the congregation had been meeting in temporary accommodation, but by 1960 Marshall's Charity had rebuilt Christ Church as an Industrial Centre. (If ever you're nearby then drop in and look at the unique stained glass windows. They illustrate the history of Southwark's industry.) Everyone assumed that Christ Church would become SLIM's headquarters, but Gibson and Weaver thought not (Torry, 1990, p. 160). SLIM remained closely in touch with South London's parishes, and there was none of the antagonism which Sheffield had experienced, but Gibson and the full-time chaplains had been sufficiently influenced by the Sheffield model to believe that industrial mission was a mission complementary to that of the parishes and wasn't itself part of the parish's work. Weaver thought his factory visiting a normal part of parish ministry. Another difference was that Weaver's style was more paternalistic than SLIM's. He was more interested in individual managers: SLIM's chaplains were more interested in the shop floor and in industry as a social structure. It was probably a wise decision to await Weaver's departure.

Comparisons

Just one brief comparison in this chapter:

It was Leslie Hunter who raised the money to found William Temple College as a memorial to Archbishop Temple, who died in 1944. The college opened in 1947 at Hawarden in North Wales, and its aim was to train women in theology and the social sciences. By the 1950s the college had moved to its own premises in Rugby and by then was running residential courses for 'both sides of industry' and also for specific professional groups (Brown and Ballard, 2006, p. 160). The industrial mission conferences which the college hosted were part of its overall strategy: to enable men and women to think about the relationship between their faith and their working lives. The content was both biblical and relevant, and the idea was to send participants away able to do their own theological thinking about the situations in which they found themselves (Claringbull, 1994, pp. 150–1).

At the college's heart was the charismatic (in the broader sense of the word) pipe-smoking Mollie Batten, who administered the residential centre and its courses and often led the courses herself.

By the end of the 1960s neither industry nor the churches were willing to fund the college or its courses, so in 1971 it moved into the new Manchester Business School and became the William Temple Foundation. Since then the Foundation has sponsored and undertaken social research (particularly action research projects from its own base in Salford), run training programmes, and published books and booklets on Christian social ethics and particularly on the relationship between the Christian faith and the economy. The first director of the Foundation was David Jenkins, who later became Bishop of Durham. Until the late 1990s the Foundation ran the three week residential training course for new industrial chaplains. Since the turn of the millennium the emphasis has been on 'the nature and structure of the postmodern city and the role of the churches in regeneration programmes' (Brown and Ballard, 2006, p. 161). As we shall see, industrial mission would undergo a similar transition from industrial to more generally urban concerns.

Conclusions: a complex secularization

During the early 1960s the industrial mission movement continued to spread. Most dioceses wanted their own missions, and an element of inter-diocesan competition was no doubt at work here. Missions in Sheffield, South London, Teesside and elsewhere developed large teams of full-time chaplains and ran busy programmes. Industrial mission looked as if it had a bright future and the period we've been studying was one of growth and consolidation. However, under the surface there were signs that things were changing, and by the mid-'60s it was becoming difficult not to notice. In particular, discussion groups, courses and conferences were declining or closing. There were a number of reasons for this. The advent of flexitime and of generally more diverse working hours meant that holding lunchtime and evening meetings was becoming more difficult, and mechanisation was reducing steelworks waiting times. People were living further from their work, and wives were going out to work so it was more difficult for men to attend evening meetings and weekend conferences. The period's practical secularization therefore had a variety of practical causes.

Institutional secularization, too, was now a major factor facing the industrial missions. Just as the Church had once provided the country's healthcare and the State had then accepted responsibility for it, so in the 1950s industrial chaplains were often industry's training, welfare and personnel officers, and during the 1960s industry decided that it was going to run these activities itself. Personnel officers, training officers and welfare officers developed their own professional qualifications and career structures, and management consultancy became a widespread profession. In a desperate effort to cling on to relevance chaplains such as Claringbull and Wright turned themselves into providers of the secular product.

Mirror Group Newspapers clearly valued Nightingale's brand of peace-making, but generally industry could now do without chaplains. They were still welcome, but management could no longer see much reason for paying for them. The problem for the missions' managements was that they now had teams of full-time chaplains to support. The churches stepped in, thus aligning the missions more clearly as agencies of the Church and less clearly as bridges across which relationships could be built. As the churches were now paying the bills, relationships between industrial missions and the churches mattered, and, as Sheffield Industrial Mission was soon to find out, no longer could industrial mission plough its own ecclesiastical and theological furrow. Many chaplains were happy enough to align their work with the work of the parish. Ivor Clemitson described his factory visiting in St Alban's during this period as 'moving about among people, talking with them, getting to know them, learning from them; [this] we must always do, whether we are involved in industrial or parochial ministry'.[4] Goodenough's industry and parish conferences were perhaps a subconscious recognition that servicing the parochial church was going to become an important task for any industrial mission that wanted to survive.

Firms were now closing so chaplaincies were lost. What the missions seem not to have noticed was that newer, smaller, more technological industries were replacing the older large-scale manufacturing industry: but perhaps they had noticed and had recognised that in the 'white heat of technology' (Prime Minister Harold Wilson's phrase) religion looked irrelevant and dull. The new industries were secular in ways in which the older ones hadn't been, and in particular there was no corporate memory of armed forces padres. Fewer established chaplaincies and even fewer new ones meant that the industrial missions were less clearly identified with industry, even more identified with the Church, and in less of a position to tackle secularization.

The outcome for many chaplains was that they internalised the deeper secularization of industry, became either specialists in a secular field or missionaries to the Church, and thus bore within their own activity the growing gulf between Church and industry. The result was apathy for some, domestication for others, and in general the pursuit of personal interests (Torry, 1990, p. 190). Valiant efforts were still being made in individual conversations and in study groups to relate the Christian Faith to industrial realities, but by now the titles of study groups were almost entirely secular. This suggests a losing battle. Religion was becoming secularized, and it is no surprise that study groups were reading Harvey Cox's *The Secular City*. The chaplains still intended a Christian prophetic stance, but, as Northcott suggests, 'because of the complete identification of the ultimates, the doctrines and symbols of Christianity with secular ideologies such as Organizational Development . . . any genuine interaction between a prophetic transcendence and secular industrial society is very restricted. In the process of engaging with industrial society the original intention of penetrating it with the prophetic ideal of Christianity is lost' (Northcott, 1989, p. 107). The chaplains' Christianity had become substantially secularized, and a number of chaplains left the Church's ministry for secular posts.

I say 'many' at the beginning of that last paragraph advisedly. There were also many chaplains content with their role, trying hard to relate the Christian Faith to the workplaces they were visiting, and relating well to local churches. They were simply thrilled to be industrial chaplains. Clemitson again: 'There is a role for the clergyman in the modern world of which industry is a part: a continuous and deepening relationship with industry is developing: the challenges and opportunities opening up are tremendous.'[5]

I suspect that the laypeople and chaplains involved in industrial mission at the time weren't aware of some of the larger shifts which we can see more easily from a distance. They noticed things changing and they reacted to each new situation as it arose, often quite successfully as far as they could tell. It's when we add up the social changes and the industrial missions' reactions that we notice a general trend. What we notice is a number of different kinds of secularization taking shape during the quite short period which this chapter is about. Already there was plenty of individual practical secularization, but now we are seeing more of this, driven by changes in how industry related to its workers; and we are also seeing increasing institutional secularization and a secularization of religion. At the beginning of the '60s our society was experiencing a greater secularization of ideas and culture and a more intense desacralisation, so six different secularizations were all reinforcing each other and industrial mission was in the eye of the storm. To many industrial chaplains it still all seemed fairly calm. It soon wouldn't.

Notes

1 This wasn't the first formal relationship between industrial mission and the Institute of Personnel Management. Following a conference of chaplains convened by the British Council of Churches in 1950 a meeting was arranged between chaplains and the Institute in 1953 to discuss the role of chaplains in industry (Hackett, 1977, pp. 54–8).

2 All of the above is based on an interview with Denis Claringbull by Peter Cope on the 27th July 2006.

3 Letter from W.H. Wright to George Snow, Bishop of Whitby, 17th January 1967, quoted in Northcott, 1989, p. 49.

4 Clemitson, Ivor, 1969, 'Report on five years as Diocesan Industrial Chaplain', unpublished paper, edited by Mike West.

5 See note 4.

6

Tensions: The Sheffield crisis of the mid-'60s and its aftermath during the '70s

Michael Jackson was the only industrial chaplain to be invited to John Taylor's enthronement as Bishop of Sheffield. The other chaplains took this as a statement that they were going to be regarded as Jackson's curates. Leslie Hunter had treated them all as autonomous specialists working together in a team. That era was at an end (Bagshaw, 1994, pp. 46–8).

Any new Senior Chaplain stepping into Wickham's shoes was going to want to chart their own course. Jackson's first change of direction looked like a minor one. Such companies as Steel, Peech and Tozer were developing dispersed organizational structures, and Jackson suggested a shift from centralised lay leader meetings to a company-based co-ordination of lay leaders. Then he suggested that 'dialogue and research' should be SIM's strategy (Bagshaw, 1994, pp. 51–2): 'an open *debate* about how we should express our response, and how we should understand the basic Christian ideas. The frontier between technological change and theological debate is . . . a difficult one for laymen and chaplains, which means that much of our work is in the nature of *research* rather than working from clearly agreed principles, and that our thinking and our organization need to be flexible' (Jackson, 1965: emphasis in the original). Wickham's theological roots had been diverse, but he had been clear that God was to be found as men explored their industrial situation in the light of the gospel and that the Church was to be built within industry rather than coming in from outside it. A new kind of Christian presence was what was required, not the gospel and the Church imposing themselves ready-made on the industrial world (Brown and Ballard, 2006, p. 117). These were the definite principles which Jackson's seemingly open attitude was setting out to question. Paul Bagshaw puts the shift like this: 'Despite all the years he had spent working in and ministering to industry, Jackson stood theologically . . . outside looking in.' (Bagshaw, 1994, p. 53) The other chaplains seem not to have understood how much of a change of direction this was, perhaps because they were still visiting factories and forming and facilitating groups much as before. For the time being the Thursday evening group continued, lay leaders' organizations continued, chaplains related to everyone in the industries they visited, and the chaplains' ministry remained both pastoral and constructively critical of industry.

Jackson's next new direction was to turn 'lay projects' into 'study groups'. Wickham had intended the lay projects to be the core of industry's new kind of Church. They were now being conscripted into the external Church's attempt to apply its Christian Faith to industry. Should the chaplains have identified this as the significant change that it was? It is perfectly possible that Jackson himself wasn't entirely clear where the small changes he was making were leading. With hindsight we can see that the imposition of particular topics for study was an attempt to fit the lay projects into the Senior Chaplain's agenda, whereas before they had pursued their own understanding of the Christian Faith in the light of the situation they found themselves in. Jackson and the other chaplains probably thought that to ask the groups to discuss working hours, the affluent society, participation in industry, and the social aims of industry, was simply the obvious thing to do.

The new 'frontier' groups were thriving. These were meetings between trade union officers, managers, local politicians and chaplains to discuss the welfare state, education, science, town planning, and other issues of the day. Bagshaw here identifies a further shift. For Wickham, the basic fact about the relationship between the Church and industrial society was the gulf between them. In the mid-'60s the basic fact for Jackson and the other chaplains was that Church and society met at a 'frontier' where a relationship could be worked out between Christianity and secular understandings of society. What emerged, of course, was chaplains seeing the world as a secular society saw it, and what evolved from that was a rather secular theology. In 1964 Jackson, Michael Atkinson, Margaret Kane, John Rogan and Ian Mackay wrote a book which Lutterworth was to publish. The book had already reached page proof stage, but at the last minute Jackson decided not to publish it. The book suggested that the Church ought to 'stain' industrial society, but it could also have been understood as a recommendation that Christian Faith should capitulate to secular ideologies. One of the chapters was quite explicit that theological language no longer had a place in apologetics or mission (Bagshaw, 1994, pp. 55–8; Atkinson, undated b).[1] The context, of course, was the controversy surrounding John Robinson's publication of *Honest to God* in 1963. The chaplains had found that particular controversy to be a useful opportunity for widespread debate about God, but we can perfectly see why Jackson might have had second thoughts about joining in the controversy itself.

Conversion

Early in 1965, while Jackson was visiting India, the chaplains discovered that he had asked a group of laypeople to review the Sheffield Industrial Mission (SIM). On his return they accused him of using the group to extend his own authority. He accused them of mediocrity and clericalism (Lurkings, 1981, p. 231–3).

Then came Jackson's sudden conversion from a theology expressed in secular terms to one expressed entirely in traditionalist theological language. Whether this was a sudden change of view, or a sudden capitulation to just one of a number of views which Jackson had previously held together in his mind, a possible cause is that he had simply run out of the psychological energy needed to cope with complexity. He was, after all, having to square a secular theology with the theology of the Church of which he was a minister, to manage a complex mission agency in an increasingly secular world, and to work with both a traditionalist bishop and a group of theologically free-thinking chaplains. Perhaps he could no longer live on both sides of all of these widening chasms. No longer was there going to be a series of complex frontiers in his mind. The gulfs had opened, and he had chosen the traditionalist sides of them. Whether he understood this I've no idea, but the consequences for the Sheffield Industrial Mission were profound. At the annual two-day staff conference in August 1965 Jackson gave all but one of the papers, set out his new theological position, discussed at length the danger that missionaries might succumb to 'loss of bearings, contamination, loss of vision, mechanisation, loss of flexibility, and scaling down of the gospel, and anxiety' (Lurkings, 1981, p. 234) and demanded the chaplains' loyalty both to himself and to his new theological understanding. There was no opportunity for discussion. Ian Mackay protested in writing and Jackson gave him 12 months' notice. This was in spite of the fact that Jackson was about to take a year's study leave so that he could take up a Stephenson Fellowship at Sheffield University, and also in spite of the fact that the previous Friday Kane and Atkinson had been appointed to lead the Mission in his absence. Without consulting the Congregational Union Jackson also gave Barry Parker three months' notice. (Atkinson's view is that Jackson picked on Parker and Mackay because he couldn't handle their close identification with a swearing and hard drinking pub culture (Atkinson).) Neither Kane nor Atkinson were told of the dismissals, but when they found out they went to see the Bishop to ask for Mackay and Parker to be reinstated. The Bishop sided with Jackson, so Kane and Atkinson resigned the leadership and Jackson had to return from his study leave (Lurkings, 1981, p. 235–8). In November local newspapers publicised Parker's and Mackay's dismissals, and the *Sheffield Telegraph* reported that a union branch at the Tinsley Park Works of the English Steel Corporation had refused to co-operate with Andrew Stokes, a new SIM chaplain whom Jackson had asked to take over Parker's work at the firm. The paper quoted Leslie Crapper, vice-chairman of the branch:

We don't really know why Barry was sacked, but I can only imagine that the senior chaplain, the Revd Michael Jackson, felt they were not concentrating on religion enough. To be quite honest, I think Mr. Jackson wants a pulpit in every department. But Barry was the sort of man who would talk about any subject you wanted to talk about, whether it was religion or not. He got on very well with the men. They liked him and respected him, and if you asked him to come for a pint he was the first to buy.[2]

Atkinson decided that the situation was of more than local significance and went to see Chris Driver, a friend from university days, who was then Features Editor at the *Guardian*. Driver sent Geoffrey Moorhouse to Sheffield for a week to write the story. Articles followed in *The Times*, *The Guardian*, *The Observer*, and all the leading Christian journals, in the UK and abroad, over several months. *The Observer*'s view was that

a row in Sheffield over the dismissal of the industrial chaplain [Mackay] at one of the country's largest steel plants has brought the Church of England into headlong collision with the Unions. It could do lasting damage to the prestige of industrial missions throughout the country.[3]

As Geoffrey Moorhouse's article two days later in *The Guardian* suggested:

Quite apart from the dissensions inside the mission, which have produced two resignations in recent weeks, and which must make its life intolerable for some time to come, the reaction from outside makes it conceivable that the mission will just cease to function. For it can only function at the invitation of industry. And the way things have been going it may not have many invitations left before long.[4]

Still Jackson wouldn't discuss the matter and was understandably accused of hypocrisy by companies in which chaplains had tried to encourage better treatment of employees. Eventually the bishop agreed to call a meeting of the Bishop's Advisory Committee on Industrial Mission. Jackson used the meeting to accuse Wickham of clericalism and of founding a sect, the bishop would hear no criticism of his Senior Chaplain, and the members passed a resolution that the meeting had ended in disagreement (Lurkings, 1981, p. 238, 246). The next meeting of the committee was equally acrimonious (Bagshaw, 1994, p. 61). The conflict spread into the diocese and the Archdeacon of Doncaster publicly opposed his bishop and supported the sacked chaplains. In November, following considerable correspondence between managers, trades unionists and the Bishop of Sheffield (Lurkings, 1981, pp. 240–43), managers from four of the companies which the dismissed chaplains had visited wrote to the Archbishops of York and Canterbury. The following April Donald Coggan, Archbishop of York, invited a Works Council deputation to see him. (He signed his letter 'Donald Ebor'. Not understanding that this is the way in which Archbishops of York traditionally sign themselves, the group wrote back: 'Dear Mr. Ebor . . .' (Atkinson, undated b).) They asked for Ted Wickham to be recalled to lead the Mission, and were understandably refused. They asked for an independent enquiry and got two of them: one convened by the Bishop of Sheffield (this one included Jackson and can hardly have been called independent), and one convened by the Archbishop of York and chaired by Edwin Barker, Secretary of the Church of England's Board for Social Responsibility. Tom Chapman, by then the Board's Industry Committee's liaison officer for industry and the trades unions, was a member. This enquiry was independent, but it was always going to be traditionalist in outlook (Bagshaw, 1994, pp. 61–3). The Barker enquiry's view of the Sheffield controversy is instructive:

The assumption is that the Church has lost contact with men in industry. It is necessary to re-establish links with them and Missioners have gone into industry to do this. They are on a razor-edge. They can become identified with the men they meet by becoming like them without influencing them. They can become additional welfare officers, or exercise a personal and pastoral ministry among them without any particular reference to industry except as a meeting place. They can be tempted to interfere in the day-to-day running of industry and its related institutions. These are some of the dangers. In addition their work can become 'over-against' the Church, developing a distinct orthodoxy leading to sectarianism.[5]

When a summary of the report was published Jackson asked Peter Todd to go. He also asked David Wright, a Methodist, to leave, and the Methodist Church put out a press release saying that they could see no reason for the dismissal. A Methodist part-time chaplain resigned in protest, and the Congregational Union publicly withdrew all support from the Mission. Ecumenical relations took ten years to recover (Bagshaw, 1994, pp. 63–4).

The Barker report declared industrial missions to be unambiguously Church agencies, and while it suggested that employment issues ought to have been kept separate from theological ones, it didn't criticise Jackson's leadership or his failure to consult over the dismissals. John Taylor decided not to publish the full report. By now only three full-time chaplains remained: Jackson, Stokes and Kane, and a few days later Kane resigned. From ten full-time staff in December 1965 the team was now down to just two. Conferences and the student summer course were cancelled, some of the lay-led groups declared themselves independent of SIM and carried on, and by the end of 1966 Jackson had the clean sheet which he'd clearly been aiming at (Bagshaw, 1994, p. 66).

Jackson wrote an article in *Theology*, 'No New Gospel', in which he compared Sheffield Industrial Mission to a bridge with one way traffic on it. The Church was reaching out to industry, but industrial workers weren't coming to church even though many of them believed in God and many of them prayed.

The task of Industrial Mission as of the whole Christian Church is to bring men to knowledge, love and vision of God as revealed in Jesus Christ. It preaches the gospel of the Kingdom of God, of God who is King. There is no Kingdom without naming the

King. The task of proclamation is to say this and of teaching to work out its implications for men in industry. There is no new gospel for them, nor is there a special theology of the Church's mission and ministry in industry . . .' (Jackson, 1966, p. 540)

In June 1967 the Bishop of Sheffield's own enquiry into the Sheffield Industrial Mission finally reported. The report's authors recognised that one of SIM's successes had been that industry now listened to the Church, but they also thought that the Mission had neglected individual conversion and had ignored Christians already working in companies in favour of building its own Church within industry. Tim Forder, the enquiry's chairman, wrote to Leslie Hunter to ask him to agree that the Mission's original aims had been to build a bridge between the Church and industry, to revitalise the Church by contact with industry, and to contribute to the conversion of England. Hunter's response was that those were never the aims and that the enquiry had taken no account of the irrelevance of the Church to industrial society (Bagshaw, 1994, p. 69).

In accordance with the report's recommendations SIM began to rebuild itself on the basis of a small team of full-time chaplains (most of them from parish ministry), rather more part-time ones (all parochial clergy), and a more conservative theology (Lurkings, 1981, p. 288). The aim was now explicitly to present the gospel in industry and to apply the gospel to society.

It is often difficult to establish directions of causality, and particularly so when we study the course of events in Sheffield during the mid-'60s. Did Jackson's religious conversion come first? If so then the tensions leading up to it were those which we often see in people approaching a conversion experience as the mind prepares itself for trauma and a new paradigm. Or was Jackson struggling with being in Wickham's shadow, with tensions between the team of chaplains and a traditionalist Church represented by a traditionalist bishop, and with the gulf between the Church and the secular world, and the theological conversion was both the result and what enabled him to resolve the tensions – a resolution which imposed difficult consequences, but consequences which in his conversion-fortified state he was now psychologically equipped to deal with? I suspect that the process was circular. Whatever the causality, by the end of 1967 the conflict was over. In 1969 Jackson moved to a parish in Doncaster and Andrew Stokes became Senior Chaplain (Bagshaw, 1994, p. 71).

By 1971 the new team was visiting 30 companies, and during the following decade factory visiting flourished, groups studied industrial and biblical themes, conferences restarted, committed Christians in industry got involved, Free Church part-time chaplains joined the team, and ministry to industry's structures dropped off the agenda. It was all beginning to look rather like 1950s SLIM. In 1974 Malcolm Grundy became Senior Chaplain after visiting industry during his curacy and being a full-time chaplain for two years. By 1979 there were seven full- and half-time chaplains and 16 part-time ones, there were again full-time chaplains from the Free Churches, Grundy's strategy to spread the Mission's work more evenly across the diocese had succeeded, and running training courses for parishes had become an important part of the Mission's work (Bagshaw, 1994, pp. 74–85).

South London: a new constitution

In 1966 John Robinson chaired a SLIM working party and gave birth to a new constitution in which paid-up members elected the majority of members of a Council. SLIM thus became independent of church hierarchies, and only the membership or the Council could close SLIM down or decide a change of direction. No doubt the crisis in Sheffield had concentrated minds. The Bishop of Southwark was able to nominate three members of the Council, and was also appointed as a figurehead President, but neither he nor his nominees could now control the organization. For the first time other denominations had the right to appoint Council members. The working party also recommended that the posts of Rector of Christ Church and Senior Chaplain of SLIM should be combined and that SLIM should move its base to Christ Church. A meeting convened to discuss the recommendations noted that the constitution would now be fairly even handed between the denominations but that the combination of the two posts would mean that the Senior Chaplain would necessarily be a priest of the Church of England. The meeting agreed that the amalgamation of the posts should be reviewed each time a new appointment was made (Torry, 1990, pp. 204–5).

A new Senior Chaplain

In 1967 Robert Gibson was appointed Dean of the Port Harcourt Project on industry and society in Eastern Nigeria, but the Biafran war intervened and after standing in for Colin Cuttell at All Hallows while Cuttell wrote *Ministry Without Portfolio* Gibson was appointed to the parish of Guisborough. Allan Weaver moved to Herefordshire, and Peter Challen was appointed to the new combined post (Torry, 1990, p. 159).

Following national service Challen worked in a steel works for a year and a coal mine for six months. At Clare College, Cambridge, he came under John Robinson's influence; and at Westcott House Theological College he persuaded the Principal to allow him to spend a year of his training at William Temple College. It was there that he met his wife Ruth. Tubby Clayton was Challen's godfather[6] and wanted him to succeed him at All Hallows, but Challen was not convinced of the continuing relevance of Toc H and, following a curacy at Goole, he went to a parish in Rotherham for five years. There he worked as a part-time chaplain with the Sheffield Industrial Mission. It was Robinson who suggested that Challen should be SLIM's next Senior Chaplain, and the General Purposes Committee agreed (Torry, 1990, p. 209).

The problem with combining two posts is that the new post-holder is expected to do two people's work. An additional problem here was that the post was a marriage of convenience. Christ Church's congregation has never had much to do with South London's industry, but with both SLIM and Christ Church now inhabiting the same building, and being served by the same person, there was bound to be a certain confusion of roles. So as well as being Senior Chaplain of SLIM Challen found himself Rector of a parish and responsible for a well-used building with inadequate caretaking arrangements. (The Rectory was only a few yards away from Christ Church so Challen frequently found himself acting as late night as well as daytime caretaker.) He edited *Over the Bridge* (by 1969 he was writing most of the articles himself because nobody else would write them), he was on numerous committees, he related to a vast number of organizations, and he was an industrial chaplain to Hay's Wharf, Metal Box, Sainsbury's, and Letts Diaries. It was the industrial visiting which suffered. Some members of the Council already thought that Challen encouraged thinking at the expense of activity, and not everyone was happy when he agreed to Robinson's suggestion that he should attend the London Business School's Sloan Programme: a one year course on business management. SLIM's Executive Committee (the new name for the General Purposes Committee) thought that his attendence would create 'an alliance with management thinking which would distort SLIM's relationship with the whole working community'. Challen loved the course. He studied accounting, industrial society, and the plays of Sophocles, and he learnt to draw diagrams: 'If you can't chart a thing, you can't understand it.' He was appalled during a computer business game to find himself selling sophisticated electronics to South Africa (and he found the game difficult, too) so he wrote an essay about human values in business which the professor ridiculed in class but privately agreed was an important corrective. Challen learnt 'to speak the various management languages: accounting to accountants, marketing to marketing men, and so on'; he left behind at the business school people willing to broaden horizons (and particularly the librarian, Ken Vernon); and he returned to SLIM speaking his own kind of management language (Torry, 1990, pp. 210–13, 221, 257).

While it is true that Challen neglected shop floor visiting, he was never going to be able to do everything which came his way. His particular gift to the Church and to the industrial world was his availability to thousands of individuals who wanted to think through the relationship between Christian Faith and the world of work. To help him to do this he developed the ideas of 'three gear mission' (mission in the personal, institutional and global

spheres) (Torry, 1990, p. 293) and of 'theological audit': a systematic application of biblical principles to people's working lives
and their contexts (Hurst, 2005, p. 40). For Challen it was always
that way round: the application of the Christian Faith to industry
and commerce. It was this traditional approach, the fact that the
Senior Chaplain was also Rector of a parish, and SLIM's new
constitution, which together insulated SLIM from the kind of crisis which hit Sheffield.

SLIM's team of chaplains

Throughout the period, industrial visiting remained 'a basic
strength of SLIM's approach' (notice the indefinite article), and
SLIM maintained a substantial full-time team throughout the
period. After standing in for Challen during the Sloan fellowship, Alan Griggs left to found a new industrial mission in Leeds;
Cecilia Goodenough's aversion to Challen's charts contributed to
her leaving SLIM in 1971 (after which she received a well deserved
Lambeth Doctorate of Divinity in 1972); Michael Butler joined the
team in 1968 (and was the last SLIM chaplain to hold a Cathedral
post); Thornton Elwyn, a Baptist, replaced Eric Blakeborough;
and Ian Taylor, a Presbyterian, joined the team because he couldn't
return to Nigeria. During the following decade chaplains came
and went, one or two new industries were added (such as construction sites in Thamesmead, visited by Paul Fuller, a Congregational minister), in 1976 SLIM's first and last full-time Roman
Catholic chaplain was appointed: Peter Fitzgibbon, who visited
Mirror Group Newspapers; and in 1973 a new post was created
for an industrial chaplain at St Thomas's Hospital and John Cribb
was appointed: an Australian United Reformed Church minister
and already a part-time hospital chaplain. Because factories were
closing, chaplains were spending longer in each company and
were becoming more knowledgeable about their industries; and
while some visiting remained of an informal and pastoral variety
(such as Bill Nightingale's in IPC and Piers Golding's in Pearce
Duff, a factory in the Bermondsey parish of which he was vicar),
some of it really was quite innovative. Ian Taylor developed a

social audit for companies, and the part-time chaplain Adrian Esdaile used it in Mullard, the electronic component manufacturer. A group of employees helped him to ask a series of questions of every department in the firm. This was perhaps the most systematic attempt SLIM ever made to relate the Christian Faith to the structure of an industry. What wasn't happening was visiting of South London new industries. This wasn't anyone's fault. Access to the large headquarters offices now populating much of north Southwark proved almost impossible to negotiate, and all that was possible was contact with individuals by getting to know one employee and then through them getting to know others: a technique employed by David Curwen in Price Waterhouse's offices. For this kind of work Challen's networking approach, undertaken from his base at Christ Church, proved well suited (Torry, 1990, pp. 214–19, 261–3).

In 1978 the 'Central Study Group' at A. J. Mills was disbanded after meeting in the same works canteen for 22 years (Torry, 1990, p. 277). It was difficult to start new groups, but there were a few. At St Thomas's Hospital Cribb got to know a wide variety of people: doctors, nurses, administrators, works department employees, porters . . . and he facilitated a monthly group to which they were all invited to discuss issues facing the hospital. A monthly group at his home gathered an even broader variety of people: a good range from the hospital, GPs, workers at the Waterloo Action Centre (a voluntary agency in the health field), and various visitors. Healthcare in all its variety was the theme.[7] This certainly wasn't purely workplace chaplaincy, nor unambiguously industrial mission, and broader urban issues were now creeping onto a number of chaplains' agendas. Paul Fuller in particular held together in one job description ministry among the construction companies building Thamesmead and ministry in the community living there (Torry, 1990, p. 273). SLIM's longstanding relationships with local churches played an important role in facilitating this expansion into urban mission.

Over the Bridge became an 'Associates' Newsletter', the SLIM dances ceased, and the industrial harvest thanksgiving moved from the Cathedral to Christ Church and by the end of the '70s was attached to SLIM's Annual General Meeting as a service of rededication for people who happened to be there. Residential conferences ceased at the end of the '70s because it had become too difficult to recruit for them (Torry, 1990, pp. 222–3, 279–80). Another rather more important shift of emphasis occurred in 1969 when the Council agreed to Challen's suggestion that 'members' should be called 'associates' (Torry, 1990, p. 207), with some being paid-up and voting (capital A Associates) and some not (small a associates). No doubt this change was driven by a genuine anxiety that membership bodies can become exclusive, and an equally genuine intention to create 'an Association of people actively concerned with the dilemmas and possibilities of urban industrial life, who together explore the relevance of Christian faith, and support each other in putting their findings into practice' (Torry, 1990, p. 251), but the result of the change was that the only people now unambiguously belonging to SLIM as an organization were Executive Committee and Council members and the chaplains (Torry, 1990, p. 258). An attempt in 1973 to recruit corporate Associates among South London's firms resulted in two responses to 70 requests: a symptom of the widening gulf between industry and SLIM.

This was a period of considerable diversity for SLIM. New activities were taken on but very little from the past was entirely lost (except for residential conferences). There is little sign of a coherent strategy, but perhaps that didn't matter. In a fast-changing and secularizing world what's required is individuals doing what looks possible at the time. That's what SLIM was doing.

Elsewhere

I have concentrated on Sheffield because that's where the crisis was, and on South London because SLIM provides a contrast to Sheffield and typifies much that was going on in industrial mission between the mid '60s and the end of the '70s. There was of course much important and changing work going on elsewhere:

As we have seen, Sheffield Industrial Mission trained Bill Wright so that he could return to Teesside to found an industrial mission;

and, similarly, Frank Scuffham undertook a two year secondment in Sheffield before going to Peterborough Diocese in 1961 to build a new team of chaplains.[8] Just as the persecution of the first Christians led to a widespread diaspora and the taking of the gospel to new places,[9] many of the chaplains who left Sheffield during its turbulent period in the late '60s took Sheffield's methods and theology across the country and beyond. John Rhodes moved to Humberside, Michael Atkinson to Northampton, Peter Dodd to Newcastle, and Margaret Kane to Hong Kong (Bagshaw, 1994, p. 65). Industrial mission throughout Britain was now even more heavily influenced by Wickham's approach than it was before. An important exception is Leeds. In 1961 the Leeds Christian Association was founded to 'raise a new sense of vocation and personal commitment' (Masumoto, 1983, p. 108) among laypeople in their working life. It quickly gathered 300 members. The organization's main function was education: in economics, sociology, and theology – the idea being that if people became more knowledgeable then they would be better able to explain their Christian beliefs and to stand up for 'Christian principles' in the workplace. Between 1968 and 1970 the organization's membership transferred by agreement to the Industrial Committee of the Leeds Council of Churches, convened by a Methodist minister, C. Groom. When Groom left in 1970, Alan Griggs moved from SLIM to Leeds, and in 1971 the Industrial Committee was renamed the Leeds Industrial Mission. Its main purpose was 'the training of people in understanding work decisions from a Christian standpoint'. By 1972 one full-time and seven part-time chaplains were working in eight companies, and study groups and weekend conferences were meeting. An unusual laity-centred initiative had become a rather more clerical one (Masumoto, 1983, pp. 110–17).

In Essex it was rather different; there was a history of part-time chaplaincies undertaken by the incumbents of small parishes. An exception was Frank Hackett's chaplaincy to the Port of London Authority: a chaplaincy close in ethos to Claringbull's and Wright's. The appointment had started as a joint one between the Essex Churches Council for Industry and Commerce (ECCIC) and the London Industrial Chaplaincy. From 1979 it was just ECCIC, which made sense because there were still docks east of the River Lee and there would soon be rather fewer to the west of it. (The Indian and Millwall Docks closed in 1980 and the Royal Docks in 1981.) The same currents which were passing through the rest of the movement were passing through ECCIC: chaplains were arguing about whether their meetings should start with Bible reading and prayer. The fact that in the workplace ' "religion" [was] of very little acceptability' (Hackett, 1977, p. 153) seems to have made it less than acceptable to the chaplains. Hackett thought that getting people to talk to each other was the important task. He organized meetings between managers, shop stewards and John Cutney, Chair of the Port of London Authority; and during strikes he would attend meetings, talk to people on all sides, and correct false information. In 1976 the closure of some of the docks was threatened, and Hackett organized a petition among all of the local churches. The docks didn't close. They closed later, though, and the Government appointed the London Docklands Development Corporation to develop the area and removed all planning control both from the local population and from their elected representatives.[10]

Hackett's work was a mixture of the reconciling and the confrontationally political, interestingly setting the scene for the Church's relationship with government during the 1980s.

Stephen Kendal's relationship with industry started as involvement with shipyard apprentices on the banks of the Tyne; and then in 1970 he was appointed to build on existing chaplaincy work to the British Steel Corporation at Port Talbot in South Wales and to establish other chaplaincies in Glamorgan. He added a gear box manufacturer and then a power station, and then started to recruit colleagues. Glamorgan Industrial Mission (Canhadaeth Ddiwydiannol Morgannwg) grew to three full-time chaplains and several part-time ones governed by an ecumenical committee. Kendal would tell church leaders that the churches were full of women and of clergy out of touch with the world, and that if they wanted the gospel to get to men then they'd better appoint some more chaplains.[11]

At Teesside Industrial Mission (TIM) chaplains were now being trained in behavioural science techniques, group work, group psychology, and organizational skills, so that they could more effectively bring management and unions together to tackle contemporary industrial problems (Northcott, 1989, pp. 55–8). By 1972 there were seven full-time chaplains and the chaplains took to their Executive Board a plan for dispensing with part-timers because part-time chaplains 'could not hope effectively to interact with the real issues of industrial life' (Northcott, 1989, p. 58). Interest in creating an active Christian laity in industry was now theoretical rather than practical. The Mission's relationship with the churches improved when it got involved with growing unemployment in the North East. TIM established the Portrack Workshop where 50 disadvantaged young workers renovated furniture. Work among disadvantaged workers was activity which churchpeople could understand. Wright handed over leadership of the team to Peter Stubley, and theological debate and worship began to appear on the agenda (Northcott, 1989, pp. 59–62).

A national organization

At various times the British Council of Churches (Hackett, 1977, pp. 45–6), the Board for Social Responsibility's Industry Committee, and Mollie Batten, had gathered groups of chaplains from around the country, but no national organization or strategy had emerged. By the end of the '60s there were 115 full-time and 175 part-time industrial chaplains – a considerable body of expertise which looked as if it needed co-ordinating.[12] The Sheffield crisis had concentrated minds, John Rogan's successor at the Industrial Committee of the Board for Social Responsibility had said that he didn't intend to convene industrial chaplains, consultations restarted, and Michael Atkinson, Frank Scuffham, Richard Taylor and others organized a postal ballot among industrial chaplains; 80.6% responded positively (the organizers had rashly adopted 80% as the necessary majority) (Atkinson, undated b), and in 1970 the Industrial Mission Association (IMA) was formed (Masumoto 1983, p. 51). This was a membership organization which any chaplain or layperson could join. Just as the bishops had not wanted to cede authority to a national secretariat, individual

industrial missions had no wish to lose any of their own autonomy even though a pooling of it might have been quite a good
idea at the time (shades of Britain's attitude to European institutions). The IMA was therefore organized regionally and a small
Central Co-ordinating Committee and an elected Moderator
were the only central organization (Torry, 1990, p. 50). This has
been a successful formula in terms of enabling chaplains to consult with each other in their regions.[13] The nationally organized
conferences once every two years, and the journal *IMAgenda*
(originally monthly, now bimonthly), have served the movement
well. Particularly useful have been the national networks for
chaplains working in the same company (such as ICI), in the same
industry (railways, the electricity supply industry, the steel industry, retail . . .), or, by 1978, on the same issues (women and work,
South Africa, social inequality, unemployment, disability) (Ross,
1997, pp. 30–1; Masumoto, 1983, pp. 58–72). Also useful to the
movement as a whole has been the IMA's Theology Development Group, established in 1975 to debate the theology underlying the movement's work, to publish (often with others), and,
from 1977, to collect the movement's archives (Masumoto, 1983,
pp. 76–7). Of long term significance has been the training course
for new industrial chaplains. (A three-week residential course,
for many years in Manchester but now based at Ushaw College
in Durham, remains the norm for new full-time and part-time
chaplains. This has now been supplemented by locally-organized
courses for volunteer chaplains using resources published by the
IMA.)[14] However, the IMA hasn't been entirely successful in giv-
ing the movement a co-ordinated voice in society, industry, or
the Church. Scotland has a national organizer for industrial mission. This is an effective role, and Scottish chaplains have often
wondered why attempts to appoint a British co-ordinator have
consistently failed (Ross, 1997, p. 31). The IMA's first national
conference in 1971, addressed by the Archbishop of Canterbury,
identified lack of feedback from the movement to the churches
as a serious problem, but then didn't ask itself what an effective
solution might look like (Hackett, 1971, pp. 62–3). There haven't
been any more crises like Sheffield's, but in many places the

denominations' loss of interest has resulted in decline and closure, and the IMA hasn't been able to do anything about it. In the absence of a coherent national voice it never will be able to.

A parallel exercise was the Churches Consortium on Industrial Mission, founded by the British Council of Churches in 1975. A particularly useful piece of work was its first paper, *Ecumenical Guidelines for the Organization of Industrial Mission*, largely a repeat of the British Council of Churches' 1958 paper, but none the worse for that. In 1979 the Consortium published *Appointments to Industrial Mission: Towards a General Pattern*. This helpfully recommended that posts should be long-term, that they should be advertised, and that the best person applying should be appointed, regardless of gender and even if they were from a different denomination from the one funding the post. A basic manual for chaplains followed in 1982, *Starting the Work*. It's interesting that it's this body, made up of denominational representatives, chaplains, and one or two others, which produced these useful documents, and not the Industrial Mission Association.

Comparisons

Non-stipendiary ministers

During the 1970s the Southwark Ordination Course was joined by a number of regional part-time ordination training courses and non-stipendiary ministers became an important component of the Church of England's ordained ministry. Most of these clergy have seen their role as predominantly parish-based. Their workplaces know that they are ordained, and they will sometimes find themselves questioned about religion or used as pastors, but it is in the residential community that most of these clergy see their ministry located. Some, though, see themselves as Ministers in Secular Employment (MSEs) and attempt to work out what it means to be clergy in the workplace. The numbers of MSEs vary from diocese to diocese, of course. In the Diocese of Southwark there were enough of them in 1968 to form a separate chapter, and in 1992 there were enough for three separate chapters in the different Episcopal Areas of the Diocese (Hurst, 2005, p. 39). My impression of more recent ordinands emerging from SOC's successor, the South East Institute for Theological Education, is that more of them see their ministries in terms of the parish. I suspect that the number of MSEs is falling.

The stories which MSEs tell are in many ways similar to those told by industrial chaplains (Fuller and Vaughan, 1986), but there are of course considerable differences between the roles. Chaplains are independent of the company, which gives them a certain freedom; but 'the advantages of independence necessarily create the disadvantages of alienation'. The MSE '*feels* the problems and tension of the workplace as his own; for the chaplain they are always someone else's': so the MSE's prophetic stance might be more relevant and more engaged but it will also carry 'the anxiety of losing the job; and with it, not only his (and his family's) livelihood but also the focus of ministry' (Forshaw, 1986, p. 69).

A question shared by both the MSE and the ordained chaplain is: What difference does ordination make? After all, there is generally no sacramental component to either of their ministries. Is there any difference between the lay Christian at work and the MSE? Is there any difference between the work of an ordained chaplain and an industrial chaplain who is a layperson? My answer to both questions is 'Yes', and it has to do with the way in which people identify the priest or minister as an authorised representative of the Church. John Davis's answer is 'No' (Davis, 1986, pp. 74–9).

A more recent development is Ordained Local Ministers (OLMs) (Torry and Heskins, 2006). Christians who have been members of their congregation for a long time, and who intend to stay where they are, are ordained to serve in their own parishes. Training is generally locally based and involves the parish as well as the ordinand. While OLMs will also see themselves to some extent as clergy at work, and people at work will know that they are priests, the focus of their ministry is firmly in their residential community. A question for industrial mission is whether a workplace equivalent might be worth pursuing.

Secularization

By the end of the '70s a new element was entering chaplains' reports: the stress which industrial visiting was generating. Sometimes there were specific reasons for this, but sometimes it was simply that the gulf between the Church which they represented and the institutions to which they were relating had got so wide that it was posing psychological difficulties. Added to this was a general feeling of decline. Groups, conferences, industrial harvest thanksgiving services: all of these were failing. Long established chaplaincies were coming to an end, it was increasingly difficult to establish new ones, and companies could see no relevance in relating to SLIM or to any other industrial mission unless chaplains were supplying a secular product which they wanted. The task of relating faith to industry was simply becoming more difficult (Torry, 1990, p. 269), and industrial mission was beginning to see its task as education in industry and in the Church rather than as the formation of a fellowship within industry. Relating the Christian faith to industry could be a purely cerebral activity with little real contact with industry itself. In 1969 SLIM's Council agreed to Challen's new aim for SLIM: 'To explore the relevance of the Christian Faith to men and women in their work and where possible to implement the discoveries made' (Torry, 1990, p. 234). A subsidiary aim was to feed back 'understanding' to South London's congregations.

Michael Northcott correctly suggests that Bill Wright needed industrial management's good will in order to undertake his organizational development work, and so 'prophecy' was not what he was doing;[15] and at SLIM practical contact with industry was sometimes more theoretical than actual. Intention and reality didn't always match, but there was still a genuine intention to build bridges. In an increasingly difficult context industrial mission remained a 'sign' of God bringing about his kingdom (Kane, 1980, p. 111), and both industry and the Church would have been poorer without it. During this period workplace visiting remained a central activity, but the world was changing, and it was about to change rather drastically. The oil price shock of the mid '70s caused economic contraction, redundancies, and unemployment. In this chapter we have discovered some of industrial mission's responses. In the next we shall discover the major change of direction into which mass unemployment led the movement, and we shall need to ask whether the loss of much of the workplace visiting has meant the movement losing its soul.

Notes

1 Atkinson writes that one of the chapters appearing under his name was in fact written by John Rogan, who didn't want his name attached to it.

2 *Sheffield Telegraph*, 28th February 1966, p. 1, quoted in Lurkings, 1981, p. 249.

3 *The Observer*, 13th March 1966, quoted in Lurkings, 1981, p. 250.

4 *The Guardian*, 15th March 1966, copy supplied by Michael Atkinson.

5 Barker, E., S.F. Linsley and T. Chapman, 1966, 'Sheffield Industrial Mission', a report to the Bishop of Sheffield, July 1966, pp. 18-19, quoted in Bagshaw, 1994, p. 63.

6 If it's of any interest, Challen is godfather to one of the author's sons.

7 Interview with John Cribb, August 2009.

8 Correspondence from Frank Scuffham.

9 Acts 8:1–4.

10 Interview with Frank Hackett, 20th August 2009.

11 Interview with Stephen Kendal by Peter Cope, 20th July 2006.

12 Church of England Industrial Council, list of industrial chaplains, August 1970.

13 The IMA has recently registered as a charity and for that purpose has had to register as a single national organisation (and for the same purpose the Central Co-ordinating Committee has become a National Executive Committee); but the organisation is still organised regionally.

14 Masumoto, 1983, pp. 85–6; *IMAgenda*, September/October 2009, pp. 16–19.

15 The contest, which took place across the pages of *Crucible* in 1979 and 1980, is recounted in Church of England 1988, pp. 39–40.

7

Issues: Strikes, unemployment, and the pursuit of justice

The steel strike

In 1980 the British Steel Corporation decided to cut one third of its workforce and to offer the smallest of wage increases to those who remained. The unions had little choice but to call a strike, and with Margaret Thatcher's Conservative Government on the side of management the dispute was bound to be a bitter one.

The morning the strike started each of the Sheffield steelworks chaplains went to the site which they normally visited. They first visited the pickets and then asked for permission to go through the lines to visit management. Permission was given. They found local managements as frustrated as the men outside the gates because negotiations were national ones and local managers could do nothing but await the outcome. Malcolm Grundy, the departing Senior Chaplain, and Raymond Draper, Acting Senior Chaplain, kept in touch with the strike headquarters in Sheffield and Rotherham, and in order to be visibly impartial they would always visit both management and union headquarters on the same day. They kept in touch with steelworks chaplains in other parts of the country, and it was under the auspices of the Industrial Mission Association's Steel Chaplains' Network that the Sheffield Industrial Mission's (SIM's) chaplains visited the British Steel Corporation's Chief Executive, Bob Scholey, to state their own concern at plans to close the steelworks in Corby and Shotton.

The Mission saw itself as pastor to both sides. The chaplains were not negotiators: their task was to listen, to keep confidences, and to offer support to everyone involved in a difficult dispute. The media understood this, except for Radio 4's *Sunday* programme and *The Church Times*, both of which tried to get the chaplains to align themselves with the unions. Chaplains saw themselves as impartial truth-tellers, not as partial advocates, and they wrote to the press and to 600 South Yorkshire clergy to explain the facts and issues behind the strike.

The strike lasted 12 weeks and ended in defeat for the steel-workers. A sign of SIM's achievement is that by the end of the strike both managers and workers regarded the chaplains as con-structive friends. One interesting result was that for the first time since SIM's internal strife during the 1960s the Templeborough plant (formerly Steel, Peech and Tozer) welcomed a chaplain onto the shop floor.

Much that chaplains had helped to achieve in the steel industry never recovered from the dispute. Works Councils weren't convened during the strike and they never met again. Clerical staff unions hadn't supported the strike, and this caused continuing bitterness between clerical staff and steelworkers. SIM's 'reconciliation' theory and practice no longer seemed quite adequate to the situation, and chaplains began to discuss how industrial mission ought to relate to the kind of entrenched conflict which was no longer amenable to consensus-building and resolution (Bagshaw, 1994, pp. 90–3).

The closure of the steel mill at Consett in County Durham was announced before the steel strike and the men there were far from happy when the strike was called. Their priority was to save the plant, not to increase the salary offer. John Eyles, the works chap-lain, remained closely in touch with the details of negotiations, with possible rescue plans, and with the feelings of everyone involved. His diary of events closes with some sharp comments on the way in which the closure happened and with suggestions as to how it could have been done better. He recommends early consultation about the possibility of factory closures because 'equality among people is of more fundamental importance than their differences . . . human dignity requires participation'.[1] The depth of Eyles' engage-ment with the people and institutions involved can only have come from what we can only call deep workplace visiting.

This wasn't the first strike and closure which Eyles had had to think about. In 1979 workers at the Caterpillar tractor factory in Birtley went on strike over the management's plan for a second shift. Eyles didn't understand the strike call, and reading his account of the issues, neither do I. The strike ended quite suddenly after 12 weeks. In 1983 Caterpillar announced the plant's closure. At the suggestion of shop stewards, Eyles joined a Birtley Council of Action set up to oppose the closure, the plant's management asked him to cease visiting the plant, the trades unions told the press, and Eyles' exclusion was briefly national news. The plant closed in September 1984. The Council of Action stayed in existence to support workers made redundant and to research the likelihood of other local plant closures.[2]

Miners

Rather counter-intuitively, the first SIM chaplain to visit coal mines was a woman, Margaret Kane. She visited Elsecar colliery weekly and also encouraged parochial clergy to visit collieries in their parishes. Leslie Hunter supported this work and also, rather typically, took his own initiative by appointing Charles Grice, a former miner, to be Rector of Armthorpe and to visit Markham Main colliery: a chaplaincy which he had negotiated without involving SIM. There was no systematic group work but there was plenty of informal conversation and pastoral care. Grice spent long hours teaching apprentices, and he would often be the one to inform a family of a miner's injury or death. When Grice moved on in 1974 SIM appointed David Lawrance, another former miner, to the full-time team with a brief to visit Markham Main. The attempt to persuade local clergy to visit pits in their parishes continued, though often without success.

In 1983 the National Union of Miners (NUM) banned overtime, and in 1984 British Coal decided to close Cortonwood Colliery without following the established provisions for consultation, the local NUM called a strike, and the strike spread, region by region, without a national ballot being called. This split communities, because some miners went out on strike and some wouldn't strike because they hadn't been balloted. It also split the union: Nottinghamshire's miners left the NUM and formed the Union of Democratic Mineworkers. The Government was determined not to allow a repeat of 1974 when a miners' strike had brought down Edward Heath's government, and they used the police to defend miners who crossed the picket lines. Violence was frequently threatened and often used (Bagshaw, 1994, pp. 117–19).

Coal mine chaplains in South Yorkshire took different attitudes. David Lawrance, who believed the strike to be unconstitutional, an industrial issue and not a political one, visited everyone involved at Markham Main, maintained a neutral stance between management and miners, and attempted industrial mission's tried and tested methods for seeking consensus. Tony Attwood, Team Vicar in Maltby, was on the miners' side. He visited pickets, management, the police, and the contractors who had been brought in to run the pit. (He found that neither the miners nor the local police were particularly keen on police from elsewhere being brought into the area, and he wasn't very keen himself after being chased from a picket line by a police dog.) He believed that the management had been wrong not to employ the normal consultation process before announcing Cortonwood's closure and that this was symptomatic of the low esteem in which miners were held. The church hall in Attwood's parish was supplying 300 meals a day to miners and their families, and his support for the miners' position was well known (Bagshaw, 1994, pp. 120–21). The difference between Lawrance's and Attwood's attitudes to the strike mirrored the diverse response throughout the Church and throughout the Mission.

In the Durham coalfield the only chaplain was Stephen Kendal. The diocese couldn't afford another one and he never liked the idea of working with part-timers. He thought they couldn't develop the necessary expertise (which is nonsense: of course we can) and because they can't follow up visits to mines and factories by visiting management associations and other such bodies – though I don't really see the logic here: why not employ a full-timer to co-ordinate part-timers and then have the full-timer follow up issues as necessary? Be that as it may: Kendal was the only chaplain in the Durham coalfield when the miners' strike started. 'I remember Mary my wife going round the corner and finding all of these miners climbing on buses all wearing masks because they were the hard lads – they were ones that were paid for going on picket lincs. But the others weren't . . .' Kendal worked closely with Bishop David Jenkins and joined other chaplains in the IMA's coal chaplains' network when they visited Ian McGregor, Chairman of the National Coal Board. 'He sacked a man while we were there on the phone, it was amazing, utterly amazing . . . he knew . . . that he had a political Master telling him what to do and that's how it worked.'[3]

Douglas Bale, a chaplain in South Wales, formulated a possible agreement which could have ended the strike. ACAS, McGregor and the unions all thought the ideas worth pursuing, and so did Peter Walker, Secretary of State: 'He said, "I like it, but it has to go to number 10" and that was the last we ever heard of it.' Winning the battle was part of Margaret Thatcher's anti-union strategy, and to end the strike by negotiation wouldn't have given her the victory she wanted.[4]

In 1985 Lawrance returned to parochial ministry, Attwood took his place as Sheffield Industrial Mission's coal industry chaplain, and in 1992 his well-researched briefings prepared churches throughout south Yorkshire for a vociferous campaign against Michael Heseltine's plan to close 31 of the country's remaining 50 pits: a closure programme which would have left only three pits working in South Yorkshire. Church leaders and laity of all denominations united to oppose the Government's plans because such massive closures would have imposed unsustainable human costs on communities and because the Government had no coherent energy policy which might get anywhere near justifying the closures (Bagshaw, 1994, pp. 122–3; Attwood, 1996, pp. 160–2). The Government promised a review, but by closing pits a few at a time it finally got its way. All of the pits on the 1992 list were gone by 1993.

The events of 1992 were important because for the first time the churches had acted as a co-ordinated pressure group in a campaign facilitated by industrial mission (Bagshaw, 1994, p. 124).

The Church can respond to major events, social issues and individual need because it exists in every community. The Church in South Yorkshire, Durham, Northumberland and Wales (to name but a few of the places involved in the strikes and closures of the 1980s) was able to respond to major national events because it existed not only in residential communities but also in many of the area's industries. Industrial chaplains had visited workplaces over many years, had got to know the people who worked in them, had understood the issues which their workforces and managers faced, and had been a faithful pastoral and prophetic presence (Attwood, 1996, pp. 167–9). Their commitment was the reason for the Church's appropriate response. In the future the same will be true. We shall be able to respond to social and economic crises to the extent that the Church as an institution is involved in social and economic institutions. Individual Christians being involved is essential, but it's not enough. Institutional involvement is crucial.

Unemployment

In 1980 Denis Claringbull moved to Birmingham, to an industrial mission post which involved workplace visiting in several companies of the Delta Metal Group, in Dunlop, and in smaller firms in the Jewellery Quarter. Other chaplains in the team visited Land Rover, Lucas, Cannings, and British Rail. Most of these firms were to close, and unemployment became the main issue for the Birmingham chaplains. In Handsworth unemployment rose to 80%, and in other parts of Birmingham it was almost as bad. The statistics are shocking enough, but the millions of individual human tragedies were infinitely worse. 'When the job is lost people not only lose their income but they also lose their identity. Sometimes this may lead to illness, mental breakdown, marriage breakdown, crime or even suicide' (Claringbull, 1994, p. 127). (I would add that it can also cause someone's children a serious loss of motivation, particularly if a parent's redundancy occurs when their children are teenagers.)

Something had to be done, and with the support of Hugh Montefiore, Bishop of Birmingham, Claringbull put together an

Unemployment Commission. This began its work with an all night vigil at St Martin's in the Bullring (Churches Industrial Group Birmingham). Montefiore and other church leaders attended. The commission published a blue leaflet on unemployment which was much copied, and it worked closely with the City Council and with the Manpower Services Commission (MSC: a government agency charged with helping people through unemployment, and especially with preparing young people for work). This partnership's main project was Inter Church Endeavour, which turned a redundant school into training workshops so that people could learn to sell themselves in the employment market. Another useful project was the Birmingham Churches Management Agency, established to manage church-sponsored projects throughout Birmingham. Chaplains and others had correctly identified a problem: that many churchpeople wanted to do something about unemployment and had the skills to run projects, but they didn't have the skills and experience to manage them. That's where the agency stepped in. The chaplains also turned to more political action: Claringbull still has the mug from the People's March for Jobs.[5]

In Scotland industrial chaplains published a leaflet asking the Government to take responsibility for regional employment, gathered groups of unemployed people for mutual support, and organized meetings with speakers and gave out the invitations to people standing in queues at labour exchanges. By 1983, there were 57 church-based MSC-funded training and employment schemes (Ross, 1997, pp. 56–61).

It was a Peterborough Diocese industrial chaplain, Frank Scuffham, who helped to found and became the first Chair of Church Action with the Unemployed (CAWTU: an organization which deserves a history of its own).[6] In South Yorkshire, Elizabeth Nash was appointed to co-ordinate the churches' work on unemployment, and in 1981 a conference sponsored by SIM and the MSC gave birth to ChUG, the Christians' Unemployment Group, which successfully encouraged Christians to meet in small groups to plan practical responses to unemployment. It was ChUG which gave birth to Unemployment Sunday (Bagshaw, 1994, pp.108–9).

With the help of a Nigerian student on placement SIM sponsored six young people for work experience in church organizations. The first larger scale project was 'Workshop 6': a small foundry to smelt aluminium. Malcolm Grundy was Company Secretary. Nobody seems to have thought about the mission rationale or the politics of any of this. Something had to be done, and even small things were worth doing. They might be tokenism in relation to the massive problem which unemployment was becoming, but there was nothing wrong with that.

In South London SLIM had already contributed to the work of the South East London Industrial Consultative Group, set up in 1969 to lobby politicians, to argue for consultation on the future of the docks, and to establish Job Creation Programmes (Church of England 1977);[7] and SLIM and the Blackfriars Settlement, a social work organization, had already acted as midwives to Elephant Jobs, an MSC Youth Opportunities Programme and then a Youth Training Scheme (Torry, 1991, p. 292). In 1984 SLIM appointed Bob Nind, formerly Vicar of St Matthew's, Brixton, to pursue the issues of employment, the future of work, and unemployment. He had already done some work for CAWTU and had himself signed on for a while: so he too was among those industrial chaplains who knew from experience the field in which they were working. He organized trips to Tyneside and Teesside for unemployed people from London, convened a regular group of unemployed church members which attempted to educate the churches, took part in a forum for unemployment action groups and claimants' unions, and organized delegations to meet politicians. He set up an MSC Community Programme in Thamesmead to employ and train local people to be community workers and to teach English, and he helped churches to establish their own similar projects. From the standpoint of his own project he and others tried to get the MSC to accept community development as one of its aims. As far as Nind was concerned, the reason for doing all this was because industrial mission's pastoral relationship with a workforce doesn't end when that workforce ceases to work (Torry, 1991, p. 348). Donald Ross's reason for the Scottish activity was that 'the Church has traditionally cared for the distressed, the elderly, and the disadvantaged. Over the years of the MSC the churches shared in many excellent projects serving people within these categories. Without funding from the MSC they would never have got going (Ross, 1997, p. 63).

By the end of the 1980s the churches and industrial missions in many parts of the country were intricately entwined with the Manpower Services Commission. They had established training and employment projects, often in church premises and often managed by clergy and other church members; they had managed the complexities of MSC rules; over and over again they had managed transitions from one set of rules to another; they had objected to such provisions as the '52 weeks rule' (which insisted that no one could be on a programme for more than a year); and they had coped with the MSC's seemingly arbitrary decisions as to whether or not to continue to fund particular schemes (Ross, 1997, pp. 62–8): but in the words of a Scottish minister, 'Had I known the time it would have taken and the amount of supervision it required of me, I might not have started the projects. But again, I would have done so. It is . . . a small price to pay to be able to give people a start again. That is what matters' (Ross, 1997, p. 68).

Normally it was workplace visiting which led to issues. In the case of unemployment – the big issue for the 1980s – it was the issue which led to significant amounts of work.

Taking sides

Ian Stubbs, Industrial Chaplain in Slough, always said what he thought. In a review of the Churches Consortium on Industrial Mission's 1982 manual for industrial chaplains, *Starting the Work*, he wrote this: 'From the annals of the wise fathers of Piggy-in-the-Middle Land the secret is at last out! How to straddle the fence without damaging sensitive parts. How to hold aloft the flag of caution while picking your way through the muddy reaches of conflicting ideologies. How to sort out where you stand, sit where others sit, but avoid identifying with the sitting or the standing. How to avoid the traps of extremism. In short – how to be an Industrial Chaplain!' (Quoted in Tonkinson, 2009, p. 37)

When Mike West arrived in 1982 as Sheffield Industrial Mission's new Senior Chaplain he brought with him experience of the European Contact Group on Church and Industry and also of Urban Industrial Mission (UIM): a network of projects in every continent. UIM's ethos was a 'bias to the poor'. After Bishop David Sheppard wrote his book *Bias to the Poor* in 1983, and the Church of England published *Faith in the City* in 1985, expressing a 'bias to the poor' became rather more acceptable. It was also a fundamental challenge to the ethos of industrial mission, which from its foundation had regarded itself as pastor and prophet to the whole of industry, to management as well as to workers, an ethos well illustrated during SIM's relationships with both sides of industry during the steel strike. West asked for a reorientation of the Mission's activity towards the promotion of a just society, and by implication away from pastoral work and evangelism. Nothing much changed initially, but as the '80s wore on and the Church became more politicised, SIM educated the Church in economic and political realities and founded projects aimed at justice for the poor (Bagshaw, 1994, pp. 95–9).

In 1985 the British Steel Corporation suggested the closure of its Tinsley Park plant, and Clifford Auckland, the plant's chaplain, publicly sided with the union campaign to save the plant. The chaplains' team supported him by publishing a paper on reasons for keeping the plant open. The chairman of SIM's Council, the industrialist Peter Lee, objected that the chaplains had no right to commit the Mission to such a position without consulting the Council. Perhaps they didn't ask because they thought the Council might not agree with them. The plant closed, the chaplains' relationships with the unions were better than ever (even being asked to count union ballots), and the relationship with local management remained good, too, because they hadn't wanted the plant to close either. (Not every dispute resulted in a closure. When Sheffield Forgemasters sacked two trade union convenors a strike broke out and management sacked 700 workers and threatened to close the plant. Gordon Wilson, Mike West, and the Anglican and Roman Catholic bishops, all talked to both sides and prepared the ground for the arbitration service, ACAS, to resolve the dispute (Bagshaw, 1994, pp 103 4).)

In Southampton, from 1964 until his retirement in 1999, Julian Eagle took sides. When he arrived as a curate in Eastleigh in 1964 British Rail was planning to close the railway workshop and Eagle joined a demonstration. The railway workers asked him to visit them. He worked as a docker for six months and went to South Africa to see for himself how the South African dockers who loaded the ships lived, and was understandably distressed when he wasn't asked to speak to Winchester Diocese's Diocesan Synod during a debate on apartheid. After all, he knew something about the subject. A particular trauma for the Southampton area was the Berlin wall coming down. Less international tension meant less arms manufacturing, so fewer jobs. Eagle got involved in the campaign to find new products for arms companies to make. He joined trades unionists on their visits to fellow trades unionists in France and Germany, and came back to try to persuade the Industrial Mission Association to get involved in issues beyond our own shores. He went to the Philippines to find out about the lives of fruit pickers and found that they were both Marxists and Roman Catholics. They picked the fruit which went into the holds of the ships which Southampton's dockers unloaded, but Eagle didn't find it easy to interest trades unionists in England in doing anything about the problems which he had discovered on the other side of the world. By then it was the 1980s and trades unions had enough of their own problems to worry about.[8]

Workplace visiting

In Sheffield chaplaincies closed as traditional industries closed, but new chaplaincies were added in retail, in the leisure industry, and in high-technology industries. In 1987 a new chaplaincy to the Sheffield Science Park proved that traditional chaplaincy methods could be applied to firms with tiny workforces. The full-time team remained strong, the number of part-timers grew during the decade, and it was mainly part-timers who became chaplains to fire stations when in 1987 the Sheffield Industrial Mission took responsibility for chaplaincy to the whole of the county's fire service. Gordon Wilson visited the headquarters, and because he was also chaplain to Sheffield Wednesday he went immediately to the ground when the Hillsborough football disaster happened. He spent the whole of the following week offering counselling to the ground staff and organizing the necessary counselling for everyone involved. He helped with the investigation of the tragedy, and he participated in memorial services – and all of this was possible because he was already chaplain to the ground and to the fire service (Bagshaw, 1994, pp. 99–103).

In South London the stories are rather less dramatic, but, as in Sheffield, workplace visiting remained the bedrock of industrial mission's activity. New chaplains arrived, some to carry on existing work and some to try new things. Richard Moberly had been in parochial ministry in Kennington and is allegedly the rector in David Hare's play *Racing Demon*. He joined the full-time team in 1980, visited Mirror Group Newspapers, and negotiated a chaplaincy to the manual workers of Lambeth Borough Council. I joined the team in 1983; in 1984 James Siddons, a layman, was appointed to work on the railways and in London Transport; and at the end of 1984 Michael Gudgeon, a United Reformed Church Minister, arrived to work among trades unions. Thornton Elwyn was still visiting the power stations and offices of the electricity supply industry, and David Curwen, who had moved from SLIM to Croydon, rejoined the team when Croydon became part of the Diocese of Southwark in 1985 (Torry, 1991, pp. 333–5, 347).

If I might be personal for a while: in 1983 I was the only applicant for the combined post of curate of Christ Church and industrial chaplain. I took over John Cribb's industrial mission work at St Thomas's Hospital and did my best to establish a networking chaplaincy in civil service offices in north Southwark. St Thomas's Hospital was an absorbing task. I started with the works department, and then added porters, kitchen staff, the linen department, administrators, finance offices, and several other departments. The issues which dominated conversation when I arrived in 1983 still did so when I left in 1988: redundancy, trades unions, loneliness, privatisation, dining rooms, low morale, death, industrial mission, new technology, the bomb, frozen posts, Jesus, administrators, being valued, and bonus schemes. The Joint Trade Union Committee, and later the Joint Consultative Committee, invited me to observe their meetings. Excellent relationships with the hospital chaplains meant that between us we could serve individuals and structures throughout the institution. For the sheer variety of people involved and issues raised it was a fascinating place to be an industrial chaplain. As far as I know only John Cribb and myself have worked as industrial chaplains in a hospital. More people should try it.

Rather different was my work in Department of Social Security headquarters buildings. When I was a curate at the Elephant and Castle, where one of the buildings was located, I got to know some of the people working there. I had worked for the department for two years before ordination, so I too had worked in the industry in which I later became a chaplain. General access to the building proved impossible to negotiate so what emerged was a group of civil servants committed to promoting debate on the relationship between Christian faith and the work of the department. We published a quarterly journal, 'Shades of Grey', and held occasional meetings.

Any chaplain who visits a workplace picks up issues which need to be discussed and worked on. During the early days of industrial mission the creation of a fellowship within industry was the major task, and the pursuit of issues was sometimes an outcome of visiting and sometimes a method by which to create a fellowship: but the pursuit of issues was never an end in itself. By the 1980s there was far more balance to the process. Workplace visiting was largely to pick up issues which could then be worked on both within the company and outside it; and sometimes the issues led to visiting.

Thus for James Siddons pastoral visiting and reconciliation between different groups of workers was still the task, but the issues facing the rail industry were high on his agenda. Group work simply wasn't feasible on the railways, so reorganizations, transport policy, privatisation, overtime, changes in trades unions, and other issues, were discussed with individuals, with the Chartered Institute of Transport, and at a 'transport forum' which Siddons and Ian Yearsley, a Reader and a SLIM Council member, organized (Torry, 1991, pp. 340, 347). My own work on issues relating to the health service gave birth to a monthly newsletter at St Thomas's Hospital, 'Questions', and to a William Temple Foundation booklet;[9] and my work on issues in the Department of Health and Social Security gave birth to long-term research on the tax and benefits system.[10] Moberly took the issues he picked up in the rather fraught Mirror Group Newspapers to a 'media group' of Associates which included Paul and Sue Eedle (Visnews and the BBC) and John Murray (counsellor, Times Newspapers). Graham Shaw, a part-time chaplain in London Weekend Television's South Bank building, also picked up media issues. Elwyn pursued the issue of acid rain, both inside and outside the offices which he visited, and he debated energy policy with the IMA's Theology Development Group. Michael Gudgeon's work in trade union offices drew him into their campaigns, and particularly their campaign against the privatisation of the water industry. So, just as in Sheffield and Southampton, chaplains were taking sides (Torry, 1991, pp. 345–8).

Women at work

More women and fewer men were now in employment, so working conditions in those industries employing predominantly women were becoming more of an issue. In Sheffield a 'Working Women's Group' was a place where women could tell their stories and study the Bible (Bagshaw, 1991, p. 107). On Tyneside, Caroline Barker Bennett was chaplain to a factory making oil seals in which women worked side by side with men, and she was also chaplain to the workforce of a women's clothing co-operative. The differences she discovered led to research into the ways in which factory work can benefit women, and particularly into how much women appreciate the extra-family community with which the factory provides them (Barker Bennett, 1996). In South London, Alison Norris joined the team to visit Freemans Mail Order. She started in the data preparation department where 250 women worked, and slowly worked her way round all of the departments, visiting at different times of day in order to meet different shifts. A common topic for discussion was the problem of combining paid work with responsibility for a family, and Norris involved herself in such difficult issues as racism. Ray Rowsell, the manager in charge of training and later a member of SLIM's Council, thought that women found Norris more approachable because she was a woman (Torry, 1991, p. 343).

A national review of Industrial Mission in 1985 singled out the issue of women at work for particular mention, discussed the interconnectedness of work and home, and asked industrial mission to do more analysis in this area (Church of England, 1988, pp. 60–8).

The review

By 1986 there were 127 full-time industrial chaplains in England, Wales and Scotland, and also 56 half-time and 220 part-time ones. The movement was 40 years old, and it was high time a systematic appraisal was carried out to review achievements so far and make recommendations for the future. There was, of course, a hidden motive. Of the full- and half-time chaplains 73% were employed by their Church of England dioceses (Church of England, 1988, pp. xiii, 121), and a number of those dioceses were wondering whether to carry on paying for them. In Peterborough the Bishop took the opportunity of a longstanding chaplain's retirement to cut other industrial mission posts without holding any kind of review of the chaplains' effectiveness. One of the part-time chaplains dispensed with was Noel Beattie, who thought that he was successfully 'keeping a rumour of God alive . . . and certainly the church had become a little more relevant for people because of this',[11] but the bishop seems to have made up his mind before asking for any assessment at all.

The review group's report, *Industrial Mission – An Appraisal*, discusses the changing nature of industry, the diversity of industrial mission responses, a variety of issues facing industrial mission, and relationships between the churches and industrial mission. The main recommendation is for a regional management structure for industrial mission in which ecumenical bodies appoint management committees (Church of England, 1988, pp. 93–105). This would have turned industrial mission more clearly into an agency of the Church and would have made it very difficult for the movement to function as a bridge between the Church and a secular industrial society. No account seems to have been taken of successful independent constitutions such as SLIM's, or of the important precedent of independently constituted mission societies such as the Church Mission Society and the United Society for the Propagation of the Gospel. It's a good thing that nobody followed the committee's recommendation.

The report begins: 'The picture of Industrial Mission which began to emerge during the Committee's discussions was colourful and complex. There was clearly enormous variety around the country, in terms of organization, ecumenism, ways of working and aims and objectives' (Church of England, 1988, p. 2).

In this chapter we have come across something of that variety. During previous decades, different industrial missions faced different situations and did things differently. During the 1980s this was still true, but, as we have also seen, there was also greater diversity within each industrial mission as well as between the missions.

Comparisons

Faith in the City

Following riots in Brixton in 1982 the Archbishop of Canterbury established a commission to examine the situation in the most deprived urban areas and to make recommendations to the nation and the Church. Sir Richard O'Brien, formerly Chairman of the MSC, chaired the commission. When the report was published in

December 1985 Conservative politicians, and particularly Norman Tebbit, attacked it as 'Marxist'. It wasn't, of course, but the attack was useful in that it helped to publicise the report and to get it read. The Government's defensiveness was understandable. The commission had gathered evidence which proved the desperate state of many inner urban areas and large housing estates. Most of the recommendations were to the Church, and two major outcomes were the Church Urban Fund and Ordained Local Ministry.

Industrial mission was well involved in the creation of the report, and it was often industrial chaplains who hosted consultation events and visits when the commission visited their parts of the country. Following publication, industrial chaplains disseminated the report widely and participated in local consultations inspired by the report. There were three reasons for this close involvement: first of all, industrial mission was now doing urban mission because it could no longer separate industry from the urban world; second, unemployment and its effects were at the heart both of the report and of industrial mission's concerns (the report recommended that more industrial chaplains should work among the unemployed (Church of England, 1985, p. 226)); and third, the method which the commission used was the same as the method which industrial chaplains had employed since the days of the Navvy Mission: going to where people were, listening to their concerns, understanding their situation, understanding social structures, providing pastoral care where required, and being prophets where possible.

There is very little contrast involved in this particular comparison. *Faith in the City* was classic 1980s industrial mission.

Secularization

As we have seen, chaplains have often been tempted to employ secular methods and ideologies in the cause of relevance in industry. Their own religion and practice has thus become secularized. During the 1980s industrial mission's close engagement with the Manpower Services Commission posed a more serious problem.

Where a religious or faith-based organization relates closely to a secular organization then it will become more secular (DiMaggio and Powell, 1983; Torry, 2005, p. 31). Fulfilling the MSC's aims and objectives became the task, and where chaplains held the MSC to task it was usually over practical difficulties which industrial missions and churches were having with the processes and rules and not over the MSC's policies. We might have expected industrial chaplains to object strongly to having to eject trainees after a year because ejection isn't what the Church does: but ejection was what the church-run schemes did because they wanted to keep their MSC funding. This constitutes both religious secularization and institutional secularization both of industrial mission and of the churches.

Industrial mission has always been the Church's 'yes' to the secular. This 'yes' became particularly visible during 1986, the year which the Royal Society for the Encouragement of Arts, Manufacturing and Commerce designated 'Industry Year'. The Royal Society was concerned that Britain had developed an unhealthy anti-industry culture. Industrial chaplains knew that there was a lot wrong with industry (Church of England, 1988, pp. 53–8), but they could also agree with Kenneth Adams' assessment that industry is 'the prime social service' (Church of England, 1988, p. 55) and so could use the year to say to the Church that industry mattered, and, by implication, that industrial mission mattered.

God also mattered to industrial mission during the 1980s, and a question sometimes debated among chaplains during the decade was: should we speak about God when we visit workplaces? Margaret Kane thought that we should:

It is possible and necessary at times to be quite explicit in speaking about God. The need is twofold. First, there is a need to clear away a mass of misconceptions and to make some basic information about Christianity available. Second, there is a need to convey the nature of God's personal invitation. (Kane, 1980, p. 166)

In my own chaplaincy work I tried to notice in which situations I spoke about God (generally in answer to questions about religious or life-stage questions) and also how I spoke about God; and during the mid-'80s SLIM chaplains were expected to say in their annual reports how and how often they had spoken about God. While it might not have been stated in these terms, this was a conscious attempt at desecularization both of the workplace and of industrial mission.

Conclusions

This chapter, even more so than the others, could have contained far more accounts of projects founded, companies visited, and campaigns and people supported. The few accounts for which I have managed to find space will need to stand for the substantial amount of intelligent and committed hard work with which chaplains faced the massive challenges posed by a fast-changing society.

During the 1980s industrial mission entered a new era. Workplace visiting had always given rise to issues which needed to be addressed, either within the company or with wider management, union or management bodies;[12] but now issues and projects were becoming a major theme and were themselves drivers of industrial mission activity. Industrial visiting was still the foundation of everything else but on this foundation was now being built a diverse construction of consultations, publications, education, partnerships, businesses, training and employment projects, and much else. Still there was no national strategy, and it's probably a good thing that there wasn't, because the dispersed nature of industrial mission management meant that teams were able to meet their unique local situations with their own pragmatic responses. There was plenty of mutual learning, not least through the IMA networks, but much of the activity was locally generated, with much trial and error and probably with the wheel being reinvented many times over.

There were plenty of challenges facing the industrial mission movement by the end of the decade. Traditional industry was closing down, existing chaplaincies were disappearing, new chaplaincies were difficult to negotiate, the churches were becoming less willing to fund full-time and in many cases part-time posts – but chaplains continued to do what they could, they continued to be available to workforces and to many who were no longer employed, and they continued to relate to institutions, communities and individuals.

If there is a serious loss during this period then it is the laity. It became more difficult to gather an industrial laity into structured activity, more difficult to recruit members of the Church's laity into active industrial mission work and management, and almost impossible to generate sustainable and autonomous lay projects. So what we had left was a smaller and more threatened group of industrial mission professionals (among whom were now a number of full-time lay chaplains) and an often lively but soon to decline group of parochial and congregational clergy visiting workplaces in their parishes or localities. *Industrial Mission – An Appraisal* had affirmed industrial mission as an important mission activity of the Church, and that's what it now was: a mission agency of the Church rather than a bridge between the Christian Faith and industrial society or a bridge between the Church and industry. Whether anybody had noticed that this was a significant change in perception I rather doubt.

Notes

1 Eyles, John, 1981, 'Diary of a Closure: B.S.C. Consett Works December 1979 - December 1980', unpublished paper.

2 Eyles, John, 1985, 'Another Year, Another Closure: Caterpillar Tractor Company Ltd., Birtley, September 1983–September 1984', unpublished paper.

3 Interview with Stephen Kendal by Peter Cope, 20th July 2006.

4 Interview with Stephen Kendal by Peter Cope, 20th July 2006.

5 Interview with Denis Claringbull by Peter Cope, 27th July 2006.

6 Correspondence from Frank Scuffham.

7 The ecumenical Employment and Unemployment Group which wrote *Work or What?* was mainly people who were or had been industrial chaplains.

8 Interview with Julian Eagle by Peter Cope, 29th May 2008.

9 Torry, Malcolm, undated, 'Health Poverty', in *Health and Poverty: A Christian Contribution*, Occasional Papers, no. 13, Manchester: The William Temple Foundation.

10 I remain Director of the Citizen's Income Trust: www.citizensincome.org

11 Interview with Noel Beattie by Peter Cope, 6th July 2006.

12 Interview with Stephen Kendal by Peter Cope, 20th July 2006, on Kendal's pursuit of issues relating to steelmaking during the 1970s.

8

Survival: Diversity and decline during the 1990s

Industrial mission's early history was one of heroes, passion, and doing new things. Then came a period of sustained growth and consolidation, followed by crisis and recovery. The 1980s was characterised by a rich diversity, and more heroes and passion. The 1990s was rather different. There was still plenty of diversity, but also decline, and not a little anxiety over the movement's capacity for survival.

London: closure and decline

We have already recorded the closure of industrial mission in Peterborough and discovered just how vulnerable a longstanding piece of work can be to the whim of an individual bishop. Shockingly, the same happened to industrial mission in our capital city.

London might have an economy larger than that of most nation states, but the Church has never spoken to it with a single voice simply because ecclesiastical boundaries have never taken any account of the modern world. Until the middle of the nineteenth century nobody would have spoken of South London. There was dense development along the south bank of the Thames, but from just south of the Elephant and Castle it was villages and farmland. The Church of England in the area we now call South London was divided between the Dioceses of Winchester, Rochester, and Canterbury. North of the river it was the Diocese of London, and to the East of the River Lee it was the Diocese of St Alban's: again, villages and farmland. When the Roman Catholic hierarchy was re-established, north of the river went into the Westminster Archdiocese and south of it into the Southwark Archdiocese. In 1905 the Church of England formed the Diocese of Southwark out of parts of the Dioceses of Winchester and Rochester, and in 1914 the Diocese of Chelmsford out of the Essex part of the Diocese of St Alban's. The result of all this was that by the time the railways had caused London to explode to its present size all of the mainstream denominations except the Baptists had ecclesiastical boundaries along the river. The Methodist Church has recently put things right by establishing a London District. The Church of England and the Roman Catholic Church have still got it wrong and thus fail to relate effectively to a major world city. One day a few people are going to have to be brave enough to do something about it.

I have said all that because it's the background to the fact that London had two industrial missions: the South London Industrial Mission south of the river, and the London Industrial Chaplaincy north of it.

Whereas the South London Industrial Chaplaincy was independently constituted, the London Industrial Chaplaincy (LIC) never was. That never stopped it from doing some useful work. At the beginning of the '90s there were half a dozen Anglican chaplains (some half-time, some full-time, and two of them were women), there was a Methodist minister, and there was a Baptist minister. The chaplains were attached to workplaces in various parts of London: Thames Gas, Heathrow Airport, large department stores, London Transport, and a number of factories, including Hoover on the Great West Road, and a biscuit factory, where Francis Jakeman was the chaplain. (He once introduced some of us to a table top training exercise in which we had to work out how to obtain the maximum production while the orders kept changing.)

Gerald Ellison had been a naval chaplain and as Bishop of London he attended LIC Annual General Meetings, told them that he didn't entirely understand what they were doing, and expressed his full support. Graham Leonard understood less and supported less. In 1993 David Hope decided that the chaplains weren't making new church members, that industrial visiting was an entirely parochial matter, that therefore curates could do it, and therefore that he no longer needed LIC. The Chaplaincy was governed by a Council, but it had no real independence. The Bishop could close the Chaplaincy, and he did.[1]

I've called this chapter 'Survival'. LIC didn't. SLIM did, just about. During the 1990s every denomination had financial problems. Because it was easier to cut industrial mission posts than parochial and congregational ones, when full-time chaplains resigned or retired they weren't replaced. Alison Norris left SLIM's employment in 1992. Then came a series of retirements: Thornton Elwyn in 1992, James Siddons in 1993, and Richard Moberly in 1995. Raymond Singh replaced Michael Gudgeon and continued to visit trade union offices, in 2000 he joined the team of chaplains working in the Millennium Dome, and in 2001 he too left SLIM's employment. None of these were replaced (Torry, 2000).

During the 1980s Merton Deanery had used one of its posts to employ an industrial chaplain to work in the borough's industrial estates. The first appointee to this post, Derek Coombes, left in 1989. The full-time post was then replaced by a joint post and Andrew Wakefield was appointed Vicar of St Andrew's, Wimbledon, and industrial chaplain in Merton. Wakefield took on a wide variety of work: Merton's industrial estates, the retail sector, the Chamber of Commerce (which he eventually chaired), the transport industry, and the local authority. He got involved with employment projects and negotiated over Lambeth Borough's regeneration strategy on behalf of the Brixton Churches. He worked with parishes on faith and work issues. He got involved with the birth of the London Civic Forum and chaired that. In 1998 SLIM's Board 'thanked him for his excellent paper, which demonstrated his enthusiasm, charisma and energy, but suggested that he might consider how his work might be more focused.'[2] Is focus a necessary characteristic of high-quality industrial mission? I think not.

In 1990 Terry Drummond, a Church Army officer, was appointed industrial missioner in Croydon. Little workplace visiting had survived, but he related to Christian Fellowship groups where he could, and worked among the unemployed and with voluntary organizations. By now the missioner was being paid as a social responsibility officer and Drummond found himself accountable in four directions: to Croydon Parish Church, the Croydon Episcopal Area Mission Team, SLIM, and Croydon's own Industrial Mission Management Group. Accountability had always been plural: to the industrial mission, to the denomination, and to workplace managements and trades unions. Such workplace multiple accountability was now being replaced by a more ecclesiastical variety.

A new development was the appointment of Mark Nicholson, a pastor of the Emmanuel Pentecostal Faith Church of God. In 1992 a grant enabled SLIM to employ Nicholson to visit in the electricity industry and British Rail and to pursue equal opportunities issues. This last piece of work blossomed. Nicholson helped to formulate the Wood-Sheppard principles on equal opportunities in the workplace, publicised the principles in companies, police forces and other public sector organizations, and in 1997 was joined by an administrator and established REEP: the Race Equality in Employment Project.

Peter Challen continued to pursue a diversity of interests, and in particular the South London Partnership Forum: a network of organizations and individuals interested in South London's communities and economy. The network ran occasional 'marketplaces': all-day events to enable people in different organizations to find out what each other were doing. Challen authored numerous papers and in the regular 'SLIMline' he took people back to his days in the coal mine and steelworks and reminded them of SLIM's method: 'visitation, association, derivation, dissemination'.[3] He retired in February 1996 after 29 years as Senior Chaplain. For a while he continued to write papers for SLIM, and then he turned his attention to the Christian Council for Monetary Justice, an organization campaigning for a debt-free money supply.

Again the pragmatic decision was made to combine the posts of Rector of Christ Church and Senior Chaplain of SLIM, and John Paxton was appointed. He had previously worked for the Greater Manchester Industrial Mission Team and then as Team Vicar in the Southampton City Centre Parish and industrial chaplain with the South Hampshire Industrial Mission. He had done a stint as Moderator of the Industrial Mission Association and so was well known in the movement.

Paxton visited the railway franchisee Connex South East's offices, extended lunchtime worship at Christ Church, organized a visit to Paris to study city-wide government in preparation for its arrival in London, taught modules for the South East Institute for Theological Education (into which the Southwark Ordination Course had been merged), taught on the Readers' training course, and attended meetings of the Board for Social Responsibility and the Woolwich Area Mission Team (which he subsequently left). There were still curates at Christ Church: Nick Harris, Christine Latham, and finally Eugeniah Adoyo, all of whom visited offices in the parish. Adoyo was the last occupant of the post.

There were short-term appointments: Elizabeth Bradley visited organizations along the South Bank and had lots of ideas for new chaplaincies, but then the funding dried up. Maureen Henderson, a member of the Community of the Sacred Passion, visited workplaces and places of worship and gathered people of different faiths to discuss economic and social issues. Tom Hurcombe, on the staff of Christ Church, East Greenwich, visited Tunnel Refineries on the Greenwich Peninsula and tried to involve local parishes in planning for the future of the riverfront. Fintan Phelan, a Roman Catholic deacon and a member of the chaplains' team who never did seem to do much that looked like industrial mission, was replaced by David Young, Parish Priest of the Roman Catholic parish of Waterloo. Young visited the Union Jack Club, a hotel and club for service men and women passing through London (Torry, 2000).

During 2000 I undertook a survey of South London's denominations and discovered eight people doing workplace visiting: Paxton, Adoyo, Young, Singh, and four parochial clergy. There were a few others closely involved with their local economies (including Wakefield and Drummond) or who supported church members in their working lives. There were bound to be many more clergy and laity doing all this than I managed to find, but what was interesting was that SLIM didn't know about quite a lot of what I did find.

By the end of the decade there were still a few Associates (but they were generally older clergy), there was no longer a 'General Team' of part-time chaplains (though as we have seen, there was a small amount of workplace visiting going on around South London), SLIM's workplace visiting was tailing off, and the chaplains had found it almost impossible to create new chaplaincies or new connections with the institutions of London's economy. While in Southampton Paxton had found himself invited to all sorts of meetings and to join all manner of secular organizations. He waited for this to happen in South London. It didn't.

An important change during the decade was that Paxton's reports to the denominations more closely reflected work actually done than work in which SLIM was peripherally involved or wished it was doing, but these more realistic reports made it fairly clear that not a lot was happening. In 1999 he suggested that 'Board meetings [had] lost some of their sparkle, and the agendas [had] become routine.'[4] Indeed, they had. The world was changing fast but SLIM hadn't innovated for years. One particular missed opportunity was that it didn't even consider extending its remit north of the river when the Bishop of London closed LIC. It takes a lot of emotional energy to innovate in a threatening industrial and ecclesiastical world, and it's even more difficult to do when there are few human or financial resources to do it with.

Nobody outside SLIM could decide to close it down, but the churches did the next best thing: they starved it of resources, gave it neither support nor encouragement, and waited for its death.

This raises the question of financial resources. If full-time chaplains are going to be paid then the money has to be found from somewhere. During the 1990s churches' budgets got tighter, and they are tightening still, not least because of the cost of pensions for retired clergy (which includes, of course, the cost of pensions for retired industrial chaplains). Charitable trusts have only ever been willing to grant short-term funding for new pieces of work. That leaves companies as the only source of funds. As we have seen, there has always been an element of this, with the payments understood sometimes as donations to the work of the industrial mission and sometimes as direct payment for the services of a particular chaplain. As we saw when we discussed Bill Nightingale's SLIM chaplaincy and the early days of the Croydon Industrial Mission, direct payments are bound to have an effect on the nature of chaplaincy. Every chaplain will self-censor because he or she is a guest in industry and needs management's agreement to be there, but that self-censorship will be even more thorough when the chaplain's income depends on management's goodwill. During the 1990s industry agreed to fund a number of previously church-funded posts. At Manchester Airport the Baptist chaplain retired and the Baptist Church decided not to renew the funding. The Greater Manchester Industrial Mission approached all of the companies on the airport site and between them they put together enough money to pay for a chaplain (Brown and Ballard, 2006, p. 307). Mike Vincer was appointed, and saw his role as 'to be with people where they are and primarily on their terms' (Brown and Ballard, 2006, p. 377). In South London no companies were offering any money so the chaplains' independence didn't need to be discussed.

Survival and more in Sheffield

London, north and south, was a rather extreme case, as was Peterborough during the previous decade. In many parts of the country the 1990s was a decade of both survival and innovation.

At its 1990 Annual General Meeting the Sheffield Industrial Mission became 'Industrial Mission in South Yorkshire' (IMSY). This more correctly describes what it was from quite early days, though it's a pity that the acronym sounds rather like 'whimsy', of which there has been rather little. IMSY maintained a strong team of full- and part-time chaplains during the decade, mostly still working in steel, engineering, and metal-based products. There were five chaplains visiting fire stations, and several in retail and distribution. There was still a coalfield chaplain, and there were chaplaincies at Trebor Bassett (sweets), Sheffield Wednesday Football Club, Sheffield Science Park, and the Workshop 6 Training Centre. By now the churches were meeting the costs of all of the salaries, and only working expenses were being met by donations from companies, trusts, congregations, and individuals. Relating to churches remained a priority, and in this the Mission took the initiative, with chaplains asking if they could visit churches and preach in them rather than waiting to be invited. In 1992 IMSY put its relationship with part-time chaplains on a more formal footing, creating a clearer relationship between workplace chaplaincy and the parish for those clergy working in both. Work on issues continued, with Elizabeth Nash working with the Low Pay Campaign and Margaret Halsey researching the consequences of compulsory competitive tendering for public services. An increasing interest in racism led the Mission into an active campaign in Cole Brothers, a member of the John Lewis Partnership; and IMSY supported the Keep Sunday Special campaign because of the effects of Sunday working on retail workers and their families. A major new approach was involvement in local economies, and Norman Young was recruited to work half-time in a parish and half-time on Doncaster's economy and its institutions (Bagshaw, 1994, pp. 126–7). Mission was now urban as well as industrial, and charitable foundations funded a community development post in Sheffield to promote local employment, self-help groups and community businesses, in collaboration with local churches. A Methodist layman, Chris Sissons, was appointed in 1992. IMSY's 1992 mission statement contained references to justice and local communities as well as to chaplaincies and workplaces (Bagshaw, 1994, pp. 128–9). A more political statement was now possible because the churches themselves had come to understand that the pursuit of 'justice in economic and social matters' was integral to the proclamation of the gospel.

In 1991 Mostyn Davies wrote a paper for the Industrial Mission Association's Theology Development Group which defined the four 'generations' of industrial mission. The first generation was the Navvy Mission and such bodies as the Missions to Seamen. These were explicitly evangelistic in intention, though they often developed a concern for social justice. The second generation was the Sheffield model of industrial mission. The Church was to be created anew in industry. The third generation was a move away from workplace visiting and towards issues and projects, particularly with unemployed people. The fourth generation is focused on the local economy.[5] No categorisation is without its problems. For instance: where does early SLIM fit? Presumably somewhere between the first and second generations. The order, too, has varied between one industrial mission and another. SLIM took the stages in the order given. Sheffield, though, started with the second generation and finally got round to the first during the mid-'60s. Nevertheless, Davies' fourfold structure is a useful summary. As we have seen, SLIM went through all four generations before it was stifled. Sheffield has successfully negotiated all four generations and continues to do so. In both Sheffield and South London the new was always added to the old. It didn't replace it. New activities and ideas were taken on but older ones were not discarded. By the end of the 1990s all four generations could be discerned in IMSY's work.

In 1994 Paul Bagshaw summed up the first 50 years of the Sheffield Industrial Mission:

> Since 1944 Sheffield Industrial Mission has bridged the gulf and explored the frontier between the Church and the world. It has contributed to the potential for Christian discipleship in the industrial, commercial, and civic life of South Yorkshire. It has enriched the discipleship of the Church in society. It has sought to discover God at work in God's world and to further God's work in a godless world. It has struggled to perceive the holy in the unholy, to evoke faith in the midst of the secular, to realise the church beyond the Church. (Bagshaw, 1994, p. 138)

Elsewhere: survival and more

It's not just in South Yorkshire that industrial mission thrived during the '90s. In 1992 Noel Beattie moved from Lincoln to Kent to revive industrial mission there. Because the Thames Gateway developments were going to affect millions of people's lives he looked for help, and the Methodist Church appointed Malcolm

Cooper, a South African, to be chaplain to a construction site in a chalk pit near to the Dartford Crossing.[6] That site is now Bluewater, a commercially successful 'destination' containing shops, restaurants, and a cinema. Families spend the day there. Cooper's work was classic workplace chaplaincy on a construction site, but it was also more than that because he related to the developer, Lend Lease, at many levels. When Bluewater opened, complete with multi faith quiet room, Cooper recruited a sizeable team of part-time chaplains to visit the many different retail outlets.

There never used to be that many shops. 50 years ago Dartford town centre contained a few dozen, each selling a limited number of products. The weekly shop was very similar from household to household: meat, vegetables, bread, and a few basic groceries and cleaning products. Now there's Bluewater, a bus-ride from Dartford: 200 shops and restaurants, three huge department stores (John Lewis, Marks and Spencer and House of Fraser), and the range of products has increased exponentially, probably literally by the looks of it. This is all the result of computerisation, mechanisation, and global manufacture, distribution, marketing, ordering, and retailing. When one shop extends its opening hours in order to increase market share then all the others have to follow so they don't lose theirs. This is why at many supermarkets we now have 24 hour opening. Shop workers are often part-time and short-term, they work diverse shift patterns, and their rare breaks from the till or shelf-stacking are 20 minutes long. This is a world away from the steelworks, engineering works and coal mines of early industrial mission, so the methods have had to adapt. Groups are still held, sometimes services take place in shopping malls, and chaplains such as Cooper still involve themselves in their industries' issues and structures. There are plenty of issues facing the retail industry. Sunday trading was once a major issue, and at the Gateshead MetroCentre, funded by the Church Commissioners, the chaplain they appointed held a service in the centre as a protest against trading on Sundays, the service became popular, it's now a regular part of what Sunday trading is all about, and it's understood as politically neutral: which is really rather a pity (Brown and Ballard, 2006, pp. 308–9). A more recent issue for

Bluewater was Boxing Day trading. When Bluewater first opened it didn't trade on Boxing Day. Then under pressure from some of the stores' managements the centre management agreed to open, but John Lewis held out. The following year it decided to join in. Cooper and others joined in this debate not because Christmas itself is special (which it is) but because retail workers need to spend time with their families. There are now just two days on which the stores can't open: Easter Day and Christmas Day. We wait to see whether these two remain sacred.

Malcolm Cooper wasn't Noel Beattie's only recruit. He recruited Dick Johnson to develop town centre ministry and industrial mission in Bexley and Bromley, added a Salvation Army officer, established a United Reformed Church post in East Kent, and appointed to a community development post in Gravesend. The chaplains established a large team of part-time chaplains, both lay and clerical. Beattie's own work was in Medway, and as well as industrial visiting he related to the local authority and all manner of other organizations responsible for the future of the Thames Gateway. He helped to found the Medway Interfaith Forum so that members of a variety of faiths could speak together to the civic authorities,[7] and Johnson found himself Chair of the Bexley Multi Faith Forum. The next decade would see some interesting questions raised about Christians working with people of other faiths, and some innovative activity was the answer: as you would expect from industrial mission.

In other parts of the country industrial chaplaincy continued, often in small pockets, and often with little publicity. In Kidderminster, in Bromsgrove and Redditch, and in Worcester, there were small teams of chaplains, each with their own management committee, and all of them (along with an agricultural chaplain) working in Worcestershire. In 1990 Stephen Kendal moved from the strike-torn coalfields in Durham and Northumberland to a rather quieter chaplaincy in Kidderminster. It was a bit of a shock visiting lots of small industrial units rather than a few large coalmines. In 1992 he became team leader and set about combining Worcestershire's industrial missions into a single Worcestershire Industrial Mission, sometimes against opposition from both clergy and laity in the local areas, not least because Kidderminster had lots of money and the other areas didn't. An important issue which they and other industrial missions had to tackle during this period of declining lay involvement in the movement was this: to what extent should laypeople be asked to give time to industrial mission management committees? Isn't their time better spent being Christians at work and preparing themselves for that task?[8] The problem is that only laity active in the workforce can manage workplace chaplaincy relevantly. In a fast-changing world the retired really can't. I don't know the answer to this one.

Corporate Responsibility

From the early 1980s a small group of Anglican industrial chaplains would visit representatives of the Church Commissioners to discuss issues relating to the stewardship of their investments. After all, they were looking after our pension funds, and we had an interest in what they were doing with them. The year that I was a member of the group one topic of conversation was the lettings policy on their rented housing estates in Waterloo and Walworth. An apparently virtuous policy of granting tenancies to the children of existing tenants in order to keep families together was causing the Commissioners' estates to become white enclaves in racially mixed areas. That couldn't be right. We also discussed whether the Commissioners were investing ethically.

The 1988 Industrial Mission Conference was a turning point for the movement. Participants passed two resolutions: one asked that all future industrial mission work should have a bias to the poor; and the other was a decision to work systematically on corporate responsibility: that is, on the ways in which companies behave. The conference had been galvanised in these directions by some international visitors, by Julian Eagle, and by a Filipino guest speaker (Tonkinson, 2009, p. 52) who spoke about what it was like to be a migrant worker. The second resolution charged Bob Nind with convening a group to tackle corporate responsibility.

The group quickly gathered members not only from industrial mission but also from such charities as Christian Aid and CAFOD.

The first decision the members took was to concentrate on corporate responsibility rather than on ethical investment: that is, on the ways in which companies treat their workers, the environment, and the communities in which they work, rather than on what they're making – though of course the two issues frequently relate to each other. In 1989 the group constituted itself as the Ecumenical Council for Corporate Responsibility (ECCR), it raised some money, it did some research into what the churches were already doing in this field, and it published the results. The Joseph Rowntree Charitable Trust gave ECCR three years' funding, Crispin White was appointed co-ordinator, a major piece of research into ICI's activities was sponsored, and in 1997 an ECCR group meeting in Oxford put to a Shell Annual General Meeting the first ever resolution on environmental matters to be brought to a transnational company AGM. Their resolution obtained a creditable number of votes (10.5%) and a number of abstentions (6.5%). ECCR has created some 'benchmarks' for evaluating companies' corporate responsibility, and these have formed the basis for continuing research work, particularly on companies' environmental policies and environmental performance. Links with similar organizations in other countries have enabled ECCR to evaluate companies' global performance as well as their performance in one country (White, 2009).

ECCR is an autonomous organization with links with all manner of church and other organizations in the UK and elsewhere. It continues to research, to publish the results, and to buy shares in companies so that it can attend AGMs, propose resolutions, and ask questions. It is no surprise that this substantial piece of work was inspired and facilitated by industrial chaplains.

Christians at Work

This book is about workplace chaplaincy, which is why I have concentrated on that aspect of industrial mission: an aspect which now encompasses the Church's laity becoming volunteer part-time chaplains. A related but different aspect of industrial mission has been workers making an impact in their own workplaces. Throughout industrial mission's history most chaplains have seen themselves as facilitators, hoping that lay leaders would emerge and would form genuinely lay projects which would become a new kind of church in industry. To some extent this has happened, but by the 1990s it was happening no longer. What was happening was activity by and with Christians at work: that is, Christians bringing their faith to bear on their working lives.

During the decade many parish churches and other congregations ran 'Christians at work' groups. These were often short-term and consisted of members of the congregation telling each other about their work. (We have held such groups in both of the parishes of which I have been incumbent). The aim of the process is to affirm people in their working life and to help us all to see more clearly how to relate our faith to what we do at work.

A particularly significant piece of work of this kind has taken place in Richmond over many years. Here Julian Reindorp has tried ten different strategies: a fortnightly group on Saturday mornings to which members bring issues from their working lives; an annual day conference, to give people a taste of the fortnightly group in case they might want to join it; evening theme meetings, which concentrate on one person's working life; one Sunday a year when members of the congregation are invited to bring to the altar some representation of their working life; the vicar visiting people's workplaces; the commissioning of people during Sunday morning worship for their daily work; bringing people together who work in the same field (for instance, those who work in education, or in healthcare); discussing workplace dilemmas at house groups and Lent groups; and during preaching and public prayer making explicit mention of people's working lives (with their permission, of course). In relation to this last method there is now a wealth of material available to help us to make public worship relevant to people's working lives: from the Industrial Mission Association, the Industrial Christian Fellowship, and elsewhere (Claringbull, 1994, pp. 157–66). (That's nine strategies. The tenth is workplace visiting in the parish, which isn't quite to the point but is of course important nevertheless.)

The theological method is inductive, starting with people's experience and then seeing whether biblical passages or theological themes shed light on them. As Reindorp puts it, the Christians at Work group helps its members to see the whole world as God's world 'by linking head and heart, faith and work, work and worship', by 'minding the gap', and by 'making connections' (Reindorp, 2000, pp. 53–6).

Comparisons

The Ridley Hall Foundation

In 1989 Richard Higginson, a lecturer at Ridley Hall Theological College in Cambridge, founded the Ridley Hall Foundation. It publishes a journal, *Faith in Business* (jointly funded by the Industrial Christian Fellowship), sponsors research, and runs seminars and public events. It invites laypeople to stay at Ridley Hall to reflect on the relationship between their faith and their daily work by reading, writing, and discussion with others. The Foundation's particular interest is the relationship between Christian faith and business practice and theory:

> Business plays an enormously important role in today's world. It creates wealth through the provision of a rich variety of goods and services which enhance the quality of life. But business is often the target of public criticism. In today's highly competitive global economy, companies are having to face searching questions such as: What balance to strike between the interests of different 'stakeholders' . . . how to secure contracts honestly in countries where bribery is rife? Christians in business often feel unsupported because of: indifference, suspicion or hostility to business on the part of church leaders; the failure to include business in the church's prayer, preaching and celebration . . . The Ridley Hall Foundation works to bridge the gap between business and the church. (Brown and Ballard, 2006, pp. 158–9)

A number of laypeople involved in industrial mission (for instance, SLIM's Ian Yearlsey) have found the Ridley Hall Foundation to be a useful context in which to think about their working life, and there are clearly significant overlaps between the aims of the Foundation and industrial mission's aims. The difference is that in industrial mission *everyone* is involved in industry, commerce, or the public services: lay associates because they work in them, and chaplains because they visit them. This is not true of the staff of Ridley Hall. This is not to say that one method of relating Christian faith to the world of work is necessarily better than another: simply that a method in which the facilitator is outside the situation will be different from one in which the facilitator relates closely to the institutions of the economy. The former is likely to generate greater objectivity, the latter a more engaged understanding.

Conclusions

In his *The Church under Thatcher* Henry Clark reports on his research into industrial mission at the beginning of the '90s:

> Some of the best theological and political/economic theorising in the Church of England arises from IM circles . . . IM is a crucial element in the overall social witness of the C of E. It is a movement that addresses both the needs and opportunities of those in power, and of those who are relatively powerless . . . IM is an exceedingly *significant specialised ministry* . . . which among other things, is able to provide adult education programmes within the churches whose intent is (at least in part) to help Christians see their daily work as a form of Christian vocation or mission.[9]

All true. In spite of the difficulties (and Clark identifies a loss of full-time posts as a serious difficulty), industrial mission was doing some significant mission work on behalf of the churches and in the churches. Against all the odds it was still doing it by the end of the decade.

It's difficult to identify any new secularizations during the 1990s. Industrial mission had already discovered them all, so during this decade it's still the same mixture which had emerged by the 1970s: practical secularization, institutional secularization, religious secularization, the secularization of ideas and culture, and all constantly reinforcing each other. There has been the occasional desecularization in one category or another, but in the other categories secularization pressures haven't subsided, so any desecularization has been short lived. What is remarkable is the commitment with which laypeople at work have carried on trying to relate the Christian faith to what they do, the persistence with which chaplains have sought new ways to relate the Christian faith to industry and commerce, the energy which management committees have expended trying to keep so many industrial missions afloat, and the way in which missions have taken on new areas of work. Work on local economies as important institutions in their own right is a colossal new agenda. Already there are other players in this particular field (Baker, 2007), and future work in this direction, in partnership with others, could be very creative, as we shall see in our next chapter in relation to a new initiative in London.

The one set of institutions which really doesn't come out of it very well is the churches. Here congregational decline and financial difficulties have led to cutting what can easily be cut, which means industrial mission posts. When industry is in financial trouble, it is sometimes tempted to stick to what it knows, to reduce research and development, to discourage innovation (because innovation carries financial and other risks), and to wait for things to get better. The companies which do well during a recession are those which look around for new opportunities and pursue them passionately. This is precisely what the Church has not been doing. The Church is not industry, and it works differently from industry, but in this respect it has something to learn. In difficult times innovation is essential. Take another example: During difficult periods, and particularly during periods in opposition and leading up to elections, it might look as if political parties have stopped thinking. Official spokespeople and prospective candidates are fed standard and rather bland messages to parrot so that they don't cause problems when it might matter. But the parties haven't stopped thinking. It's just that they have outsourced the task to think tanks such as the Fabian Society, the Institute for Public Policy Research, the Centre for Social Justice, and the Bow Group, where the most important and the most difficult issues can be debated at one remove from the party itself. In such groups creative things can happen because the parties can disown all of it if necessary, nobody needs to feel committed to any of it, the debate generated will tell party officers how both public and parliamentary opinion are evaluating new ideas, and useful new ideas can be turned into legislation when the time is politically right. Yes, this is a difficult time for the churches – which makes it even more important to try new things. The most serious issue facing the Church is secularization, but this is such a huge problem that it's been easier for churches to do nothing much about it and to carry on doing what they've always done. During the 1990s the churches could have renewed industrial mission, asked it to treat secularization as a major issue needing attention, encouraged it to do new things, persuaded Christians with skills to get involved, and resourced the movement: not necessarily with the same number of full-time chaplaincy posts as in the past, but by appointing in every area full- or part-time co-ordinators able to gather, train and deploy voluntary chaplains. But they didn't.

Notes

1 Interview with Frank Hackett, 20th August 2009.
2 Minutes of the Board, 20th October 1998.
3 'SLIMline', February 1996.
4 Minutes of a joint meeting of the Board and chaplains' team, 13th July 1999.
5 Davies, Mostyn, 1991, 'Towards a Strategy for the Fourth Generation of IM', in *Local Economy Based Industrial Mission*, published by the Theology Development Group of the Industrial Mission Association, summarised in Brown and Ballard, 2006, p. 395.
6 Interview with Noel Beattie by Peter Cope, 6th July 2006.
7 Interview with Noel Beattie by Peter Cope, 6th July 2006.
8 Interview with Stephen Kendal by Peter Cope, 20th July 2006.
9 Clark, Henry, 1993, *The Church under Thatcher*, London: SPCK, London, pp. 83, 84, 86, quoted in Tonkinson, 2009, pp. 56–7.

9

Chaplains for everyone: Chaplaincy in the new millennium's plural world

New directions in Greenwich

In 1996 we moved to the Parish of East Greenwich, and on the day the Bishop of Woolwich licensed me to serve the parish we were told that the Millennium Exhibition was coming to the Greenwich Peninsula. It didn't take long for the building to start. We watched the steel uprights slowly raised, the wire mesh take shape like a spider's web, and the tent roof spread across everything except the Blackwall Tunnel air vent. The Millennium Exhibition opened on time: a stunning high-wire show, a Blackadder film, and zones to represent the planet, time, transport, the body, the mind, work, communities, money, rest, communication, learning, the seaside, and faith. Yes, the BBC might have been right to celebrate the 2000th anniversary of Jesus' birth in 1996, but we were going to be celebrating it when the clock ticked over to 2000 so the Faith Zone had a Christian heart to it and the team of chaplains was a Christian one. We're no longer a Christian country, we're a multi faith one, so the Prayer Space was used by people of all faiths and the Faith Zone had glass columns round it showing different faiths celebrating birth, marriage, death, and other life stages. (The National Lottery paid for the Millennium Dome, so we perfectly understood when the Muslims built their own Mosque outside it.)

After leaving SLIM's full-time team in 1988 I had moved to New Cross where the only industry in the parish was a banana distribution warehouse. I visited it until it closed and yet more flats were built on a London industrial site. Chaplaincy in the Millennium Dome was rather different. There were about 20 of us, all volunteers. We worked two shifts a day, and there always two of us on duty whenever the Dome was open. We were there for both visitors and staff, and we led prayers in the Prayer Space twice a day. We all did it differently. Some of us spent most of our time in the Diner, where the staff took their breaks; some of us preferred the Prayer Space, waiting for visitors to find us; some of us wandered the Dome, talking to staff and whoever else we met; and some us did all three. We had radios and palmtops (new wizardry then) so that Dome staff could contact us. Occasionally Nicholas Rothon, our Roman Catholic co-ordinating chaplain, would raise issues with the management. More often it was affirmation that we offered. The exhibition and its staff were brilliant, and the press treatment was quite unjust.

Was this workplace chaplaincy? Yes, after a fashion. It only lasted a year, there were no groups, meetings or conferences, and we ran a Prayer Space and organized services in it. This was a mixture of airport, hospital and workplace chaplaincy: a unique approach for a unique event.

It was really quite sad to watch the Millennium Exhibition being demolished and everything portable being auctioned off. I continued to visit the Dome after it closed. Security and maintenance staff were still looking after it, and there were a few people planning what to do with it next.

Like John Eyles, I've just experienced my second closure. When I arrived in the parish I took over from Tom Hurcombe the chaplaincy at Amylum (Torry, 2006b), formerly Tunnel Refineries. This was classic workplace chaplaincy, and for 13 years I visited everybody on the site, talked about what they wanted to talk about, and sometimes took issues in an anonymous form to management. There was never any formal group work: simply a visit once a month, for as long as it took to get round all the departments. The subject matter remained diverse: life, death, bereavement, marriage breakdown, relationship difficulties, difficulties at work, the economy, society, religion, God, Jesus, crossword clues . . . One of the things I learnt early on as an industrial chaplain was not to have anything in the diary immediately following a planned visit to a workplace. The visit might take much longer than I'd thought. For the first few years visits got longer and longer as I got to know people and they wanted to talk about things that were important to them. Then the redundancies began and visits got shorter simply because there were fewer people around. My first few years there were rather like 1940s Sheffield. Workers had time to talk and would enjoy heated discussions in the canteen or in their own departments' rest rooms. As the workforce shrank such meetings became shorter or they didn't happen at all.

Tate and Lyle bought the plant from Amylum; Syral, part of the French Tereos group, bought it from Tate and Lyle; and Syral closed it in September 2009. It's a matter of justice, in a way. It's only right that developing countries can now export to Europe refined sugar products as well as the raw material, sugar cane: but the consequence is that food manufacturers in the UK are substituting imported products for the glucose and other sweeteners made at the Greenwich refinery. The European Commission is paying companies to close plants like ours, so no one's surprised that Syral decided to close it. I continued to visit staff at the Millennium Dome when it closed. I continue to visit demolition staff at the refinery, and I watch them demolishing what I think was the last major manufacturing industry on the south bank of the Thames. I'm not sure that anyone has noticed that this particular closure might be a significant event.

It's not that we're short of other opportunities for workplace chaplaincy. When in 1994 the Archdeacon of Lewisham discussed with me the possibility of moving to East Greenwich, half of the territory of the parish, the Greenwich Peninsula, was a derelict wasteland. The borough council had fought for a station to be built on the Jubilee Line extension running under the site and we knew that it was a possible site for the Millennium Exhibition, but, as for the Peninsula as a whole, masterplans had come and gone. (It still says 'Port Greenwich' on a gas company gate in Millennium Way because that was the name of one of those plans.) Because the site had hosted Europe's largest gas works and other toxic industries, the land had to be cleaned up, mains services put in, and roads built, so whatever happened was going to be expensive.

North Greenwich tube station was opened in 1999, the Millennium Dome opened, and later in 2000 tenants occupied the first dwellings of the Greenwich Millennium Village (GMV): a housing development at the southern end of the Peninsula. Then after the Millennium Exhibition closed we waited. We waited for nearly two years, and then Meridian Delta Ltd's masterplan won the planning competition: ten thousand new dwellings, enough office space for two and a half Canary Wharf towers, a hotel, a higher education college, a relocated secondary school, and the dome turned into a 20,000 seat arena and an entertainment district of restaurants, bars, and cinemas.

Lend Lease is the lead partner in Meridian Delta, and Susie Wilson had worked for it when it built Bluewater. She had consulted with the local community then and was now charged with doing the same for the Greenwich Peninsula. She had worked closely with Malcolm Cooper, and when I phoned her she was more than happy to discuss chaplaincy. A single one hour meeting between Susie and representatives of Greenwich's faith communities and the Borough Council laid plans for the next 20 years: a multi faith chaplaincy for every aspect of the new community, a temporary building for the chaplaincy and Greenwich's faith communities to use for their own work and for community development, and then a permanent building. (There was no space in the masterplan for religious buildings: yet another institutional secularization.) (Torry, 2007)

The Millennium Dome became The O2, we survived an unintentionally rather public dispute with Anschutz Entertainment Group, managers of The O2, over their desire to locate a regional casino in it (Torry, 2007, pp. 122–4, 128–30), and we put together a team of eight chaplains to visit the construction site. We now have five pairs of chaplains visiting staff in the restaurants, bars and nightclubs in the Entertainment District round the outside of the arena. Particularly helpful with our negotiations with the many different venue managements has been Malcolm Tilsed: he too had experienced industrial chaplaincy before. So it has always been. Works managers in South London in the late 1940s had known armed forces padres, and it was across networks of managers and shop stewards that SLIM's early chaplaincies were organized. New chaplaincies will continue to happen most easily where the people involved have already experienced good chaplaincy.

We now have seventeen chaplains (Muslim, Sikh, Hindu and Christian) governed by a board of trustees (Jewish, Baha'i, Sikh, Muslim and Christian). Chaplains are working in The O2, on construction sites, and in a nearby retail park. (A new piece of work is among Greenwich's police officers – of which more below.) The developer will soon be constructing the temporary building for the chaplaincy to manage for its own work, for Greenwich's faith communities, and for community development. Up until now we've had no base. Our only activities have been regular workplace visiting, the occasional conference, regular meetings for trustees, chaplains, and our Council of Reference, and training courses (we recently organized one on 'Skills for Chaplaincy Work' with Greenwich Community College). We're waiting to see what difference having a building will make to our work.

There are two unique aspects to this particular piece of chaplaincy: First, chaplains and trustees are from a number of different faiths. We do together everything which everyone in good conscience can do together, and separately everything else (Torry, 2008b). Second, we are serving the whole diverse community as it evolves: workers in The O2, retail workers, office workers, students, residents, visitors to the Peninsula, commuters passing through it . . . This is no longer sector ministry: this is ministry to diversity in which workplace chaplaincy has a role within a larger whole.

Getting it Together: Mission in London's Economy

By the turn of the millennium it didn't look as if industrial mission in London was going anywhere. The Bishop of London had closed the London Industrial Chaplaincy, and south of the river John Paxton, Eugeniah Adoyo, Raymond Singh, Terry Drummond and Andrew Wakefield were the only chaplains still working for SLIM. They all had other responsibilities. There was, of course, workplace chaplaincy elsewhere. I attached to my survey of workplace chaplaincy a suggestion that Michael Dent, who was working part-time for Kent Workplace Chaplaincy, should establish some new chaplaincies in South London: something he'd been rather good at doing around Tonbridge and Tunbridge Wells. SLIM's Board eventually agreed that he should, so he did. He found South London rather more difficult to do it in.

Singh left in 2001, Adoyo left, Drummond became chaplain to the Bishop of Southwark, and in 2003 Paxton left for a social responsibility post in the Diocese of Worcester. The Bishop of Southwark, Tom Butler, asked Marshall's Charity to appoint a Rector of Christ Church who would also be his advisor on regeneration projects in the diocese. They agreed, and Tim Scott arrived. One of his early tasks was to help me to locate SLIM's archives at Christ Church (they were under a pile of jumble in the balcony) so that I could lodge them in Southwark's local history library. The marriage of convenience was at an end. However, SLIM was still a company and a charity. Chairs of the Board came and went (one suggested that there should be a club for Chairs who had resigned). Finally Marcus Beale, who had very much valued Peter Challen's ministry, was in charge of the small Board and the website. The Board was responsible in a somewhat undefined manner for Andrew Wakefield's work, and that was all.

I think it was in 2004 that I was party to a conversation at the back of a church hall during an interval in a Diocesan Synod meeting. We bemoaned the fact that London is our capital city and that the Church was now left with no voice in its economy and workplaces. Clearly something had to be done, and Mission in London's Economy (MiLE) was the result. There was no money so it had to be volunteers doing the work. We called them 'practitioner groups': groups of people actively involved in London's economy who were willing to give their time to relating the Christian Faith to the economy. One group has worked on economic policy and has responded to the Greater London Authority's and others' consultation documents, another has mapped workplace chaplaincy and is doing what it can to support chaplains, another creates educational material for churches, another supports lay-people in their places of work, and the group pursuing relationships with other faiths is now particularly active and goes under the name of FiLE: Faiths in London's Economy. (FiLE recently ran a consultation and issued a document on the faith communities' response to the economic crisis.) With Marcus Beales' help MiLE took over and renamed SLIM's non-profit company structure, we found enough money to employ David Driscoll part-time to co-ordinate MiLE's activity, and the Royal Foundation of St Katharine at Limehouse offered a base. It's still early days, but at least there is now an institution to which people at work can relate, which can support workplace chaplains, which can respond to issues facing London's economy, where churches can find educational material, and which can work with people of other faiths on London's economy and its institutions.

Just as the Greenwich Peninsula Chaplaincy has tried to keep together a few activities which had previously been done separately, so MiLE is trying to do the same; and one particular aspect of this togetherness is the involvement of the London City Mission (LCM). This is older than the Navvy Mission. Its aim has always been evangelism, and since 1835 it has provided evangelists in London's parishes, on London's streets, in its own mission centres, and for the last hundred years in workplaces: at Smithfield Market, in police stations, and on the railways, buses and tubes (Thompson, 1985). Relationships between SLIM and LCM had always been distant or worse, mainly because both thought themselves responsible for workplace visiting in London. Things are now different. Three LCM evangelists were members of the Millennium Dome chaplaincy, and from the beginning of MiLE LCM has been thoroughly involved. Those involved in MiLE might differ over emphases, but we all agree that the Christian Faith needs to relate to London's institutions and their workers.

A previous Bishop of London closed the London Industrial Chaplaincy. The current Bishop of London, Richard Chartres, has appointed his own chaplain to Canary Wharf, Fiona Stewart-Darling. This is a ministry of availability and networking rather than of visiting workplaces to see who might want to talk to the chaplain: but in this situation that's all that's possible. Before being appointed to Canary Wharf Stewart-Darling was a higher education chaplain. Some of us on the Greenwich Peninsula might be moving in the opposite direction when the relocated Ravensbourne College – a design and communication college – opens on the site. Yet more boundary-crossing.

Resurgence

So new things have happened during the past few years, but, as in previous periods, tried and tested methods remain the foundation on which new work has been built. New chaplaincies in traditional industries still happen. In 2005 the Industrial Mission Association collected stories from teams around the country into a booklet, *This is our Story* (White, 2005). In Scotland chaplains were still visiting shipyards, engineering works, ports, airports, oil fields, local authorities and shops. In Basingstoke, Andover, and North Hampshire, full-time chaplains were visiting in manufacturing, distribution, public services, and local authorities; volunteer chaplains were visiting mainly shops; and chaplains were relating to a variety of organizations involved in the economy. The aim was 'to make connections and enable good relations between Church and Business, Commerce and Industry; to relate the Gospel to Work and Economic Life; and to promote Christian faith values.' In Birmingham new chaplaincies started at Jaguar car plants in 2002,[1] chaplains still visit retail stores and the jewellery trade and provide a multi faith team at the airport. There are now chaplains working in the National Exhibition Centre and in business parks, and the issues which the Churches Industrial Group Birmingham tackles are migrant workers, unemployment, the recession, business ethics, and the environment.[2] In both Birmingham and Worcestershire chaplains were closely involved with people made redundant when MG Rover closed, briefing church leaders, and supporting individual workers. In Derbyshire traditional industries have been disappearing for years, but in 2005 there were still volunteer chaplains visiting in the manufacturing, agricultural, retail and leisure sectors; Sussex had chaplains in manufacturing, pharmaceuticals, railways, the emergency services, at Gatwick Airport, and in all of the county's ASDA stores; and Mission in the Economy on Merseyside had chaplains in retail and at Liverpool's John Lennon Airport and now has a larger team of part-time and volunteer chaplains working mainly in retail and on establishing quiet spaces in retail areas and a business park.[3] In 2005 Telford had chaplaincies at GKN, the shopping centre, the power station, and to the police, and Cambridge had chaplaincies in retail, the emergency services, and the football club. Cambridge has now added a chaplaincy in the courts service and is adding further town centre and science park businesses.[4] As in other areas, it's now mainly volunteer chaplains with a full-time co-ordinator.

In the Black Country the former steelworks chaplain is still visiting the Merry Hill regional shopping complex (a sign of the times) and local churches organize Sunday worship there. In response to local need the Baptist chaplain has adapted his church to make room for a youth training centre, and other chaplains are doing what we can only call community development work.[5] The report of a recent review of the Black Country Urban Industrial Mission's work describes 'significant grass roots engagement and strategic networks with which [the chaplains] are involved. The scope is remarkable and demonstrates the ability of the Church to reach sections of society – often very influential in shaping the lives of huge numbers of people and communities – through such involvement . . . The work reflects many years of building up trust and understanding, being alongside those on the shaping as well as those on the receiving end of economic change' (Diocese of Lichfield, 2008, p. 6). The review group's report bears out this assessment.

This is our Story shows that in 2005 in Bristol social concerns and the economy were still being tackled together. There were traditional workplace chaplaincies, and a recent addition was a chaplain to the economic life of Swindon. Chaplains in the Southampton area were working in airports and retail, pursuing environmental issues, and networking with organizations involved in the area's economy; and in Northumbria chaplains were visiting factories, retail stores, bus garages, fire stations, the airport, and call centres. The Essex Churches Council for Industry and Commerce was working across Essex and up to the Chelmsford Diocesan boundary at the River Lee, which runs through the Olympics construction site. (Wouldn't it have been better to move the diocesan boundary? Or do ecclesiastical authorities find it metaphysically impossible to give up territory?) The Essex team's name will soon be 'Workplace Chaplains, Essex and East London'.[6]

In 2005 Hertfordshire and Bedfordshire chaplains were still finding themselves working for reconciliation in manufacturing firms, and they had recently added chaplaincies in retail and in the emergency services. When the Buncefield Oil Refinery disaster at Hemel Hempstead wiped out small firms in which several hundred people were employed, the Mission's chaplains were soon on the scene. In Coventry and Warwickshire chaplains were visiting in manufacturing, financial services, a major utility, automotive research and manufacture, transport, logistics, the public sector, and emergency services. The main task for two of the three half-time co-ordinators was to seek out new clients for the Mission's work: the team still modelled their work on Australia and New Zealand[7] where companies pay fees for defined services from the paid and volunteer chaplains. (As we have seen, such fee for service arrangements aren't new. Defence Research complexes - now largely privatised as QinetiQ - have always paid for their chaplains.) There was once a coalfield chaplain: in 2005 there was a Communities Regeneration Officer funded by the Coalfields Regeneration Trust.

The stories told in *This is our Story* reveal a substantial diversity both between and within chaplains' teams. Another typical case is Selby. Here industrial mission started with a single coalfield chaplain in 1978. A chaplain to work in agriculture followed, and then a power station chaplain. By 1983 flour mill and paper mill visiting had been added, and the name became 'Selby Coalfield Industrial Chaplaincy'. In 1984 the mission recruited lay chaplains to work among the unemployed and on youth and community issues, and later on homelessness, community education, and drugs. During the following decade more part-time chaplains made it possible to visit more power stations, more coal mines, a shipyard, some newer small-scale industries, adult further education colleges, and local authority workers. In 2000 the name changed to Selby Coalfield and District Industrial Mission. In 2004 the closure of the coalfield led to the most recent name change: The Selby Communities and District Industrial Mission. Everything else carries on, and the chaplains know that they are only scratching the surface.[8]

What do we notice here? There are now workplace chaplains in all manner of organizations: manufacturing, local authorities, shops, airports, emergency services, offices, call centres . . . in fact, anywhere where people work. Most of the chaplaincy work is now being done by volunteers, and in 2006 David Welbourn created a six-module training package on CD for volunteer chaplains who weren't able to undertake the residential training course.[9] Chaplains still pursue issues vigorously. The issues arise from the visiting, but sometimes the issues (such as environmental concerns) motivate the activity (White, 2005). Recession and redundancy have of course returned as issues, and fair trade has emerged as an important concern.[10] Relationships with denominations are generally good, but there's now little money from that direction: hence the small but growing amount of activity now funded by the companies visited. A particularly significant growth area is chaplaincy to the emergency services, and there are signs outside London that multi faith activity is now on everyone's agenda (White, 2005),[11] particularly in airport chaplaincy.

This is all better described as workplace chaplaincy than as industrial mission. The stated aims are still to relate Christian Faith and the Church to people at work, but there is now little sense that a new kind of Church is to be created within the institutions of the economy or that the gospel confronts society's industrial structures. The approach is a pastoral one: an ethos which attracts parochial clergy and other volunteers into chaplaincy. Group work and other corporate activity is now rare, and any application of 'values' or 'faith' happens in conversation between the chaplain and the individual worker, or perhaps with a small group in the canteen. An important continuity is chaplains contributing positively during a crisis because of their existing relationships with institutions and their workforces; and another is that even though most of the activity is now pastoral in nature, prophetic responses are still possible, even though Sunday trading protests haven't always worked out entirely as intended. Services in shopping centres and prayer spaces in airports are evidence of a trend towards taking the explicitly religious into workplaces: a significant desecularization.

The pattern now emerging is of sizeable teams of part-time volunteer chaplains co-ordinated by full-time or half-time chaplains who still do some workplace visiting. This is surely right. There will never again be large numbers of paid posts, but neither should groups of committed volunteers be co-ordinated by people who aren't themselves active in workplace chaplaincy. The Methodist Church's stated policy is to equip the Church at large for workplace chaplaincy; to encourage laypeople, deacons and ministers into part-time chaplaincy; and to focus central resources on providing training for the Church generally and for chaplains appointed locally (Methodist Church, 2003). It would be no bad thing for all of the denominations to adopt similar national policies.

Where chaplains are paid, serious consideration now needs to be given as to how that's to be done. In the United States a number of organizations contract with companies to supply them with 'corporate chaplains', and Douglas Hicks estimates that there are now between 2000 and 4000 such chaplains, either paid by an agency or paid directly by the company in which they work. 'Marketplace Ministries' markets itself as a 'faith-based employee assistance program' which takes 'the gospel of Jesus Christ to the frontier of Christian ministry: the modern workplace' (Hicks, 2003, p. 127). Hicks' research reveals that companies like having chaplains around because their work promotes productivity, employee loyalty, lower staff turnover, and mediation in place of lawsuits (Hicks, 2003, p. 130). These were some of the benefits for which South London and Croydon firms were hoping when chaplains first started work there. Whatever the benefits of such contractual arrangements in the States, Croydon, or defence research establishments, the disbenefits in terms of lost autonomy are clearly sizeable. The issue is well overdue for a discussion across the workplace chaplaincy movement.

Comparisons

Hospitals, prisons, courts, police

There are now chaplains everywhere. Health authorities employ chaplains to serve patients' spiritual needs: both full-time chaplains and part-time ones, Christian ones, Muslim ones, Sikh ones . . . (Flagg, 2006). These chaplains are now having to justify the money spent on them because previous specifically religious justifications don't tick the funding boxes. The Home Office employs multi-faith teams of chaplains in prisons (Tyler, 2006). Here chaplains have statutory duties and also explicitly religious ones, and their contribution to prisoners' wellbeing and rehabilitation isn't too difficult to argue. Hospices, too, often employ their own chaplains. Chaplains help patients to prepare for their deaths and help patients' families to cope with bereavement. A rather generic 'spirituality' is what's on offer.

The fact that all of these chaplains are employed by their institutions, or are in some cases contracted volunteers, doesn't remove all autonomy. The right to comment on issues facing the institution, usually in private, is often earned and is as often exercised. The same is true of police chaplains and of chaplains to the fire and ambulance services. The brief is to support police officers, fire officers, ambulance drivers, and paramedics: people who often face traumatic situations and who find it important to be able to share their feelings with someone they know. Yes, the growing number of counselling services now available to employees can provide people to listen to workers' concerns, and their promise of confidentiality is as good as a chaplain's: but the important combination provided by chaplaincy is that the person keeping confidences is someone the police or fire officer, patient or nurse, prisoner or prison officer, has got to know and trust.

A newer venture is chaplains in the courts,[12] available to courts staff and to anyone involved in court cases, including the jurors (as long as the chaplain doesn't discuss the evidence before the jury gives its verdict). Police, fire, ambulance and courts chaplains are volunteers and receive no payment.

There is a spectrum, from the hospital or prison chaplain employed by their institution, to the courts chaplain who is a volunteer from a local church, and somewhere on this spectrum we find workplace chaplains. Some workplace chaplains are paid by the companies they visit, some by an industrial mission paid by the company, some by an industrial mission with funding from the churches, some by their denominations, and some aren't paid at all: though where the volunteer is a paid member of the clergy their denomination might be counting their chaplaincy work as the denomination's contribution to the workplace chaplaincy team. None of these workplace chaplains have lost all of their autonomy. They can all criticise their institutions if they feel they need to. For those employed by their institutions public criticism of their employer might be a resigning matter entailing loss of income as well as loss of access to the institution, whereas public criticism by a volunteer might mean simply the end of their chaplaincy work. Any chaplain will censor themselves to some extent if they want to remain a chaplain, so the difference made by payment by the institution will be a matter of degree rather than a difference in kind. An interesting research project would be a study of the different levels of autonomy which chaplains in different situations experience. To what extent does a prison chaplain censor themselves? And a workplace chaplain? Is private comment to management self-censored as much as public comment is? An interesting comparison would be with chaplains in higher and further education (Collier, 2006). Sometimes universities employ and pay their chaplains, sometimes they don't have them, sometimes it's the incumbent of the local parish and the diocese pays, and sometimes it's on an entirely voluntary basis. It would be interesting to know the difference which the financial arrangement makes to the chaplain's autonomy and their sense of their autonomy.

Equipping the laity for being Christians at work

The Methodist Church's stated strategy for relating to the economy and its institutions is to 'equip Christians to develop their theological understanding and to link it to issues that arise from economic life . . . equip Christians to bring the challenges of the Gospel into economic debate . . . help Christians witness to their own faith among those with whom they work' (Methodist Church, 2003, p. 7). In our last chapter we discovered substantial investment in this process in Richmond. One of Mission in London's Economy's practitioner groups supports Christians in their places of work, and another produces resources for the churches to help them to do this too.[13] An indicator of people's interest in relating their faith to their work and their workplace is the volume of literature now published on the subject. To take just two examples: Antony Hurst's *Rendering Unto Caesar* grounds an 'exploration of the place of paid employment within the framework of Christian belief' in the Genesis creation stories and in Christology (Hurst, 1986, p. 131); and Ken Costa's *God At Work* sets out from biblical texts and offers lots of good advice about work, ambition, making decisions, work-life balance, managing stress, coping with failure, hope, and generosity: all in the cause of 'a fresh lay initiative . . . to reconnect the workplace with Christianity' (Costa, 2007, p. 192).

There is no copyright in titles, and David Miller's *God At Work* is largely a history of the empowerment of the Church's laity to work out the relationship between faith and work in their own workplaces. The 'God at work' in both Costa's and Miller's books is largely the God on whom business executives rely to help them to make decisions and cope with the pressures of the workplace. Miller himself notes a major difference between this 'faith at work' movement and the work of workplace chaplains (or 'corporate chaplains' in his American context): 'Workplace chaplains largely although not exclusively attend to the spiritual needs and problems of hourly and lower- to middle-management employees. In contrast, the [Faith At Work] movement also has solo practitioners, similar to consultants or executive coaches, who work with a select group of business leaders' (Miller, 2007, p. 115). One of the important virtues of the industrial mission movement has always been its concern for everyone in the workplace. There always has been, and there still is, a bias to the poor.

The Spirit at Work movement

In 2000 David Welbourn went on sabbatical to California to research the Spirit at Work movement in the United States. There he found firms making use of 'spirituality', and on his return he and Dermot Tredget, a Benedictine monk, founded the Spirituality in the Workplace network. The 'Spirit in Work' journal followed, and then Howard and Welbourn's book: 'While some [Spirit at Work] authors regard God or the Divine as a fundamental component of spirituality, the current use of the term "spirit at work" is most often not associated with any specific religious tradition' (Howard and Welbourn, 2004, p. 42). At this movement's heart is a generic 'spirituality': 'the basic feeling of being connected with one's complete self, others, and the entire universe. If a single word best captures the meaning of spirituality and the vital role that it plays in people's lives, that word is "interconnectedness".'[14] Spirit at Work practitioners, by conversation, group work, and the creation of quiet places in the workplace, help workers to discover 'spirit' within themselves, and thus to connect with self, others, nature, and a 'higher power' (Howard and Welbourn, 2004, p. 83). The results are fulfilled employees, corporate vision, company transformation, and the application of values. Howard and Welbourn discuss some 'spirit-led companies' (Howard and Welbourn, 2004, pp. 169–79): which all rather suggests that 'Spirit at Work' is quasi-theological language for a management and human resources approach which values employees and their aspirations. It is one of the 'somewhat shallow and undemanding spiritual options' (Taylor, 2007, p. 513) which Charles Taylor finds to be characteristic of the spirituality of our times.

It's a pity that among the spirit-led companies mentioned in the book Welbourn doesn't discuss QinetiQ, the 'UK science and technology organization' (Howard and Welbourn, 2004, p. i). It was while he was chaplain to this privatised part of the Government's defence research activity that he worked out his commitment to 'Spirit at Work'. Welbourn had initially been unsure about becoming chaplain to a defence research establishment, especially one which was paying for his services. His conscience became less troubled when QinetiQ described the industrial chaplain's role as that of a 'critical friend', when his increasingly honest and sometimes critical annual reports were well received and acted upon, and as QinetiQ increasingly worked on non-weapons products.[15] However, if 'spirituality' is the foundation of an industrial chaplain's rationale, then a question surely needs to be asked: If there is no reference outside the individual, then how can the chaplain's pastoral activity ever become prophetic? In the field of weapons research, isn't a prophetic edge rather important? Does 'Spirit at Work' run the risk of making it all rather comfortable for both workers and chaplain?

'Spirit at Work' is a long way from historic industrial mission, from today's workplace chaplaincy, from 'faith at work' groups, and from 'God at work' literature. All of these are founded on particular religious traditions, and in particular on biblical literature full of prophetic challenge. In today's multi faith workplace chaplaincy the major differences between the religious traditions of the chaplains are fully recognised and the pastoral work which chaplains undertake together is well understood to emerge from the chaplains' particular and different religious commitments. Workplace chaplains don't proselytise, but their religious commitments inform their pastoral work and they are always willing to hold specifically religious conversations. For Howard and Welbourn the role of religions is different: it is to 'give more regular expression to the wisdom that we have . . . been examining' so that Spirit at Work practitioners might be 'more in tune with modern people's spiritual quest, more sympathetic to their needs' (Howard and Welbourn, 2004, p. 113). This is a secularization of religion to make religion marketable (Hicks, 2003, p. 38), and will surely only serve workplace chaplaincy's traditional purpose if regarded as one step in the direction of the justice demanded by a religion with prophetic challenge at its heart.

I very much hope that workplace chaplains will continue to relate to industries which raise acute ethical questions, as Welbourn has done. I also hope to see a lively debate about the adequacy or otherwise of 'Spirit at Work' as a basis for workplace chaplaincy.

Conclusions

Again we have discovered important continuities with previous periods. Workplace visiting has remained the foundation of what many still term 'industrial mission' ('Worcestershire Industrial Mission', 'Basingstoke, Andover and North Hampshire Industrial Mission', 'Industrial Mission in South Yorkshire'), and now the terms 'workplace' ('Sussex Workplace Ministry') and 'chaplaincy' ('Chaplaincy to People at Work' in Cambridge) are becoming more common. This suggests that workplace chaplaincy is what it's all about. However, that isn't the only thing it's about, as 'Mission in the Economy' and 'Mission in London's Economy' indicate. The kind of diverse activity which we have discovered in London is now fairly widespread, and those organizations which describe themselves as 'workplace chaplaincies' often regard chaplaincy as a core activity and empowerment of the Church's laity, the education of churches, and relationships with the institutions of the local economy, as at least as important. An additional diversity is provided by multi faith chaplaincy. This has for a long time been common in hospital, educational, prison and airport chaplaincy, and it is now becoming more common in chaplaincy to the emergency services. The first multi faith workplace chaplaincy is now at work on the Greenwich Peninsula.

The Industrial Mission Association has been trying to keep up with all of these changes. At the time of writing it is consulting its membership about its own name, and its next national conference will be discussing multi faith workplace chaplaincy. We await the outcomes of these important discussions: but whatever the outcomes, the movement is alive and well. There is lots of chaplaincy, a lay-led relationship between Christian faith and the workplace is still the aim, and relationships between workplace chaplaincy and the churches, both locally and regionally, are generally good. The movement is not the same as it was, of course. Chaplaincy is now more likely to be done by volunteer laypeople and clergy than by full-time chaplains; it's more likely to be in department stores than in coal mines, steel works, and factories; and there is less group work and there are fewer conferences: but in many places urban and workplace ministry are the partners which they ought to be and the economy as an institution is taken seriously. The movement has changed with the times, but it has consistently built bridges and has itself been a bridge across which the Christian Faith and industrial society can relate to each other.

Whatever each local manifestation of the movement is called, and whatever its chaplains are called, we have now seen 65 years of modern industrial mission in Britain. Both its history and its current health and activity need to be better known. A widely read recent report on the relationship between government institutions and the Church recognises that congregations on their own aren't particularly well suited to relate to major social institutions, and the authors ask: 'What significant assets [does] the wider institutional . . . structure [of the Church] bring into play for both state and Church?' (Davis et al, 2008, p. 19) They then spend much of the rest of the report discussing cathedrals and diocesan staff. There's no mention of industrial mission. This is really rather a pity, because the movement is well practised at enabling communication to occur between the Christian Faith and a secular institutional world: precisely the kind of communication which the report's authors are looking for.

There is still plenty of secularization in our society. Whether there is less religious belief or sense of the sacred than there was before remains an open question, but what is certain is that a number of secularizations have deepened during the past 60 years: the secularization of ideas and of culture, practical secularization, state secularization, religious secularization, and particularly institutional secularization. This does matter because such secularizations evacuate our ideas, culture, state, institutions, religion and individual practice of hope for a community of justice and peace which can only come to us as a gift. Secularization impoverishes all of us. We still need the bridges: we all need the bridges, so that the churches don't become ghettos and the world doesn't lose a transcendent reference-point.

Notes

1 Churches Industrial Group, Birmingham, 'A Brief History of CIGB', unpublished paper.

2 Correspondence from the Churches Industrial Group, Birmingham.

3 Correspondence from Mission in the Economy, Merseyside.

4 Correspondence from Chaplaincy to People at Work, Cambridgeshire.

5 Correspondence from the Black Country Urban Industrial Mission.

6 Correspondence from ECCIC.

7 Hackett, Frank J., 1983, 'Ports and Industrial Chaplaincy in the Far East, Australia and New Zealand', dissertation written when he was a Churchill Fellow during 1983, p. 47.

8 'A History of the Industrial Mission in the Selby Area', unpublished paper.

9 David Welbourn, 'resumé of industrial mission career', prepared for his interview by Peter Cope, 28th May 2008.

10 Correspondence from Mission in the Economy, Merseyside.

11 Faith and Work groups are now sometimes multi faith (Correspondence from the Churches Industrial Group, Birmingham).

12 A talk given to the London and South East Region of the Industrial Mission Association on the 7th July 2009 by Andrew Drury.

13 www.mile.org.uk.

14 Mitroff I. and Denton, E., 1999, 'A Study of Spirituality in the Workplace', *Sloan Management Review*, 40 (4), p. 83, quoted in Howard and Welbourn, 2004, p. 47.

15 David Welbourn, Resumé of Industrial Mission Career, prepared for his interview with Peter Cope, 28th May 2008; interview with David Welbourn by Peter Cope, 28th May 2008.

Conclusions

Fresh expressions

Have I answered my own question? Has industrial mission been an appropriate response to secularization? Is workplace chaplaincy still an appropriate response? My answer to both of those questions is 'yes'. Industrial mission has been a significant response to institutional secularization, a partial response to state secularization (because of industrial mission's work on local economies and their institutions), and something of a response to the secularization of ideas and of culture; and it has occasionally reconnected individuals' working lives with their Christian faith, thus desecularizing their beliefs and resacralising their working lives. The movement hasn't had much of a direct impact on practical secularization and has probably contributed to the secularization of religion. If you build a bridge into a secular world then a certain amount of travel from a secular world into the Church and its religion is inevitable. Some of my readers won't think that's a good idea, some will regard it as a price worth paying for something of the Christian gospel rubbing off on the working world, and some will think that a secularization of religion fits rather nicely with an incarnational faith. In a society and in a Church in which religion is increasingly privatised and commodified, industrial mission has stood for religion as fellowship, as reconciliation, as institutionally relevant, and as finding God active in the world and in its institutions. This is a proper secularization of religion.

Institutional desecularization in factories after the Second World War was helped along by working men's familiarity with armed forces chaplains. Some practical desecularization happened, too, because although the lay projects, canteen courses and residential conferences weren't congregations in the traditional sense, they were the Church, and today we would recognise them as valuable 'fresh expressions'. These desecularizations were possible because the chaplains were working in those parts of the social structure which were not yet seriously secularized. Many of those men would have experienced religious activity as children as well as in the army, and while they might have regarded their parish church or their local chapel as not for them, they didn't find religious activity itself alien or oppressive. It was as the traditional heavy industries closed and their workforces were dispersed, and as longer travelling times, increasing home responsibilities and longer and less predictable working hours made it more difficult for anyone to participate in voluntary activity of any kind – and as memories of armed forces padres faded - that industrial missions found it more difficult to tackle either institutional or practical secularization and turned their attention to educating the churches in the realities of the workplace and the economy. This was both a displacement activity and an attempt at survival in a difficult funding climate. The unfortunate consequence was that it was now clear to the denominations that industrial missions were what they had in fact always been: agencies belonging neither to industry nor to the Church (Torry, 2005, pp. 51–3). Industrial chaplains were freelance bridgebuilders, and many in the Church didn't see why they should be funding them. At the same time, many chaplains became experts in secular fields: in personnel management, industrial organization, and counselling. So by the late 1960s there were chaplains building on the secular side of the gulf, chaplains building in the middle of the river, and a few chaplains building on the Church side of the river. The bridge was being built, but it wasn't clear that it was the Church that was building it.

Lots of small changes create major social revolutions. In Britain's urban areas reliable contraception meant that women were more likely to stay in the labour market for longer, have fewer children, and re-enter the labour market; chaplains found it more difficult to visit office blocks than engineering works; and flexitime brought to an end the standard one hour lunch break and the standard finishing time. So by the 1960s both workplace visiting and lunchtime, evening and weekend meetings were becoming difficult to organize. Whereas during the 1950s a chaplain could spend a day in a factory which employed several thousand men, she might now spend a morning visiting half a dozen shops employing 50 people between them. Industrial mission's impact on institutional and practical secularization was bound to decline, and it did. The issues-based and local economy work of the past couple of decades, while valuable, can't hope to match the effect on secularization which chaplains achieved while visiting large industrial workforces and convening large numbers of groups, courses, and conferences. The workplace chaplain today visits workplaces, but holding individual conversations with workers is generally the sum total of the activity. One of the results of all this for industrial missions is the loss of the laity's involvement, an increasing clericalism, and thus even less ability to build bridges between the Church and the rest of the world.

What has saved industrial mission is that in many places it has continued to do what it has always done, and while numbers involved might now be rather small, workplace visiting, group work, publishing and discussion have continued to build bridges: bridges, and not just structures on the banks. At various times and in various places the movement has done new things, but methods and intentions from the past have never been entirely lost. Interestingly it has often been part-time lay and clerical chaplains who have done the necessary new and risky things: they are the ones who have been willing to relate to today's institutions in order to converse on the shop floor, in canteens, in small companies, and on construction sites. SLIM's Adrian Esdaile was innovating when many full-time chaplains weren't, it's the entirely volunteer Greenwich Peninsula team which has created the first multi faith workplace chaplaincy, and it's Mission in London's Economy's volunteer practitioner groups, co-ordinated by a very part-time postholder, which have tried to integrate a variety of aims and objectives into a strategy to relate the Christian Faith to London's economy.

So bridges have been built: between the Church and secular institutions, between secular institutions and the Christian tradition, between individuals and the Christian Faith, between the Church and individuals, and more recently between people of different faiths. Much of what has travelled across those bridges is lost to history, but the bridges themselves are not. Almost as significant are some of the movement's other achievements: an empowered and articulate laity, improved relationships within a number of industries, early involvement in lay training and in the ministry of women, contributions to social and economic justice, appropriate responses to major crises, workers facing redundancy supported, and the Church reconnected with the realities of the industrial world, of unemployment, and now of the diverse working world and of the economy . . . the list could go on.

Above all, industrial mission has exemplified the connectedness of life. As Paul Ballard argues: in a world in which life is 'dispersed' everything is a 'sector', including the domestic. Therefore every ministry is a sector ministry (Ballard, 2009, p. 18). I would add that ministry in a congregation or parish church based in a residential community is now more of a 'sector ministry' than workplace chaplaincy is, for the simple reason that workplace chaplains concern themselves with every aspect of people's lives whereas the residentially-based activity of the Church often doesn't. Similarly, we only have to look at the 'five marks of mission' worked out by the Anglican Consultative Council and adopted by the Lambeth Conference in 1988 to understand the breadth of the mission undertaken by workplace chaplaincy and mission in the economy:

- to proclaim the Good News of the Kingdom
- to teach, baptize and nurture new believers
- to respond to human need by loving service
- to seek to transform unjust structures of society
- to strive to safeguard the integrity of creation, sustain and renew the life of the earth[1]

A combination of workplace chaplaincy and mission in the economy ticks all of those boxes. The same combination also conforms well to David Bosch's description of our participation in

God's mission as 'a multifaceted ministry, in respect of witness, service, justice, healing, reconciliation, liberation, peace, evangelism, fellowship, church planting, contextualization, and much more' (Bosch, 1991, p. 512), so such a combination could properly be regarded as a normative ministry. Bosch's thesis is that the Church's mission belongs within God's mission. I would add that God's mission is best described as building bridges and crossing them, that that's what mission should be for us, and that industrial mission has been a classic example of this kind of mission. Similarly, God's mission is an 'embedded' mission, the workplace chaplain's ministry is similarly embedded in a complex world, and so again workplace chaplaincy is the Church's mission properly located within God's own mission (Ballard, 2009, pp. 20–21). Our world is a world of institutions so we shall only relate to it by building 'mediating institutions' (Torry, 2009, pp. 439–42) across which the world and the Christian Faith can relate to each other. Once we've built such mediating institutions we must make sure that they don't wander too far either from the Church or from the economy and its institutions so that they can continue to be the bridges we need (Torry, 2008a, pp. 17–19).

At its best industrial mission has been a servant of both the Church and the world, and it can therefore properly be called 'diaconal', or 'serving' (Clark, 2005, 217–31). 'Christendom' can be defined as 'a society where the historic Christian faith provides the cultural framework for social living, as well as the official religious form of the State'.[2] Clark thinks that the Church is still operating in that mode and that it needs instead to be a 'Diaconal Church', 'a kingdom community-centred church. As such, it is called by God to make manifest the kingdom community's gifts of life, liberation, love and learning within its own life' (Clark, 2005, p. 70). This is what industrial mission has always tried to be, as Clark recognises. (He thinks that industrial chaplains should be ordained deacon - *diakonos* means 'servant' - and should be neither laity nor priests or ministers (Clark, 2005, p. 231).) But the movement has also tried to do something else: to shape society and its institutions in accordance with the coming Kingdom of God, a Kingdom of peace and justice in which 'King-' means

'Servant', *diakonos*. This requires not the abandonment of the 'Christendom' terminology, but rather its rescue. Industrial mission has wanted to positively influence society, the economy, and society's institutions, so that they might conform more closely to the Kingdom of God. It has quite properly tried to 'influence the influences' (Wickham, 1964, p. 19). A 'Christendom Church' is therefore required, with 'Christendom' defined as 'the shaping of society according to Jesus' vision and embodiment of the Kingdom of God': so truly a 'Christ-en-dom'. It is such a Christendom which will prove to be the basis for our future response to diverse secularization, and, by pursuing such a Christendom, workplace chaplaincy and mission in the economy will contribute to that necessary response.

Recommendation

So my single recommendation is this: more of the same. We need more empowerment of the laity, more relating of the Christian Faith to the economy and its institutions, more discussion groups, more people responding to consultation documents, more education of the churches, more workplace chaplains, more local chaplaincy organizations, and more chaplaincies: so training in how to establish chaplaincies will be as important as training in how to be chaplains. Unlike Ted Wickham and his 1959 report (Church of England, 1959), I'm not going to recommend a national strategy. We don't need one. Local autonomy is essential for experimentation. The Industrial Mission Association's regional structure is OK. One thing we do need, though, is a voice for the movement, so there is a case for the IMA's National Executive Committee[3] appointing and paying an executive officer so that the churches know who to talk to.

What I'm really not sure about is whether we need full-time workplace chaplains. This is a question which Peter Cope raised quite sharply during his retirement sermon in July 2007: 'We are getting the balance of emphasis in ministry wrong. The message we are sending out is both very depressing, and (I would argue) untrue to the gospel. Let me explain. When people outside the

Churches see that an appointment like mine – Industrial and Town Centre Chaplain in Telford – is being shut down, while other parochial-based jobs are being maintained or increased, they are surely entitled to think that the Churches are looking after themselves.'4 There is some justice in this complaint. You can tell an organization's priorities by the posts which it establishes and by those which it abolishes. We all know what it means when a company closes its research and development department and tells everyone that it's everybody's task to do research and development. The message is clear: research and development don't matter. The economic reality is that in the medium term there won't be the money for a large number of workplace chaplaincy full-time posts, as there was during the 1950s and '60s. Volunteer part-timers will from now on be the normal way of doing both workplace chaplaincy and mission in the economy. However, for this to be an effective strategy, we shall need full-time or at least half-time co-ordinators to recruit, train and supervise part-time chaplains, to negotiate new chaplaincy opportunities, and to convene groups to work on local economies. Such paid posts will encourage into Christian mission substantial amounts of expertise and many hours of volunteer chaplaincy activity. So I share Cope's concern and would offer the same challenge: Any church which is serious about joining in God's mission in the world needs to be willing to pay for co-ordinating chaplains. It needn't be expensive, because it can be done ecumenically, and it might increasingly be done in a multi faith manner: but it needs to be done, and it needs to be a priority.

Multi faith chaplaincy

A major issue for the IMA and for the movement generally is whether multi faith workplace chaplaincy should be regarded as normative or as an aberration. We now live in a secular multi faith society (Cooper and Lodge, 2008, pp. 13–14, 61–70) and it is now difficult[5] and will soon be impossible for purely Christian bodies to appoint workplace chaplains to industry, commerce, and public services. The Christian Faith is the major cause of the equality and inclusion which are now inalienable expectations in civil society, so we can hardly complain when companies and local authorities say that they want the faiths to work together to serve the spiritual and other needs of their workforces and communities. We are faced with a choice: either we shall have to work in multi faith teams or eventually we shall not be workplace chaplains at all. I understand some of the anxieties surrounding the idea of multi faith work, but our experience on the Greenwich Peninsula is that all that's required is an agreement that we do together everything which everyone can agree to do together and separately everything else. Our experience is that multi faith work needn't compromise Christian Faith's distinctiveness. Far from it: it makes those of us who are Christians more aware of who we are, of what we share with people of other faiths, and of what we don't.

By taking the multi faith road, workplace chaplaincy will be doing something which industrial mission has always done: it will be creating reconciliation. During the 1950s that meant reconciliation between trades unionists and managers. Today one of our major tasks is reconciliation between people of different faiths.

Prophecy

In the Old and New Testaments, prophecy is a God-inspired judgment on the state of the world. Industrial mission has always been both pastoral and prophetic: sometimes more of one, sometimes more of the other, but always there has been something of a prophetic edge to the activity. Michael Northcott suggests that during the period 1958 – 1979 Teesside Industrial Mission identified Christian values with chaplains' acceptability to the personnel and organizational functions of industry and thus lost its ability to speak prophetically to the totality of industry's activity. 'The more effective chaplains become at legitimating the ideologies and power figures in the organizations they serve, the more they subvert their ultimate prophetic and theological intentions' (Northcott, 1989, p. 104). What he writes might or might not be true of public prophetic comment, but what he can't know is how much critical comment went on privately in managers' offices.

In our multi faith society, and in the context of increasingly multi faith workplace chaplaincy, we now need to look at this issue from two different perspectives. First, can specifically Christian industrial mission publicly prophesy in relation to companies which they visit? My answer is that they can, provided they discuss the issue first with the firm, make clear that they intend to make a public stand, and explain the theological reason for it. They still risk being ejected from the firm, but that's a risk worth taking. It is, of course, a risk which a part-time volunteer chaplain is more likely to take than a full-time paid one: which is a good reason for preferring part-time and volunteer chaplains to full-time ones. Second, we need to look at this issue from the perspective of chaplaincy work in multi faith teams. If there is an issue facing the chaplaincy – as there was in 2006 for the Greenwich Peninsula Chaplaincy when the London Borough of Greenwich and Anschutz Entertainment Group wanted to locate the country's largest casino in The O2 – then wide consultation among the chaplaincy's trustees, the chaplains, and also local faith communities, can result in a solid consensus. This can then provide a good basis both for debate with the company and for any necessary public comment – in that order. Such comment needn't damage the relationship between the chaplaincy and the company: though, again, it might result in the end of the relationship, and this possible cost will need to be carefully weighed by the chaplaincy's trustees.

A secular theology?

Northcott also criticises the Teesside Industrial Mission, and the movement as a whole, for secularizing its theology. There is some justice in this. I would say first of all that a proper secularizing of theology is a good thing: our theology needs to be inspired by the Word made flesh (John 1:14), by God's creation of a material world, by our responsibility for stewardship of the created order, and by the Christian hope for God's kingdom coming 'on earth as in heaven' (Matthew 6:10). But that's not what Northcott is complaining about. He's complaining about a theology evacuated of all transcendent reference. I have found working in a multi faith team to be immensely helpful here. It forces us to be clear about our theological commitments. In today's multi faith chaplaincy Northcott would find rather less secularization of Christian theology than he found in a purely Christian context on Teesside during the 1970s.

Constitutions

Multi faith teams raise an interesting question: To what extent are such organizations agencies of the Church? The answer is that they are not. Such organizations are bridges between the Church and other faiths just as much as they are bridges between the Church and the economy and its institutions. (Traffic will, as always, be in all possible directions.) In this new context chaplaincy will be seen to be what it has always been: an independent exercise of the mission of God, and, for Christians, of the God we meet in Jesus Christ. It is God's mission which is primary, and this relativises both the Church as it is and the work of chaplaincy, both of which stand judged by the God who is at work among us. This suggests that the way ahead has to be independently constituted multi faith chaplaincy organizations and not industrial missions constitutionally bound to particular Christian denominations. An alternative would be the London solution: an independent Christian organization which gives birth to an autonomous multi faith organization which it continues to work alongside. A related question then becomes: To what kind of area should a multi faith team relate? Clearly not to an area defined by the Church of England's diocesan boundaries. The best option has to be teams drawn from within a borough or a combination of boroughs and serving the industry, commerce and emergency and public services within the borough boundary.

As for governance: independence requires a charitable trust or a charitable company, and the board of trustees or the board of directors will need to be drawn from multi faith forums and similar bodies. Where faith communities have structures which can deliver representatives then that's how trustees and directors should be appointed. However, some faith communities don't have governance structures suitable for appointing trustees to external organizations, and the nearest we can get to representative people is those members of faith communities who attend meetings of the local multi faith forum. They will generally have the respect of their own faith communities and will already be practised at working with people of other faiths.[6]

Other structural issues which once exercised the minds of industrial chaplains and their denominations and management committees now seem rather less relevant. Whether individual chaplains should be deacons is up to them, and similarly if some chaplains wish to form or join a religious order then again that's up to them. In the future, chaplains will be mainly part-time, they will generally be volunteers, they will be appointed by the trustees of their local multi faith team rather than by their denomination, and they might or might not be supported by paid full- or part-time paid chaplains. The most important requirement in each area is therefore a constitutionally independent charitable trust or company to which workplaces can relate, to which the churches can relate, and to which other faith communities can relate. These will be the mediating institutions that we need, and their objectives will be that same wide diversity of tasks which have always been at the heart of industrial mission practice: workplace visiting with both pastoral and prophetic motives, reconciliation within the workplace and between people of different faiths, education and empowerment of the laity for relating their faith to their work and their workplace, education of the churches and of faith communities in the realities of economic life, and responding to major issues in industry, commerce and other social institutions from within faith perspectives, with faith communities working both separately and together as the occasion demands.

Julian Reindorp thinks that supporting Christian laypeople as they relate their faith to their work is the essential task for industrial mission. I agree. One of the dangers of the now more common designation 'workplace chaplaincy' is that it is about chaplains visiting workplaces and it isn't obviously about other related activity. 'Industrial mission' could encapsulate the empowerment of a Christian laity, and 'mission in the economy' can do so too: but the problem with 'mission' in a multi faith context is that it is even more of a Christian term than 'chaplain' is. 'Chaplain' is now more acceptable because prison, university, hospital and hospice chaplaincies involve practitioners of a variety of faiths so the term is now well understood in many faith communities. 'Mission' is a much more difficult word in a multi faith context. One of the options for the Industrial Mission Association's change of name is 'Ministry among people at work' ('map @ work'). There is much merit in this suggestion as it can be used for multi faith work and it can encompass the wide variety of activity in which industrial mission, mission in the economy, and workplace chaplaincy, are now involved.

There is a huge agenda awaiting workplace chaplaincy and mission in the economy. The problem is going to be making it happen, and, in particular, funding it. This is going to be a real problem. Financial independence from the companies which chaplains visit is essential to the prophetic task, so while I can understand Australian, Coventry and other chaplaincies seeking fees for services rendered, such chaplaincy is more likely to be co-opted by the institutions to which it relates than chaplaincy funded in other ways. Simply being present in an institution is sufficient of a problem, because not wanting to be thrown out tempts us to self-censorship. For salaries to depend on continuing good relationships with powerful figures in those organizations surely compounds that problem. It really is time that we decided that we are going to take no more money from industry.

Where we need physical space for our work, and the only way we're going to get it is for the organizations to which we relate to provide it, then that's the way it will have to be; but just as management agreement to our presence is bound to compromise us, so accepting physical space will do the same. We must therefore be aware of that danger and must consciously address the collusion which is likely to result. In the end, we must be willing to hand back the space if that's what's required in order to maintain independence of speech and action. Receiving money for salaries is a step further than receiving a welcome or being lent space to use, and I would say that it's a step too far.

Grant-making trusts can sometimes be persuaded to fund new work, and this will be particularly helpful as we establish the many multi faith teams which we're going to need: but such sources will rarely fund ongoing work, and it's long term commitment that we require. Having already discounted receiving money from the institutions in which we work, the only funding option left is the faith communities themselves. We must vigorously ask for such funding from the churches on the basis that workplace chaplaincy and mission in the economy are between them a normative ministry. Trustees and chaplains of other faiths will need to offer their own rationales to their own faith communities. As the British Council of Churches' 1958 report put it: 'If the Churches really care unselfishly and responsibly about the "Church and industry" had they not better start by paying for any gesture they propose to make?' (British Council of Churches, 1958, p. 37)

However, even willing faith communities are in financially straitened times, and there is never going to be very much money from this direction. We must therefore learn to live within our means. This means teams of unpaid part-time chaplains supported and co-ordinated by part-time and half-time faith community post-holders who can agree with their faith community leaderships that spending time on such work is a good idea.

Until now the Roman Catholic Church has stood on the edge of industrial mission. As we have seen, there have been the occasional Roman Catholic industrial chaplains, but the Church's official view has always been that it's the laity who are the Church in industry and that it's such lay organizations as the Young Christian Workers and the International Christian Union of Business Executives which should co-ordinate the lay witness.[7] Who can disagree with that? What we might wish to disagree with is the idea that chaplains shouldn't be involved as well. After all, the Roman Catholic Church is more than willing to involve itself in higher education chaplaincy. If teams of part-time lay and clerical volunteer chaplains are to be the future for workplace chaplaincy, and if a broader mission in the economy is also the future, then a new relationship between the movement and the Roman Catholic Church is clearly both desirable and possible.

The basis on which this new relationship might be built could be the same that we might recommend to every church and to every faith community: that whenever a faith community is about to appoint to a post or office then the question should be asked: Are there institutions to which this new office- or post-holder could relate? Are there people at work in them who could be visited? Is there a local team of workplace chaplaincies to which this new post-holder or office-holder could be linked? If the answers to these questions are 'yes' then everyone and everything will benefit: the people and institutions visited, the post- or office-holder themselves, other workplace chaplains, and the local mission in the economy. Both faith communities and chaplaincy teams will need to facilitate this process, and they will also need to provide the necessary initial and ongoing training and support which new workplace chaplains will need. As we have discovered in the Greenwich Peninsula Chaplaincy, providing such training is an invigorating process for everyone involved.

Still doing everything

There have been periods during the history which I have recounted in which particular activities or ideas have come to the fore, but even when that has happened the necessary diversity has never been entirely lost. Workplace visiting, groups, conferences, ideas, theology, networking, education, political action, and comment and activity in relation to the wider economy . . . it is this diversity which has contributed to the health of the movement. We shall in the future need activity and ideas to be even more diverse. Another source of the movement's health has been its ability to innovate, and innovation must surely continue to characterise the movement. If such diversity and innovation continue then workplace chaplaincy and faith communities' other activity in relation to the economy and its institutions will be an effective response to secularization.

I think I've answered my questions.

Notes

1   www.cofe.anglican.org/faith/mission/missionevangelism.html

2   Nichols, Aidan, 1999, *Christendom Awake*, Edinburgh: T. and T. Clark, p. 1, quoted in Clark 2005, p. 58.

3   The IMA is still organized regionally but it is now registered as a single charity and thus has a National Executive Committee rather than a Central Co-ordinating Committee.

4   Peter Cope, retirement sermon, 16th July 2007.

5   Peter Cope, 'Reflections on leaving industrial mission in Telford', *IMAgenda*, September/October 2007, pp. 42–43.

6   Such a structure isn't that dissimilar to the ecumenical structure for industrial mission governance recommended in Church of England 1988, p. 102.

7   Muir, Kevin, 1987, 'Industrial Mission – Catholic Style', in *Industrial Mission and the Churches in Britain Today*, paper 4, London: Board for Social Responsibility, quoted in Brown and Ballard, 2006, p. 144.

Bibliography

This bibliography contains

1 published works
2 dissertations and theses available in university libraries,
3 documents available on the website www.industrialmission-history.org.uk (marked with an asterisk).

Each chapter's other sources will be found in its endnotes

Acquaviva, S.S., 1979, *The Decline of the Sacred in Industrial Society*, tr. Patricia Lipscomb, Oxford: Basil Blackwell

Atkinson, Michael, undated a, 'Theological Influences in the Early Years of Industrial Mission', in *Thinking in Practice: Theology and Industrial Mission*, Working papers from Industrial Mission, no. 3, Manchester: William Temple Foundation, for the Industrial Mission Association's Theology Development Group

* Atkinson, Michael, undated b, 'Industrial Mission 1944–1979, Memoirs', unpublished paper

Attwood, Tony, 1996, 'The Coal Campaign 1992–93: The interaction of faith and economics', in Rogerson 1996

Bagshaw, Paul, 1994, *The Church Beyond the Church: Sheffield Industrial Mission 1944–1994*, Sheffield: Industrial Mission in South Yorkshire

Baker, Chris, 2007, 'Entry to Enterprise: Constructing Local Political Economies in Manchester', in Atherton, John and Skinner, Hannah (eds.), *Through the Eye of a Needle: Theological Conversations Over Political Economy*, Peterborough: Epworth Press

Bardsley, Cuthbert, 1967, *Him We Declare*, Oxford: Mowbray

Barker Bennett, Caroline, 1996, 'Speaking as we Find: Women's experience of Tyneside industry', in Rogerson 1996

Bell, Catherine, 1997, *Ritual: Perspectives and Dimensions*, New York and Oxford: Oxford University Press

Berger, Peter, 1970, *A Rumour of Angels: Modern Society and the Rediscovery of the Supernatural*, Harmondsworth: Penguin

Berger, Peter, 1995, *The Social Reality of Religion*, Oxford: Oxford University Press

Berger, Peter, 1999, *The Desecularization of the World: Resurgent Religion and World Politics*, Grand Rapids, Michigan: Eerdmans, for the Ethics and public Policy Centre, Washington DC

Bloy, Philip, 2001, *The Call to Mission Answered: Ted Wickham and the Sheffield Industrial Mission, 1944–1959*, 2nd edition, Northampton: Disciple Press

Bogle, James, 2002, *South Bank Religion: The Diocese of Southwark 1959–1969*, London: Hatcham Press

Bonhoeffer, Dietrich 1953, *Letters and Papers from Prison*, edited by Eberhard Bethge, translated by Reginald H. Fuller, London: SCM Press

Bosch, David J., 1991, *Transforming Mission: Paradigm Shifts in Theology of Mission*, Maryknoll: Orbis Books

British Council of Churches, 1958, *The Church and Industry*, London

Brown, Callum, 2001, *The Death of Christian Britain: Understanding Secularization 1800–2000*, London: Routledge

Brown, Malcolm and Ballard, Paul, 2006, *The Church and Economic Life: a documentary study: 1945 to the present*, Peterborough: Epworth Press

Bruce, Stephen (ed.), 1992, *Religion and Modernization: Sociologists and Historians Debate the Secularization Theory*, Oxford: Clarendon Press

Bruce, Stephen, 1995, *Religion in Modern Britain*, Oxford: Oxford University Press

Buber, Martin, 1966, *I and Thou*, Edinburgh: T. and T. Clark, originally published in German

Buchanan, Colin, 2003, *Cut the Connection: Disestablishment and the Church of England*, London: Darton, Longman and Todd

Chadwick, Owen, 1975, *The Secularization of the European Mind in the Nineteenth Century*, Cambridge: Cambridge University Press

Chaves, Mark, 1993, 'Intraorganizational Power and Internal Secularization in Protestant Denominations', *American Journal of Sociology*, 99 (1)

Church of England: The Archbishop's Fifth Committee of Inquiry, 1918, *Christianity and Industrial Problems, being the Report of the Archbishop's Fifth Committee of Inquiry*, London: SPCK

Church of England, 1943: *Towards the Conversion of England: Being the Report of a Commission on Evangelism appointed by the Archbishops of Canterbury and York pursuant to a Resolution of the Church Assembly passed at the Summer session, 1943*, London: The Press and Publications Board of the Church Assembly

Church of England, 1959, *The Task of the Church in Relation to Industry*, London: Church Information Office

Church of England: Employment and Unemployment Group, 1977, *Work or What? A Christian examination of the employment crisis*, London: Church Information Office

Church of England: The Archbishop of Canterbury's Commission on Urban Priority Areas, 1985, *Faith in the City: A Call for Action by Church and Nation*, London: Church House Publishing

Church of England, 1988, *Industrial Mission – An Appraisal: The Church's Resonse to the Changing Industrial and Economic Order*, London: Board for Social Responsibility

Churches Consortium on Industrial Mission, 1977, *Ecumenical Guidelines for the Organization of Industrial Mission*, London

Churches Consortium on Industrial Mission, 1979, *Appointments to Industrial Mission: Towards a General Pattern*, London

Churches Consortium on Industrial Mission, 1982, *Starting the Work – A Basic Manual for Industrial Chaplains*, London

Claringbull, Denis, 1994, *Front Line Mission: Ministry in the Market Place*, Norwich: Canterbury Press

Clark, David, 2005, *Breaking the Mould of Christendom: Kingdom Community, Diaconal Church and the Liberation of the Laity*, Peterborough: Epworth Press

Cleal, C. H., 1945, *The Chaplain in the Factory*, London: SCM Press

Coggan, Donald, 1989, *Cuthbert Bardsley: Bishop, Evangelist, Pastor*, London: Collins

Coleman, T., 1968, *The Railway Navvies: A history of the men who made the railways*, Harmondsworth: Pelican

Collange, André, 1961, in Edwards, David L., *Priests and Workers*, London: SCM Press

Collier, Paul, 2006, 'Serving in a Learning Community: The Chaplain in Higher Education', in Torry 2006a

Cooper, Zaki and Guy Lodge (eds), 2008, *Faith in the Nation: Religion, identity and the public realm in Britain today*, London: Institute for Public Policy Research

Costa, Ken, 2007, *God At Work: Living every day with purpose*, London: Continuum

Cox, Harvey, 1968, *The Secular City: Secularization and Urbanisation in Theological Perspective*, Harmondsworth: Penguin

Cox, Jeffrey, 1982, *The English Churches in a Secular Society: Lambeth 1870–1930*, Oxford: Oxford University Press

Cuttell, Colin, 1962, *Ministry without Portfolio*, London: Toc H

Davie, Grace, 1994, *Religion in Britain Since 1945: Believing Without Belonging*, Oxford: Blackwell

Davie, Grace, 2000, 'Religion in Modern Britain: Changing Sociological Assumptions', *Sociology*, 34 (1)

Davie, Grace, 2002, *Europe: The Exceptional Case: Parameters of Faith in the Modern World*, London: Darton, Longman and Todd

Davies, Rupert E., 1963, *Methodism*, Harmondsworth: Penguin

Davis, Francis, Paulhus, Elizabeth and Bradstock, Andrew, 2008, *Moral, But No Compass: Government, Church and the Future of Welfare*, Chelmsford: Matthew James Publishing, for the Von Hügel Institute, Cambridge

Davis, John, 1986, 'Lay and Ordained in the Workplace', in Fuller and Vaughan 1986

DiMaggio, Paul, and W. Powell, 1983, 'The Iron Cage Revisited: Conformity and Diversity in Organizational Fields', *American Sociological Quarterly*, 48

* Diocese of Lichfield, 2008, 'Report of the Review Group: Commissioned by the Diocese of Lichfield to Examine the Work of the Black Country Urban Industrial Mission', unpublished paper

Edwards, David L., 1984, *Christian Britain*, vol. 3, London: Collins

Elwyn, T., 1996, 'Industrial Mission: A Reflection', *Baptist Quarterly*, 1996, quoted in Tonkinson 2009

Erlander, Lillemor, 1991, *Faith in the World of Work: On the Theology of Work as lived by the French Worker-Priests and British Industrial Mission*, Uppsala: Uppsala University

Flagg, David, 2006, 'Serving in a Healing Community: The Hospital Chaplain', in Torry 2006a, pp. 171–84

Forshaw, Eric, 1986, 'Industrial Chaplaincy and Ministry in Secular Employment', in Fuller Vaughan 1986

Fuller, John and Patrick Vaughan (eds.), 1986, *Working for the Kingdom: The Story of Ministers in Secular Employment*, London: SPCK

Gill, Robin, 1992, 'The Empty Church', in Bruce, Stephen (ed.), 1992, *Religion in Modern Britain*, Oxford: Oxford University Press, pp. 90–117

Gill, Robin, 2003, *The 'Empty' Church Revisited*, Aldershot: Ashgate

Golding, William, 1980, *Rites of Passage*, London: Faber and Faber

Goyder, George, 1961, *The Responsible Company*, Oxford: Blackwell

Hackett, Frank J., 1971, 'The Role of the Industrial Chaplain', unpublished Diploma in Management Studies dissertation, Wolverhampton Polytechnic

Hackett, Frank J., 1977, 'The Role of the Industrial Chaplain', unpublished M.A. dissertation, University of Birmingham

Harcourt, Melville, 1953, *Tubby Clayton: A Personal Saga*, London: Hodder and Stoughton

Hastings, Adrian, 2001, *A History of English Christianity, 1920–2000*, fourth edition, London: SCM Press

Heskins, Jeffrey and Baker, Matt., 2006, *Footballing Lives*, Norwich: Canterbury Press

Hewitt, Gordon (ed.), 1985, *Strategist of the Spirit: Leslie Hunter, Bishop of Sheffield, 1939–1962*, Oxford: Becket

Hicks, Douglas A., 2003, *Religion and the Workplace: Pluralism, Spirituality, Leadership*, Cambridge: Cambridge University Press

Howard, Sue and David Welbourn, 2004, *The Spirit at Work Phenomenon*, London: Azure

Hunter, Leslie, 1931, *A Parson's Job*, London: SCM Press

Hunter, L., 1941, 'Evangelism', *Sheffield Diocesan Review*, 15th November 1941, quoted in Masumoto 1983, pp. 8–9

Hunter, L., 1943, *Christian Newsletter*, supplement, no. 249, 12th December 1943, quoted in Masumoto 1983, p. 7

Hunter, Leslie, 1966, *The English Church: A New Look*, Harmondsworth: Penguin

Hurst, Antony, 1986, *Rendering Unto Caesar: an exploration of the place of paid employment within the framework of Christian belief*, Worthing: Churchman Publishing

Hurst, Antony, 2005, *The Diocese of Southwark, 1905–2005, A Centennial Celebration*, London: Diocese of Southwark

Jackson, Bob, 2002, *Hope for the Church: Contemporary Strategies for Growth*, London: Church House Publishing

Jackson, Michael, 1965, 'Major Issues in Industrial Mission', *International Review of Missions*, pp. 151–160, quoted in Bagshaw 1994, pp. 62–3

Jackson, Michael, 1966, 'No New Gospel', *Theology*, 69 (558), London: SPCK

Kane, Margaret, 1980, *Gospel in Industrial Society*, London: SCM Press

James, Eric, 1987, *A Life of Bishop John A.T. Robinson*, London: Collins

Kierkegaard, Søren, 1940, *The Present Age*, translated by Alexander Dru and Walter Lowrie, London: Oxford University Press

Kane, Margaret, 1980, *Gospel in Industrial Society*, London: SCM Press

Lloyd, Roger, 1946, *The Church of England in the Twentieth Century*, vol. I, London: Longman, Green and Co.

Lurkings, E.H., 1981, 'The Origins, Context and Ideology of Industrial Mission, 1875–1975', unpublished Ph.D. thesis, London School of Economics and Political Science, University of London

MacIntyre, Alasdair, 1967, *Secularization and Moral Change*, Oxford: Oxford University Press

MacIntyre, Alasdair, 1967, *Secularization and Moral Change*, Oxford: Oxford University Press

McLeod, Hugh, 1974, *Class and Religion in the Late Victorian City*, London: Croom Helm

McLeod, Hugh, 2007, *The Religious Crisis of the 1960s*, Oxford: Oxford University Press

Mantle, John, 2000, *Britain's First Worker-Priests*, London: SCM Press

Martin, David, 1969, *The Religious and the Secular*, London: Routledge and Kegan Paul

Martin, David, 1978, *A General Theory of Secularization*, Oxford: Blackwell

Martin, David, 2005, *On Secularization: Towards a Revised Theory of Secularization*, Aldershot: Ashgate

Masumoto, Shigeko, 1983, 'A Critique of British Industrial Mission as a Response of the Church to Modern Industrial Society', M.Phil. thesis, University of Leeds

Melton, Violet, 1961, in Edwards, David L. (ed.), *Priests and Workers*, London: SCM

Methodist Church, 2003, *Let Your Light Shine: A Strategy for the Methodist Church's Engagement with Economic Life*, London

Miller, David W., 2007, *God at Work: The History and Promise of the Faith at Work Movement*, Oxford: Oxford University Press

Miller, Spencer Jr and Fletcher, Joseph 1930, *The Church and Industry*, New York: Longmans, Green and Co.

Norman, Edward, 2002, *Secularization*, London: Continuum

Northcott, Michael, 1983, *The Church and Secularization*, Frankfurt am Main: Verlag Peter Lang

Otto, Rudolf, 1923, *The Idea of the Holy*, London: Oxford University Press

Paradise, Scott I., 1968, *Detroit Industrial Mission*, New York: Harper and Row

Percy, Martyn, 2006, *Clergy: Origin of Species*, London: Continuum

Perrin, Henri, 1947, *Priest-Workman in Germany*, tr. Rosemary Sheed, London: Sheed and Ward

Perrin, Henri, 1965, *Priest and Worker*, London: MacMillan

Phipps, Simon, 1966, *God On Monday*, London: Hodder and Stoughton

Putnam, Robert, 2000, *Bowling Alone: The Collapse and Revival of American Community*, New York: Simon Schuster

Reindorp, Julian, 2000, *Equipping Christians at Work*, London: Industrial Christian Fellowship

Riordan, Patrick, 2008, 'At a Loss for Words', in Riordan, Patrick (ed.), *Words in Action: Finding the Right Words*, The Institute Series, no.11, London: The Heythrop Institute for Religion, Ethics and Public Life

Robinson, John A. T., 1960, *On Being the Church in the World*, London: SCM Press

Robinson, J. A. T., 1963a, *Liturgy Coming to Life*, 2nd edition, Oxford: Mowbray

Robinson, John A. T., 1963b, *Honest to God*, London: SCM Press, London

Rogerson, John W. (ed.), 1996, *Industrial Mission in a Changing World: Papers from the Jubilee Conference of the Sheffield Industrial Mission*, Sheffield: Sheffield Academic Press

Ross, Donald M., 1997, *God It's Monday*, Edinburgh: St Andrew's Press for the Scottish Churches Industrial Mission

Sheppard, David, 1983, *Bias to the Poor*, London: Hodder and Stoughton

Siefer, Gregor, 1964, *The Church and Industrial Society*, London: Darton, Longman and Todd

Snape, M.F., 2003, *The Church of England in Industrialising Society*, Woodridge: The Boydell Press

Southcott, Ernest, 1957, *The Parish Comes Alive*, London: Mowbray

Stacey, Nicholas, 1971, *Who Cares*, London: Anthony Blond

Stockwood, Mervyn, 1982, *Chanctonbury Ring: An Autobiography*, London: Hodder

Studdert Kennedy, G. A., 1941, *The Unutterable Beauty*, London: Hodder and Stoughton

Studdert-Kennedy, Gerald, 1982, *Dog-collar Democracy: The Industrial Christian Fellowship, 1919–1929*, London: MacMillan

Symanowski, Horst, 1966, *The Christian Witness in an Industrial Society*, London: Collins

Taylor, Charles, 2007, *A Secular Age*, Cambridge, Massachusetts: The Belknap Press of Harvard University Press

Taylor, Richard, 1961, *Christians in Industrial Society*, London: SCM Press

Thompson, Phyllis, 1985, *To the Heart of the City: The Story of the London City Mission*, London: Hodder and Stoughton

Tillich, Paul, 1952, *The Courage to Be*, London: Fontana, Collins

Tillich, Paul, 1962, *The Shaking of the Foundations*, Harmondsworth: Pelican

* Tonkinson, David, 2009, '60 years: Some Views of Industrial Mission', unpublished paper

* Torry, Malcolm, 1990, 'The Practice and Theology of the South London Industrial Mission', unpublished Ph.D. thesis, University of London

* Torry, Malcolm, 1991, 'Over the Bridge: A History of the South London Industrial Mission, 1942–1987', an unpublished extended version of the unpublished Ph.D. thesis which includes new material from 1980 to 1987

* Torry, Malcolm, 'A Change of Gear', 2000, an unpublished supplement to 'Over the Bridge' which brings the story up to 2000

Torry, Malcolm (ed.), 2004, *The Parish: People, Place and Ministry: A Theological and Practical Exploration*, Norwich: Canterbury Press

Torry, Malcolm, 2005, *Managing God's Business: Religious and Faith-based Organizations and their Management*, Aldershot: Ashgate

Torry, Malcolm (ed.), 2006a, *Diverse Gifts: Varieties of Lay and Ordained Ministries in the Church and Community*, Norwich: Canterbury Press

Torry, Malcolm, 2006b, 'Serving in the Economy: The Workplace Chaplain', in Torry 2006a

Torry, Malcolm and Heskins, Jeffrey (eds.), 2006, *Ordained Local Ministry: A new shape for ministry in the Church of England*, Norwich: Canterbury Press

Torry, Malcolm, 2007, 'Starting from Scratch: The Greenwich Peninsula', in Torry, Malcolm (ed.), *Regeneration and Renewal: The Church in New and Changing Communities*, Norwich: Canterbury Press

Torry, Malcolm, 2008a, 'Voluntary, Religious and Faith-based Organizations: Some Important Distinctions', in Riordan, Patrick (ed.), *Words in Action: Finding the Right Words*, The Institute Series, no. 11, London: The Heythrop Institute for Religion, Ethics and Public Life

Torry, Malcolm, 2008b, 'Starting Out Together: The Greenwich Peninsula Experience', in Torry, Malcolm and Sarah Thorley (eds), *Together and Different: Christians Engaging with People of Other Faiths*, Norwich: Canterbury Press

Torry, Malcolm, 2009, 'On Building a New Christendom: Lessons from South London parishes', *Theology*, 512 (870)

Truss, Richard, 2007, 'Renewing the Culture: The Church on the South Bank', in Torry 2007

Tyler, Alison, 2006, 'Serving in a Walled Community: The Prison Chaplain', in Torry 2006a

van Buren, Paul, 1963, *The Secular Meaning of the Gospel*, London: SCM Press

Ward, Maisie, 1949, *France Pagan? The Mission of Abbé Godin*, London: Catholic Book Club

Wesley, John, undated, *The Journal of John Wesley*, edited by Percy Livingstone Parker, Chicago: Moody Press

White, Crispin (ed.), 2005, *This is Our Story*, Industrial Mission Association

* White, Crispin, 2009, 'Building a Network: The Initiation and Development of the Ecumenical Council for Corporate Responsibility', unpublished paper

Wickham, E. R., 1957, *Church and People in an Industrial City*, London: Lutterworth Press

Wickham, E. R., 1961, 'Appraisal', in Edwards, David L., *Priests and Workers*, London: SCM Press

Wickham, E. R., 1964, *Encounter with Modern Society*, London: Lutterworth Press

Wickham, E. R., 1966, 'What should be the new look?' in Hunter 1966

Wilkinson, Alan, 1978, *The Church of England and the First World War*, London: SPCK

Wilkinson, Alan, 1986, *Dissent or Conform? War, Peace and the English Churches 1900–1945*, London: SCM

Wilson, Bryan, 1966, *Religion in Secular Society*, London: C.A. Watts

Wilson, Bryan, 1976, *Contemporary Transformations of Religion*, Oxford: Clarendon Press

Wilson, Bryan (ed.), 1982, *Religion in Sociological Perspective*, Oxford: Oxford University Press

Winter, Gibson, 1961, *The Suburban Captivity of the Churches*, Garden City, New York: Doubleday

Wootton, Janet, 2009, 'Saving the Soul of Anglicanism: The Nature and Future of the Anglican Communion', *Modern Believing*, 50 (3), pp. 49–61

Yeo, Stephen, 1976, *Religion and Voluntary Organizations in Crisis*, London: Croom Helm

Youings, K. M., 2008, 'A Comparative Study of Mission at Chelmsford and Southwark Anglican Cathedrals 1930–1970', unpublished Master of Research dissertation, University of Keele